The Camino Compendium

A Historical and Cultural Exploration of the Camino de Santiago

Dave Whitson

Contents

Introduction

Does the world really need another book about the Camino Francés, the most-well-known and most-written-about branch of the Camino de Santiago, in 2025? The market isn't just saturated; it's flooded, with new memoirs, guides, personalized journals, fictional accounts, and even coloring books popping up constantly. This isn't inherently a bad thing, of course. Pilgrims are moved to share stories from their powerful experiences on the road, in many different formats, and the self-publishing boom has made that easier than ever. With all that literary traffic, though, it can be difficult to find fresh ground to explore.

Like many pilgrims, I started out on the Camino Francés, completing four pilgrimages along that bustling route before mostly leaving it behind in order to explore other tracks. My own publishing journey followed in those footsteps, leading to three guidebooks focused on less popular Caminos in Spain and France.

But you never forget your first. Even as my attention shifted elsewhere, the Camino Francés continued to hold a prominent place in my mind. The layers of history, piled across the centuries and millennia by the millions of pilgrims and other travelers passing along this holy ground, have left behind remarkable stories. And clearly, those continue to accrue in the present, as new waves of contemporary pilgrims make their mark.

As a guidebook author, it has been an honor to make a contribution to so many pilgrims, helping them find their way on such a transformative journey. At the same time, though, as the years have passed I've also begun to chafe against the limits of the genre. Inevitably, a guidebook, especially one trying to outline an 800-kilometer route in 300 pages or less, has to take a mile wide and an inch deep approach, rarely pushing much beyond the surface in its discussion of even the most important sights along the way. This isn't a condemnation; I love guidebooks, even more as a reader than as a writer. It's merely an honest acknowledgement of what the format can offer–and can't.

My early walks on the Camino Francés were shaped, of course, by traditional guidebooks, but even more profoundly by David Gitlitz and Linda Davidson's *The Pilgrimage Road to Santiago: The Complete Cultural Handbook*, which remains the definitive work on the route. As a young teacher preparing to bring my first group of high schoolers on pilgrimage–something that became a fixture in my life over the following decades–I found the most exemplary of role models in David and Linda. How many times did I read this passage in their introduction? "When our group stopped for a lesson, most walked on by. But every so often some fellow pilgrims would pause as we stared at a line of rocks in a seemingly empty field [...] Sometimes we drew a small crowd as we recited a medieval poem that recounted events that took place in the very building we were looking at. The urging behind all those pilgrim voices saying, 'I wish we knew more,' is why we have written this book." As an educator, that is exactly who I wanted to be, and in time it shaped my thinking as a guidebook author as well. As a writer, though, their book also felt limiting; after all, what more could be said about the Camino Francés, when the greats had already crafted their masterpiece?

Still, one of the most consequential lessons I've learned as a history teacher is that, beyond anything else, it's the appealing narrative that makes the facts-and-figures medicine go down. We learn best from stories, from seeing how those details cohere together in some sort of meaningful package. When I set out as a teacher on the road, I had lengthy lectures prepared, eager to download the extensive information I had assembled upon my tired, footsore students in our evening meetings. They tried their best, but that approach didn't set them up for success; at some point, all those details simply washed over them. In time, I learned to trim, trim, trim, homing in on the heart of the story, and preserving only the core elements that were critical to narrative integrity. Along the way, I realized that I was developing something that somehow didn't yet exist among all the pilgrim publications out there. The guidebooks offer a 10,000-foot view; more specialized texts home in closely on specific topics. Not much exists in the middle range, though, offering a satisfyingly deep dive into issues of broader significance, in a reasonably compact package. That's where this book comes in.

The Camino Compendium is designed with the pilgrim on the road top-of-mind. Like a guidebook, it's organized into stages, with full acknowledgement that these shouldn't be prescriptive, and everyone walks at their own pace. They're merely an organizational aid. Within each stage, I've found one important story to tell that is grounded in the places you're walking through. The range of subjects has made the research process equally exhilarating and challenging. (Fun fact: While working on this project, I discovered that Google Docs has a limit of 1,024,000 characters, when my research notes document threatened to blow well beyond that.) In the pages that follow, you'll encounter important literature from the way, including Ernest Hemingway, Emilia Pardo Bazán, and Concha Espina, along with the two great epic heroes, Roland and El Cid. Significant architectural works feature prominently as well, including León's Basilica of San Isidoro, Frómista's *Iglesia de San Martín*, and Torres del Río's *Iglesia del Santo Sepulcro*, along with the distinctive Galician *hórreo*. Miracle stories are highlighted, of course, from Santo Domingo de la Calzada, O Cebreiro, and Santiago de Compostela, as are military encounters ranging from the Templars to Napoleon to Franco. Most important to many of us, of course, are the stories related to food and drink, including bread, wine, and chocolate. I haven't even mentioned the exploding monastery, the dumpster-diving storks, the underwater ghost town, or the prehistoric cannibals. Even if you're already familiar with many of those topics, stick around. One of the great thrills of this project was discovering, time and time again, evidence that challenges conventional wisdom.

The vision is that each day on the Camino, a pilgrim can sit down with a café con leche in a bar or recline in their bunk, flip open the book to the next day's stage, and enjoy a story that will enhance their understanding of what they will soon encounter. Most chapters can be consumed in fifteen minutes or so, making them perfect for a break, or just short enough to complete before keeling over into a deep slumber at day's end. Of course, binge-reading is encouraged as well!

A book like this is only possible due to the dedicated work of professors and other academic researchers around the world. As I moved from topic to topic, I was consistently amazed by the wealth of resources available; often, I found a dissertation or specialized academic text dedicated precisely to the issue I hoped to examine. Alas, all too often that great work remains sequestered in its own world, largely beyond the reach of contemporary pilgrims. My hope is not only to share some of the insights from those many writers, but also to direct more readers to their work.

I haven't walked the Camino Francés in its entirety since 2014, though I've revisited the beginning and ending when completing other routes. Nonetheless, it remains vivid in my mind, and the process of writing *The Camino Compendium* exemplified why. The abundance of resources available underscores just how much there is to discover along these nearly 800 kilometers. As a walker, though, it can sometimes be difficult to access those deeper stories at the end of a long day. My hope is that this book makes those stories more accessible, and in so doing contributes in a modest way to an even more profound, life-changing experience.

The Song of Roland and Basque Erasure

Stage 1: Saint-Jean-Pied-de-Port to Roncesvalles

On behalf of historians everywhere, I ask you for one courtesy: don't learn history from Hollywood movies. Having said that, kudos to *The Way* for its curious but informative decision to spotlight the erasure of the Basque people from *The Song of Roland* in the dinner scene in Akerreta, when the *hospitalero* infuriates his French guest with his revisionist history. In that case at least, Hollywood trumped a literary classic in reliability. Let's not count on that to happen again any time soon.

Despite its dubious accuracy, *The Song of Roland* is worth knowing, as this first day's walk on the Camino Francés leads you into the heart of that narrative. As the work begins, we learn that Charlemagne, the French monarch who would become Holy Roman Emperor, has been on campaign in Iberia for seven years. (Mark Kurlansky, in *The Basque History of the World*, points out quite fairly that the poem couldn't even make it through the first sentence without a glaring inaccuracy.) His forces surround the city of Zaragoza, and its Muslim ruler, King Marsilie, is panicking. Charlemagne, by contrast, "is confident and joyful," having sacked Cordoba, leaving every Muslim in his wake either dead or converted to Christianity.

The desperate King Marsilie finds a lifeline in Ganelon, a Frenchman in Charlemagne's army who, driven by bitter jealousy of the emperor's beloved nephew Roland, betrays God and kingdom. When Marsilie seeks insight into what might halt the implacable monarch's military endeavors, Ganelon asserts that nothing will, at least "as long as his nephew is alive, for there is not such a vassal under the vault of heaven. Exceedingly valiant, too, is his comrade Oliver; the twelve peers also whom Charles loves so dearly and who form the vanguard with twenty thousand knights. Charles is safe for he has no one to fear." Conveniently enough, then, Ganelon has a plan to isolate Roland and the twelve peers, manipulating the honor-hungry young noble into taking the lead of the rear guard, as the bulk of the French army passes back over the Pyrenees. By persuading Charlemagne of his earnest desire to follow the emperor back to his capital, in order to submit to him and God alike, Marsilie could thus set his downfall in motion.

First through keen intuition and later by divine inspiration, Charlemagne sees through Ganelon's deceit, and yet for all his might, he is unable to alter the course of history as it unfolds before him. While the emperor denounces Ganelon from the moment the villain nominates Roland to oversee the rearguard—"You are a living devil. Deadly rage has taken possession of you"—Roland insists that he must accept the position. It's a matter of duty: "May God confound me if I belie my lineage." That night, Charlemagne's dreams are disrupted by an angelic vision, causing him to declare the following morning that, "I have such great grief that I must give vent to it. France will be ruined by Ganelon." Nonetheless, the plan is the plan, and he carries on with the journey home.

It doesn't take long for the betrayal to be revealed; in short order, Roland and the rear guard are surrounded by King Marsilie's forces. Roland's loyal comrade Oliver quickly exhorts him to take decisive action: "The heathen are in great force, and it seems to me there are very few of our Frenchmen! Comrade Roland, sound your horn (known as 'Oliphant'); Charles will hear it and the army will return." Roland, to put it mildly, dislikes the suggestion: "I should act like a madman! I should lose my renown, in sweet France." On the surface, this seems to establish Roland firmly as a tragic hero, doomed to die because of a defining flaw—an excessive sense of honor that overrides any rational appraisal of the conditions on the ground. Without question, it all but guarantees the deaths of Roland and his men; they are so wildly outnumbered that they have no hope of winning a traditional victory.

Roland and Oliver are joined in this fatal showdown by Archbishop Turpin, who frames the struggle to come as a pivotal one for Christianity. "Help to maintain the Christian faith! You will have battle, you are quite certain of it for with your own eyes you see the Saracens." He calls upon his fellow Frenchmen to prepare accordingly: "Confess your sins and pray God for His mercy. I will absolve you for the salvation of your souls. If you die you will be holy martyrs; you will have seats in greater paradise." As if that message isn't clear enough, Turpin reiterates later that, "one thing I can guarantee to you: Holy paradise awaits you and you will be seated there amongst the Innocents."

As the battle unfolds, the French peers acquit themselves well, demonstrating remarkable valor. The Muslim forces, though, are hundreds of thousands strong, and their victory is imminent. At last, Roland decides to blow the horn, calling back the main contingent of the French army. Oliver is outraged, appalled that only now, when it is far too late, would his friend make this decision. He asserts that "Your prowess, Roland, has been our undoing." Turpin quickly intercedes, reconciling the two men, and encouraging Roland to proceed, so that Charlemagne might avenge them. And indeed, once the emperor hears the horn–despite Ganelon's best efforts at dissembling–he rides angrily, despairingly, to Roland's aid.

It's too late, of course. Still, Roland stands tall to the end, rallying his men with gusto: "We shall obtain martyrdom here, and I know well now that we have not long to live. But cursed be he who does not sell himself dearly first!" When Oliver falls, he can think only of his loved ones: "He prays God that he will grant him paradise, that he will bless Charles and sweet France, and his companion Roland above all other men." In Roland's final moments, meanwhile, he makes a hasty confession. Collapsing to the ground, the young man "held out his right glove to God, and Saint Gabriel took it from his hand. His head was resting on his arm and his hands were clasped, and thus he went to his end."

An outraged Charlemagne would not be denied vengeance. On the contrary, God aided him in his pursuit, by making the sun stand still while the French hunted down the fleeing Muslim forces. Finally, when he "sees that all the heathen are dead, some killed and many drowned," he falls to the ground and gives thanks to God. That night, God sends the angel Gabriel to watch over the emperor, offering the troubled man what protection and comfort he could. The battle, however, is not over; King Marsilie still lives. And in the final confrontation, Charlemagne is nearly slain, when he suffers a blow to his head that cracks his helmet open. "Charles tottered and all but fell," the poem relates, "but God

willed not that he should be killed or conquered."
Reinvigorated, the emperor strikes forth "with the sword of
France" and slays his hated rival. Far from achieving some
semblance of a happy ending, though, poor Charlemagne is
called forth by the angel Gabriel in the final moments,
summoned to fend off the "heathen" in the "land of Bire,"
causing the exhausted, heartbroken emperor to push once
more unto the breach.

While The Song of Roland narrates events that
ostensibly occurred in 778, the pronounced religiosity in the
account speaks to its much later authorship–somewhere
around 1040-1130. With Pope Urban II's call to crusade in
1095 ushering in a new era of Holy War, this timing then
allows some to claim the chanson de geste as inspiration for
and/or the consequence of these changing motivations. As
will be discussed further in Stage 12, with Spain's Roland
equivalent, El Cid, medieval Iberian conflicts were hardly distinguished by religious purity; Christians and Muslims fought
Christians and Muslims alike, and were as likely to form
alliances as enmities.

Charlemagne's march into Iberia–which did, in fact,
occur–was inspired by such internecine squabbles within
Andalusia. To understand this rivalry, some context is required. Shortly after the death of Muhammad, the Umayyad
dynasty had risen to assert control over the Islamic world. In
750, though, a new dynasty, the Abbasid caliphate,
overthrew the Umayyads. One lone descendant of that fallen
family, Abd-al-Rahman, managed to escape to Iberia, where
he founded the Emirate of Córdoba and in 756 reestablished
the western version of the Umayyad dynasty. Some of the
peninsula's Muslim rulers were less than thrilled with this
development; in particular, Sulayman al-Arabi, the governor
of Barcelona, opposed Umayyad expansion and was alarmed by the participation of other formerly pro-Abbasid Arab

leaders in the area. He turned to the only man in the wider region capable of offering resistance to such a movement–the Carolingian monarch and future Holy Roman Emperor. Al-Arabi was joined in this initiative by Husayn of Zaragoza and Abu Taur of Huesca, promising their collective submission to the rule of Charlemagne, in exchange for military support.

For Charlemagne, this was an offer he couldn't refuse. After lengthy battles north of the Pyrenees, he believed that he had finally bested the Saxons, and thus had the military capacity for a new initiative. And al-Arabi persuaded him that Andalusia was the ripest of fruits, just waiting to be plucked. Despite those sweet assurances, though, betrayal came quickly. When Charlemagne reached Zaragoza, believing he had arrived to join an ally, he instead met stiff resistance. Husayn denied ever agreeing to join the alliance, though some suspect he was turned by the intimidating Umayyad force to the south. Regardless, Charlemagne did not enjoy the welcome he had anticipated, and he responded by besieging the city. After a month of absolute futility, and with word coming that those pesky Saxons were at it again, the emperor decided to cut bait on an embarrassing boondoggle, heading back north to France.

Far from the glorious seven years of conquest and plunder boasted of by the *chanson*, then, this failed foray was a much shorter debacle. *The Song of Roland* was accurate enough, at least, in highlighting that the trip home would be equally unpleasant. The portrayal of Muslims as the villains behind this duplicitous attack is a laughable caricature, one suggesting remarkable ignorance of Islamic practice. Of course, accuracy was not the goal here, not at all. As Fuat Boyacıoğlu discusses, the poet faced a distinct challenge in his portrayal of Muslims in the narrative, in that "he must make them unquestionably evil and agents of

Satan, clearly less noble, less manly, and less brave than the Christians, but nonetheless a worthy enemy." His solution, then, "is to make the Saracens the reverse image, the evil twins, of the Christians." As one example of this makeover, the poet creates a parallel Islamic trinity–Mahomet, Tervegant and Apollin–but one distinguished by evil idolatry. We have already seen how Roland, Oliver, Turpin, and Charlemagne were all unswerving in their faith, assured even in the face of imminent death of their promised salvation. By contrast, the Muslims talk a good game, but lack any semblance of conviction: "The heathen cry: 'Help us, Mahomet! Ye, our gods, save us from Charles who has left such felons in this land of ours that they will never quit the field for fear of death.' Then said one to another: 'Let us flee!' At this word a hundred thousand turn in flight and they will never come back." Later, when Charlemagne wreaks vengeance, they turn upon their gods: first Apollin, whom "they abuse [...] and disfigure [...] savagely," then "they deprive Tervagant of his carbuncle-stone." They save the worst for Muhammad, who they thrust "down into a ditch; there the swine and the dogs bite and trample him." Such is the weakness of their faith.

This is also why many reject the notion of Roland as a tragic hero. On the contrary, this argument goes, he is a martyr. His resistance to calling for help isn't driven by misplaced honor. As Robert Harrison explains, only Roland "understands what must be demonstrated." There could be no compromise with these "heathens," for it would only prolong the suffering for all involved. Instead, matters must be brought to a head, as only a "bold sacrifice would force the Franks to make a decisive strike against the Moors." This is, essentially, a call to crusade, a demand for Holy War.

Of course, none of that happened. Instead, a frustrated Charlemagne and his soldiers marched back to the

Pyrenees, carrying some measure of gold provided by Husayn to help persuade them to leave. Whether a matter of blowing off steam or laying the groundwork for a future return, it appears that the Franks razed some of the towns in the area. They saved their worst for Pamplona, though, tearing down the city's walls, and by some accounts ravaging the city itself. Far from a Muslim city, though, Basques populated Pamplona. It's too simplistic to present them as Christian, though certainly some of them had converted by this point. The widespread adoption of Christianity by the Basque people–and, more to the point, their elevation into some of the most dedicated Catholics in the region–would unfold over the centuries between Charlemagne and the *chanson*–but they certainly weren't Muslim. And they had ample reason to be outraged, given the harsh treatment they received at the emperor's hands.

It's no surprise, then, that payback was in order, nor that they knew exactly the most vulnerable point at which to strike the superior forces. What is completely unclear, though, is the nature of that attack. The historical records are just so thin on this point, and certainly Charlemagne lacked incentive to accurately document such a setback. Perhaps the Duke of Vasconia was involved and commanding a formal Basque force in pursuit of vengeance; perhaps this was primarily a group of brigands seeking plunder. Regardless, the Frankish rearguard was slaughtered, and ample reason exists to believe a lord named Roland–though certainly not the emperor's nephew–died among them. By all accounts, this represented the most significant setback of Charlemagne's prolific career.

All of that makes the fictional *hospitalero's frustration* with the *chanson's* erasure of Basques from the narrative easy to understand. Not only does this obscure Charlemagne's villainous act (and a short-sighted one, to boot, as the compromised Pamplona became easy pickings for Muslim forces shortly after his departure), but it also masks the Basque accomplishment of being the authors of his greatest failure. It's an all-too-familiar position for Basques, having their notable accomplishments hidden from the historical record or overlooked entirely, and one that Mark Kurlansky worked to remedy in his classic account.

This was hardly an unprecedented event for the Basques, staring down a superior military force. When the Romans swept through Iberia, they reached the Ebro River and called it a day, establishing a peaceful coexistence alongside the Basques, instead of trying to root them out from the mountains. When the Visigoths took over, they were far less amenable, and "Domuit Viscones," "Dominate the Basques," became a rallying cry—albeit a totally ineffective one. The Basques instead defied their efforts for centuries. After an early Umayyad invasion pushed into France, culminating in the Battle of Tours or Battle of Poitiers in 732, Islamic rule settled in south of the Pyrenees, content once more to leave the Basques to their own devices. As Kurlansky notes, these waves of invasion and resistance served to galvanize a group of clans into a cohesive people, building a strong sense of Basque identity that would prove key to their persistence into the present. It would have behooved Napoleon to respect it more than he did—more on that to come in Stage 3.

The Basques as inconvenient truth and equally inconvenient presence shows up in Camino history as well. The fourth book of the Codex Calixtinus, the original Camino guidebook published in the 12th century, was essentially Charlemagne fan fiction, imagining a world in which Santiago came to the emperor in a dream, calling upon him to avenge Roland's defeat and liberate Compostela from the Moors. The fifth book, meanwhile, goes out of its way to disparage the Basque residents of Navarre, clearly emerging from a society without libel laws. The kindest part of the description is the first sentence: "This land, whose language is barbarous, is wooded, mountainous, devoid of bread and wine, and all sorts of food." What kind of hospitality can pilgrims expect? "In the Pyrenees, Navarrese and Basques used not merely to rob pilgrims going to Saint James, but also to ride them as if they were asses and before long to slay them." The people can't be that bad, can they? "If you saw them eating, you would take them for dogs or pigs in the very act of devouring; if you heard them speaking, you would be reminded of the barking of dogs. Their language is, in fact, completely barbarous." I'm not the cleanest eater, I confess, and my speech can be a little lazy. Let he who is without sin... "This is a barbarous nation, distinct from all other nations in habits and ways of being, full of all kind of malice and black color. Their face is ugly and they are debauched, perverse, perfidious, disloyal and corrupt, libidinous, drunkard, given to all kind of violence, ferocious and savage, impudent and false, impious and uncouth, cruel and quarrelsome, incapable of anything virtuous, well-informed of all vices and iniquities." OK, that doesn't sound great. But maybe–"The Navarrese also make use of animals for incestuous fornication. He affixes a lock to the behind of his mule or horse so that no one else but he may have access to them." Oh. It turns out, I suppose, that bigoted representation can be worse than erasure.

In any case, while most pilgrims today prefer the higher-level Route Napoléon, the alternative approach is the more historic, leading you through Valcarlos, or the Valley of Charlemagne. Regardless, provided that you take the gentler descent from the Napoléon path, the trail will deliver you to Ibañeta, claimed to be the place where Roland blew Oliphant. Today, a modern chapel has replaced the 12th-century structure that once existed here, and a monument stands to commemorate the hero. The horn itself–or, at least, what is claimed to be Oliphant–is housed in the small museum of Roncesvalles. Meanwhile, the so-called Silo de Carlomagno, located next to La Posada, is believed to be the place where Roland sought to break his sword, Durandel, so that it wouldn't fall into Muslim hands. The site also claims to be the burial ground of the twelve peers, and some suggest that the name–Roncesvalles–is linked to that, associating the French adjective "rounceval" (something very large) with the giant bones of Charlemagne's great knights. And thus, in all regards, the myth persists in Roncesvalles today, indelibly etched in the landscape, and perpetuating the glorious fiction over the more sordid truth.

Keep reading...

Fuat Boyacıoğlu (trans.), "The Historical Anachronism In The Song Of Roland," *Das Erste Internationale Symposium Zu Den Deutsch-Tüekischen Historischen Und Kulturellen Beziehungen*, 2009

Glyn Burgess (trans.), *The Song of Roland*, 2010

Mark Kurlansky, *The Basque History of the World*, 1999

Robert Harrison (trans.), *The Song of Roland*, 1970

William Melczer (trans.), *The Pilgrim's Guide to Santiago de Compostela*, 1993

How Hemingway Changed Spain and How Spain Changed Hemingway

Stage 2: Roncesvalles to Zubiri

"It was baking hot in the square when we came out after lunch with our bags and the rod-case to go to Burguete." So begins Bill Gorton and Jake Barnes's short journey from Pamplona to Burguete in Ernest Hemingway's *The Sun Also Rises*. Along the way, they take in the scenery, enjoying views that remain familiar to most pilgrims: "we could see the country spread out below. Far back the fields were squares of green and brown on the hillsides. Making the horizon were the brown mountains. They were strangely shaped."

As they neared Burguete, the landscape changed: "we could see other mountains coming up in the south. Then the road came over the crest, flattened out, and went into a forest. It was a forest of cork oaks, and the sun came through the trees in patches, and there were cattle grazing back in the trees. We went through the forest and the road came out and turned along a rise of land, and out ahead of us was a rolling green plain, with dark mountains beyond it."

Their journey finished where yours originates today: "As we came to the edge of the rise we saw the red roofs and white houses of Burguete ahead strung out on the plain, and away off on the shoulder of the first dark mountain was the gray metal-sheathed roof of the monastery of Roncesvalles."

Jake and Bill found a room at Hostal Burguete, and they proceeded to spend five days fly-fishing in the area (though not as close to the center of Burguete as is often imagined). The experience, in Hemingway's characteristically economical portrayal, is convivial and refreshing: "The nights were cold and the days were hot, and there was always a breeze even in the heat of the day. It was hot enough so that it felt good to wade in a cold stream, and the sun dried you when you came out and sat on the bank. We found a stream with a pool deep enough to swim in. In the evenings we played three-handed bridge with an Englishman named Harris, who had walked over from Saint-Jean-Pied-de-Port and was stopping at the inn for the fishing." Standing in the midst of the peaceful beech forest, Jake has a spiritual experience, and echoes Hemingway's sentiments when he observes that, "This is about the last good country there is left..." Indeed, the author later acknowledged that he "felt almost holy" in describing the scenery around Burguete.

The quiet respite, the meditative state of nature that Hemingway found in the Pyrenean foothills complemented the chaotic revelry of the fiesta of San Fermín in Pamplona and its defining event, the running of the bulls, with which the author would become inextricably linked. His first experience with *los Sanfermines* occurred in July 1923, but it certainly wouldn't be his last, as it was through the bullfight, more than anything else, that he gained access to some of the most profound insights he would discover about man's relationship with mortality.

Early in *Death in the Afternoon,* Hemingway writes that, "I went to Spain to see bullfights and to try to write about them for myself. I thought they would be simple and barbarous and cruel and that I would not like them, but that I would see certain definite action which would give me the feeling of life and death that I was working for." Having experienced death firsthand while serving as an ambulance driver in Italy during World War I, including suffering a serious injury from mortar fire, Hemingway never shook the hold it had upon him. Reflecting upon that fearful time, when he thought he might lose his leg, he remarked that, "When you go to war as a boy you have a great illusion of immortality. Other people get killed; not you [...] Then when you are badly wounded the first time you lose that illusion and you know it can happen to you." As his good friend José Luis Castillo-Puche would later write, "The mystery of the beyond was more than terrifying to him," and it would hound him at different points throughout his life.

The bullfight, Edward Stanton argues, offered something unique and something essential for Hemingway, as it represented "the only place in the modern world where a man could observe death at first hand, often surrounded by the most astonishing beauty, and thus come to terms with his own mortality." The bull captured his imagination, alternately "beautiful," "terrible," "wonderful," and "pre- historic," but above all "absolutely deadly and absolutely vicious." Like the landscape around Burguete, this, too, inspired a palpable sense of awe in Hemingway. At the same time, he was taken in by the audience, admiring the "Spaniards' common-sensical acceptance of death as a natural function," which he determined empowered them to live more richly than other people he had witnessed. The Spanish poet Pedro Salinas picked up on this idea of a "culture of death," asserting that it centered on "a conception of man and his earthly existence, in which the awareness of death functions with a positive sign; it is a stimulus, and not a hindrance, to living and acting, and it makes possible an understanding of the full and total meaning of life." The French philosopher Georges Bataille would add, after his own experience with a bullfight, that he "then began to understand that uneasiness is often the secret to the most intense pleasures [...] this is exactly the feeling that is given when the bull's horns miss, by an inch, the body of the bullfighter."

Contrary to Hemingway's expectations, the bullfight defied any notion of immorality: "I know only that what is moral is what you feel good after and what is immoral is what you feel bad after and judged by these moral standards, which I do not defend, the bullfight is very moral to me because I feel very fine while it is going on and have a feeling of life and death and mortality and immortality, and after it is over I feel very sad but very fine." What made this most powerful to Hemingway, Castillo-Puche suggests, is the duality of the event. At one moment, a bullfight could offer "trancelike moments of great valor, an instant of serenity when the bull brushes past the cape, the beautiful sensation of pure courage." At another, though, perhaps only seconds apart, it might transform into "helplessness, a ridiculous lack of guts, craven cowardice in the face of the brave bull, a sword flung in the air, an ignominious retreat, a grotesque leap, livid shame." A brutal honesty cut through all of that, an earnest reality that stood alone in the modern world.

At the center of this, the greatest of all human dramas, stands the matador–the artist engaged in creating his masterpiece from the medium of his life. Ben Stoltzfus writes that in bullfighting, "a superior performance is both art and tragedy because it ends in the death of the bull and because it reenacts in ritual form the mystery of life and death. The matador performs a work of art, and he plays with death, bringing it closer and closer with each veronica (pass with the cape) which, if he is an artist, shows his domination of the bull. These are moments of immortality that the matador proves to himself and to the observer."

When Hemingway arrived in Spain, he was still finding himself as an artist, and in the country he discovered, as Stanton puts it, "a territory that had not been claimed, incredibly, by any other major author." María de Guzmán reiterates this sentiment, noting that "Spain functioned [for expatriate American authors] not as a well-charted colony [...] but as a last frontier, a land to be discovered." The Hemingways were at the forefront of this trend, among the first English-speaking tourists to attend San Fermín. This was a place where he could make his mark and be indelibly marked. He wasn't alone in this pursuit; other modernists joined him in Iberia, and collectively they tended to ascribe a mythic quality to the land and a primal, authentic quality to its people. Not everyone appreciated their efforts; Ezra Pound, never one to hold back, wrote that Spain functioned as "an emotional luxury to a gang of sap-headed dilettantes."

Setting aside accusations of intellectual colonialism, inauthenticity posed the biggest threat to Hemingway's project in Spain, and for that reason–like many pilgrims today, I suspect–he sought to distance himself from tourism. Stuart McIver underscores Hemingway's hatred for tourism, and particularly "its inevitable end-product, tourists," and Kevin Maier illustrates how Hemingway repeatedly ran into difficulty when trying to distinguish his own European pur-suits from mass tourism. At times, it has to be ack-nowledged, this smacked of the poseur. For example, Russ Pottle describes how, after first arriving in Paris in 1921, Hemingway acquired a guide to the city's history, quickly internalized the information–in private–and then subsequently presented it as his own personal insights into the city.

In Spain, Miriam Mandel argues, Hemingway practiced "a kind of anti-tourism, in which the traveler 'passes' as a native in the settings he visits, changing himself from outsider to insider." The risk to this kind of approach, Pottle adds, is a phenomenon Alan Brien has labeled 'tourist angst,' which involves "a gnawing suspicion that after all [...] you are still a tourist like every other tourist." Ultimately, perhaps it's an unavoidable transitional stage for those aspiring to some semblance of cultural assimilation or integration, and Hemingway appears to have persuaded many Spaniards of his success in that regard. To offer one prominent example, the Spanish historian Salvador de Madariaga sang his praises: "He was that rare thing, a human being; open-eyed, open-handed, open-hearted, open-minded, a man ready to learn, to understand, to appreciate, to see beneath the surface." The journalist Rafael Hernández expressed gratitude to Hemingway for his perceptive interpretation of Spanish life, writing that, "The work he has undertaken to combat the errors and legends invented about the bullfight outside of Spain is more than enough reason for us to be grateful to him."

It's impossible to question the sincerity of Hemingway's affection for Spain, which he called "the country that I loved more than any other except my own." He made two visits to the country as it collapsed into Civil War, throwing his support behind the fight for democratic liberalism. The author Bernice Kert would later reflect that, "I think it was the only time in his life when he was not the most important thing there was," while the Spanish journalist José Delgado commended Hemingway's "great and unselfish love" for Spain. When Franco won the war, Hemingway lost Spain, at least for a time, as he refused to enter the country as long as his friends continued languishing in the dictator's prisons.

Neither Hemingway nor Spain were the same when he finally returned in 1953. Franco remained in power, but Spain's relationship with the United States was thawing, and Hemingway's love for the country trumped whatever ethical opposition he had previously asserted. Certainly never a friend of the dictatorship, Hemingway nonetheless allowed himself to be co-opted, refraining from ever making critical remarks against Franco. In the process, he was removed from the country's censorship lists, resulting in *The Sun Also Rises* finally being published in Spain in 1948, and used instead as one of the great international promoters of Spain, helping to rekindle interest in the country abroad.

"My return to Spain," Hemingway wrote, "is a pilgrimage of loving devotion." As happens sometimes, though, the pilgrim found himself awash with tourists. Pamplona, he discovered, was filled with Americans, many of them lugging around *The Sun Also Rises* as a pseudo-guidebook. Twomey describes how Hemingway, growing ever more irate, "as though he were offended and infuriated and scandalized," would periodically "get up out of his chair and bellow at them to drive them all away." Even his beloved San Fermín had become a spectacle, Suzanne del Rizzo writes, and the "bullfight itself had become heavily commercialized and, as far as Hemingway was concerned, artistically compromised." Robert Daley, writing in the New York Times about the Pamplona festival in 1959, noted that "In the old days, the fiesta was for the locals [...] Today there are more than 40,000 tourists in town, many of them young Americans." Hemingway had no one to blame but himself; his own writing had transformed his shrine into an attraction. Even worse, as María de Guzman observes, despite Hemingway's constant mission to distinguish the real from the fake, his novel "codifies" Pamplona's "rituals and makes them eminently reproducible."

We can never recapture our past, and Hemingway's pursuit in 1959 proved particularly futile. In reporting the work that would ultimately be published as *The Dangerous Summer,* Hemingway returned to bullfighting, and in so doing, William Kennedy suggests, he sought to recreate a time when he was excelling as an author and living the best version of his life. Hemingway turned 60 that summer, and he was grappling with the harsh reality best characterized by Stanley Cooperman, who observed that "the virtues of the Hemingway hero had always been the virtues of the young." The "hyper-masculine" ideal that Hemingway had cultivated in his earlier years, which had been central to his rise as a celebrity and idol, ever more appeared to be a trap in which the older author now found himself ensnared.

Castillo-Puche, later reflecting on Hemingway's death, recalled the man he met in Hemingway's last year in Spain, one who bore limited resemblance to the younger author. Beyond anything else, he writes, "perhaps the most telling and fateful sign of the change in Ernesto was that writing had become an enormous struggle that left him anxiety- ridden and depressed." Hemingway had hoped, consciously or not, to tap into that same Spanish profundity that had shaped him so fundamentally as an artist. Far from the "delirious frenzies" and "frenetic joys" that had once marked his Spanish forays, though, the country now functioned as "a spiritual handhold for a shipwrecked man who had been flourishing for years in a valiant, vain attempt to fight off the terror of death."

Just two years later, Hemingway died by suicide at his home in Idaho. "Why," Castillo-Puche pondered, "did the death of others–the very word–make his hair stand on end, while he bore his own death about him as reverently as though it were a holy tabernacle?" So troubled, so bereft was Castillo-Puche upon Hemingway's death that he retraced the places they had visited together in Spain, revisiting their conversations each step of the way, struggling all the while to understand what had brought about the loss of his dear friend. Arriving no closer to the answer after nearly 400 pages, he could offer only one conclusion: "Man is the victim of this duel he cannot resist fighting. And even if he is the victor, in the end all that remains is the acrid taste of his own destruction."

More than a century removed from his first visit to Pamplona, Hemingway endures as a tangible presence in the region. Hostal Burguete remains open; you can stay in room 23, as Hemingway did, and sample the Hemingway Soup as part of your evening meal. His signature, of questionable authenticity, is etched into the piano. In Pamplona, a bust of Hemingway rests outside the Plaza de Toros, while a full statue maintains the pose he often held, leaning against the bar at Café Iruña in the Plaza del Castillo. If he never reconciled the terror engendered by his own mortality, or the complicated impact he made upon his beloved *sanfermines*, he did achieve some measure of immortality, and a permanent connection to this second home.

Keep reading...

Ben Stoltzfus, "Bulls, Art, Mithras, and Montherlant,"
    Hemingway's Spain: Imagining the Spanish World, 2016

Edward Stanton, *Hemingway and Spain*, 1989

Ernest Hemingway, *Death in the Afternoon*, 1932

Ernest Hemingway, *The Sun Also Rises*, 1926

José Luis Castillo-Puche, *Hemingway in Spain*, 1974

Lisa Twomey, "Ernest Hemingway—¿Amigo de España?," *Hemingway's Spain: Imagining the Spanish World*, 2016

María De Guzmán, "Hemingway in the Dirt of a Blood and Soil Myth," *Hemingway's Spain: Imagining the Spanish World*, 2016

Miriam Mandel, "Configuring There as Here: Hemingway's Travels and the 'See American First' Movement," *Hemingway Review*, 1999

Russ Pottle, "Allegories of Travel and Tourism in 'Hills Like White Elephants,'" *Hemingway's Spain: Imagining the Spanish World*, 2016

Suzanne del Gizzo, "It was all there . . . but he could not see it," *Hemingway's Spain: Imagining the Spanish World*, 2016

Beware the Land Pirates!

Stage 3: Zubiri to Pamplona

Sure, you've heard of the Trojan Horse. But what about the Pamplona Snowball Fight? I bet you've missed out on that one.

It's difficult, upon arrival in Pamplona, to not become so enraptured by the tightly-packed streets in the old town, ornamented by the solemn cathedral, the vibrant Plaza del Castillo, and the flag-laden *ayuntamiento* (city hall), that one never goes beyond it. Tired legs and sore feet don't help matters. For those reasons, most pilgrims won't encounter my favorite place in the city until they're already on their way out, before the caffeine in their morning *café con leche* has even kicked in. No, I'm not talking about the El Corte Inglés, though I once spent a few slack-jawed hours wandering its floors. Keep going, just a little further.

Before too long, the office buildings and apartments give way, and the world opens up to a sprawling field of green. In the midst of that is a massive stone structure. The Ciudadela, the 16th-century fortress, is impressive enough when viewed from the side, with sheer walls giving way to sharply protruding towers. Take a moment, though, to view the pentagonal star fort from above; Google satellite view will suffice. Even today, having been converted to a recreational space, its intimidating, magnificent glory has been preserved. I can only imagine what it might look like under a fresh coating of snow.

The French forces under command of General Jean Barthélemy Claude Toussaint d'Armagnac in 1808 were more fortunate than I, though perhaps only in that regard. On the morning of February 9, they entered Pamplona the same way that pilgrims do, through the aptly named Portal de Francia, after having traveled over the preceding two days from Roncesvalles. They quickly found themselves in a messy, complicated, and potentially dire situation.

Why would that be so? Technically, the French forces were visiting an ally, bringing support that had been explicitly approved by the Spanish government, to bolster the defense against English invasion. To call that alliance tenuous, though, would be an overstatement. The two had clashed between 1793 and 1795, but who hadn't warred with France in those revolutionary years? Over the next decade, Napoleon rose to power, and the Spanish watched in growing concern as his imperial ambitions swelled. Opportunity knocked in 1806, when Napoleon's forces were drawn into Prussia, followed by further conflicts in Russia the following year. Spain, under the leadership of King Charles IV and First Secretary of State Manuel Godoy, made a hamfisted effort to break free from the French-imposed Continental System. While they quickly backtracked soon after, Napoleon's faith in Charles and Godoy had shattered. The alternative, though, wasn't much better from France's perspective, as Charles's son, Ferdinand, was expressing interest in alliance with England. Allies or not, a regime change was deemed necessary.

Portugal offered a legitimate target and a convenient excuse. By 1807, it represented the lone continental entrypoint free from Napoleon's control, but to reach it he would need to march his forces clear across Spain. This was, of course, approved by his nominal ally, and within the year the Portuguese royal family was high-tailing it across the Atlantic to Brazil. The French, though, were in no hurry to leave Spain, and the people grew increasingly antsy with the arrangement. An uncanny series of manipulative moves followed. First, Napoleon engineered a coup in the capital, helping to bring about the fall of Charles and the rise of Ferdinand VII. Next, he sweet-talked both Charles and Ferdinand to join him in dialogue, across the border in Bayonne. What could go wrong? For Spain, a lot. Both Spanish rulers were convinced to abdicate, yielding the throne to Napoleon's brother, Joseph Bonaparte.

That background helps to explain why d'Armagnac and his men were on edge, as the entire city of Pamplona was a tinderbox in search of a spark. The streets were filled with angry crowds, as orators exhorted them to rally and drive the French from the country. Instead of throwing open its gates in welcome, the Ciudadela prepared for battle, its garrison having been called to arms. The star fort was designed to be impregnable. While it had never actually been tested since its construction in 1571, most believed the truth of this, the French as much as anyone.

A week following their arrival in Pamplona, the French forces were encamped outside the Ciudadela, but arrangements had been made for them to approach the gate every four days in order to receive bread from the fortress's bakery. That's exactly what 60 French soldiers were doing on February 16, when General d'Armagnac unleashed a scheme so utterly implausible that it remains difficult to believe that it worked. With snow falling heavily on that cold winter morning, some French troops engaged in a seemingly spontaneous snowball fight. The Spanish soldiers at the gate were... amused, entranced, befuddled? They were certainly distracted. And in the meantime, the bread crew had already passed unnoticed onto the drawbridge, from which point they swiftly disarmed the guards, opening the way for the 100 other soldiers, secretly stashed in the general's house across from the gate, to charge. Before any sort of defense could be mustered, they had already taken the armory. The snowball had become an avalanche.

General d'Armagnac earned little praise for this maneuver, and instead became a figure of loathing within the city. He didn't like his position much better, referring to the operation in Pamplona as a "vile mission." Napoleon replaced him soon after. Little could they know that this would be the high-water mark for the French occupation of Navarre.

In his book, *The Fatal Knot: The Guerrilla War in Navarre and the Defeat of Napoleon in Spain,* John Lawrence Tone devotes the initial chapters to explaining the distinct geography and history of Navarre, as that context is essential to understand what happened next. First, Navarre proved to be one of the most staunchly loyal regions of Spain, rallying in support of the Crown, though that was due largely to reasons of self-interest. Navarre had finally yielded to Spanish rule in 1513, but in the process King Ferdinand swore to protect its institutions and identity, while the Castilian viceroy swore to respect the fueros, or local laws. Those fueros were imbued with a certain reverence that citizens of the USA often associate with the constitution—laws that are more than laws, hinting at a rare moment when humans transcended their baser limitations. More pragmatically, those fueros included the exemption of Navarre from taxes and customs duties. Given its position on the border, this translated into significant wealth for the region, a right and privilege that would be difficult to relinquish.

Second, Navarre's nobility and churchmen were distinct from their peers across much of Europe. The unique history of Navarre, never conquered north of Pamplona by Moors or Romans, with a significant contingent of Basques, resulted in a different, more commonplace sort of nobility. As Tone writes, "The value of a thing [...] falls when it is super-abundant," and in the valleys west and north of Pamplona 60-80% of the population qualified as nobles. Most of these were *hidalgos*, the lowest rung of the nobility, with little tangible difference separating them from peasant comm-oners. Indeed, they lived quite similarly, with most adhering to a subsistence economy that, while demanding hard work, provided an otherwise comfortable and consistent lifestyle. Navarre's ecclesiastics, meanwhile, comprised more than 2% of the region's total population, outpacing Spain's other regions. However, they made far less of an economic impact, controlling only 1% of the total land (in contrast to 8% in other regions) and yielding only 11% of the region's agricultural product via tithe (whereas it absorbed as much as half the product elsewhere). In many places, the ecclesiastics were elites, but in the mountainous parts of Navarre they blended right in with the peasants, "playing billiards, smoking, and drinking liquor in public houses."

Third, family estates in Navarre followed a strict practice of primogeniture, with the oldest child—male or female—taking it all. In the mountainous areas, this resulted in a mix of small agricultural areas, often worked by the *laya*, an old-fashioned spade, as opposed to a plow. This required coop-eration between families, which had positive consequences for the collaborative nature of communities, and it also empowered women to take a more active role in the labor. The system of primogeniture also meant that younger sons often had to pursue economic opportunities elsewhere. Northern Navarre didn't export much, but it certainly exported people.

Finally, the geography of the region requires comment. There were effectively two Navarres, the "Montaña" and the "Ribero." The former comprises the northern half of the region; as the name suggests, the terrain is more rugged, shaped by the Pyrenean foothills and heavily treed in many places. You'll be pleased to know, or at least I was, that the Camino Francés is limited to this part of Navarre. The latter, meanwhile, is flatter, more open, and more conducive to large-scale agriculture.

The table-setting is now complete; here's the point. Well, two points. First, Navarre was perfectly designed to defy Napoleon's playbook for domination. All across Europe, he capitalized on long-standing grievances, attacking noble privilege, ecclesiastical exploitation, and royal greed. None of that worked in the Montaña region of Navarre. On the contrary, Napoleon's plan to absorb Navarre into France represented an existential threat, stripping the region of its privileged economic place within Spain and making it just another province.

Second, while the Ribero could be secured easily by formal armies, the Montaña posed far greater complications. Small villages scattered across unforgiving topography made it challenging for Napoleon's forces to tax the population and commandeer supplies. And strategically, these lands were essential to control, as they provided a critical link between the French forces in Spain and Portugal and the home country. At the same time, the Navarrese had self-sustaining populations with an abundance of extra men available. The border region had a long history of smuggling, and as a consequence it contained more guns per capita than any other part of 19th-century Spain, along with a population endowed with an intimate understanding of every nook and cranny in the area.

The Navarrese couldn't hope to match the French forces head on, but they could try something different. As the resistance took shape, it became known as the *corso terrestre*, or "land pirates." And really, what Napoleon's forces faced was the birth of guerrilla war as we know it today. The efforts originated in Galicia, after General Soult's forces had chased Sir John Moore and his English army from the continent (more on this in Stage 24). Instead of feeling triumphant, the general was soon discouraged, noting that this particular brand of Galician resistance would "make warfare in this country extremely bloody, infinitely disagreeable, and seemingly endless."

While Galicia was fungible, Navarre was essential, so no matter how "disagreeable" the French were forced to maintain control. The earliest guerrilla efforts in Navarre, led by Javier Mina and the priest Casimiro Javier de Miguel é Irujo, were like flies harrying a bull–annoying for sure, but of limited consequence. For a time, they enjoyed success around Los Arcos, chasing off a French force and establishing a base of operations in the town, while also harassing soldiers near Burguete and Roncesvalles. They benefited from the support, as well, of nearby Estella, which was always ready for a fight. A strong French counterpunch, though, resulted in Mina's arrest, Miguel's departure, and the arrival of a harsher commander, Georges Joseph Dufour. Instead of grinding all resistance to a halt, though, his oppressive tactics only served to reignite the embers.

A new leader, Francisco Espoz y Mina, soon emerged to elevate the Navarrese resistance to greater heights. By this point, effective guerrilla tactics were well understood. Espoz y Mina and his men sought to isolate French forces in vulnerable positions–when they were outnumbered and exposed–and avoid direct engagement at all cost. The ultimate goal was simple: let nothing be easy for the French. Every time they departed a fortified position, they needed to feel like eyes were watching from the woods, as though an attack could come from anywhere–because it could. French morale declined; soldiers in the area, as well as their leaders, hated the assignment. And at the same time, larger and larger numbers of soldiers needed to be assigned to otherwise mundane operations, to ensure their security.

The French Colonel Joseph Conrad Marnier reflected in his memoirs that, "A new kind of war began for us, a war of constant ambush, murder and extermination [...] a daily struggle against invisible enemies, thousands of them: hidden in the wilderness, in the bottom of gorges, guerrillas ready to fight in every corner of every building, with neither truce, nor rest; and always the fear of betrayal day and night, at any point, at any bend of a trail, even while we were in bed." The psychological toll of this is impossible to measure, but it must have been steep.

Guerrilla forces need to walk a fine line when it comes to local populations. On one hand, they have to demonstrate that they can keep the people safer than the occupiers can. Many people aren't political; they just want stability, to be able to go about their lives. A lot can be tolerated if the trains run on time. As such, Espoz y Mina needed to be able to rally to the defense of towns when French oppression surged. On the other, though, guerrillas have to discourage collaboration; loyalty in such situations often requires as much fear as love, especially when the other side has few qualms about the employment of terror. On many occasions, they killed, branded, mutilated, and tortured collaborators–their fellow Navarrese. As grizzly as this was, it proved effective. One French soldier, cited by Fernando Martínez-Laínez, wrote later that, "The guerrillas were never where we were looking. The peasants protected and supported them, and gave them vital information about us, and our movements." The guerrillas won the intelligence war.

Pamplona suffered the worst of both worlds. By the summer of 1811, General Honoré Charles Reille had drawn the short straw of leading the French occupation, and he earned the distinction of being the most brutal of them all. The picture painted by Andrés Martín captures the climate of fear that dominated the city: "In the streets the people hear the heartrending cries of their friends taken to prison and torture. If they flee the city, they see the high gallows on which innocent Spaniards hang. Everywhere, there is nothing but prison, exile, and death. And in this terrible situation, the expression of grief is forbidden. A simple complaint or glance of compassion is cause enough for imprisonment."

Later that year, Espoz y Mina responded with a complete economic blockade of Pamplona, cutting off the city from the rest of Navarre. He declared the inhabitants–all of them–to be enemies for the remainder of the war. Guards surrounded the city, with very clear rules: "if they see anyone approaching," they were expected to "fire without delay." That wasn't the end of it: "whether the culprit is wounded or not, he will be hanged immediately in a tree." (Tone adds that Espoz y Mina was sometimes more lenient, generously letting violators go with only their ears or nose chopped off, instead of a hanging.) This policy didn't just damage Pamplona; it risked economically crippling the entire region. But by this point Espoz y Mina had the manpower to make this work, and he saw the endgame in reach. By 1812, the French could no longer take the offensive; they could barely gather sufficient wood to keep the fires burning in Pamplona. And before long, they had far bigger concerns–Arthur Wellesley, the future Duke of Wellington, was making his presence known. In early 1813, the English forces struck northward from Burgos, routing Joseph's army at the Battle of Vitoria in June, before pushing onto Pamplona. By November, his forces would break into France.

One of history's oft-repeated refrains is that one should never invade Russia in the winter. And that's good advice; I have no immediate plans. This is inspired, of course, by the difficulties encountered by Napoleon's forces there, which are often associated directly with his eventual demise. Obscured in that, though, is the pivotal role played by Spain generally, and Navarre specifically. The casualty count generated by the guerrillas in Navarre might not jump off the page, but the roughly 50,000 French soldiers killed, captured, or wounded over the conflict's six years is nearly 75% of what Wellesley's forces accounted for across all of their operations. That's only part of the story, though. One of the major impacts of the guerrilla resistance was merely keeping French soldiers busy, guarding terrain and seeing ghosts, instead of doing something more useful. If the 19,000 soldiers tasked with tracking Espoz y Mina could have instead been added to the force confronting Wellesley at the Battle of Vitoria, how different might the outcome have been?

Keep reading...

John Lawrence Tone, *The Fatal Knot: The Guerrilla War in Navarre and the Defeat of Napoleon in Spain*, 1994

José de la Pisa, *Napoleon´s Nightmare: Guerrilla Warfare in Spain (1808-1814) – The French Army´s Failed Counterinsurgency Effort*, 2011

THE CAMINO COMPENDIUM

Mark Kurlansky, *The Basque History of the World*, 1999

V. Echarri & A. Galiano, "The controversies between Jacobo Fratín and Vespasian Gonzaga on the project of the citadel of Pamplona in the late sixteenth century," *Transactions on The Built Environment*, 2014

Tilting at Turbines

Stage 4: Pamplona to Puente la Reina

On the fourth day of my first Camino, I crossed what felt in the moment like one of the defining sights of the pilgrim road. After an easy start, strolling from Pamplona to Cizur Menor, I soon found myself huffing and puffing through a sharp ascent. Like so many other pilgrims, I had a Don Quixote moment as I rose towards a line of turbines ahead, dotting the ridge overlooking the valley. When I finally reached the top, crossing at the Alto del Perdón, I found a marvelous series of pilgrim sculptures. By design, they were rust colored, but this conveyed a sense of permanence, as though the view I was enjoying–sculpture and turbine alike– was somehow quintessential to the Camino.

Vicente Galbete, the artist responsible, called the collection of sculptures the "Monumento al Peregrino." He sought to capture the history of pilgrims over the hilltop. On the far right, you'll see a simple pilgrim, searching for the Camino, an image that speaks to the earliest days of walkers on the way (and maybe you in a difficult moment). A pair of trios follows, the first speaking to the Camino's growth in popularity, and the second–a pack of merchants–highlighting the commercialism that, while bemoaned today, has been central to the pilgrimage from its earliest days. (Indeed, many medieval merchants dressed as pilgrims when traveling along the Camino, in order to escape tolls.) A lone pilgrim follows, distant from its predecessors, reflecting the Camino's decline after the Reformation. Finally, two modern-day pilgrims illustrate the Camino's resurgence (though maybe 200 would have been more appropriate). Inscribed across the statues is a message: "Donde se cruza el camino del viento con el de las estrellas," or "where the path of the wind crosses with that of the stars."

Of course, none of this existed before 1996.

Even the current name, the Alto del Perdón, is a change from its earlier association with the Reniega Fountain, also known today as the Fuente de Gambellacos, which still stands along the trail, shortly before the pass. An important legend is linked to that fountain. On a hot day, a parched pilgrim staggered along the Camino towards Puente la Reina. Perhaps you can empathize. The devil came along and knew a ripe target when he saw one. He offered to quench the walker's thirst for the low, low price of renouncing God. The pilgrim denied the devil. Entering negotiation mode, the devil dropped the price from God to the Virgin Mary. Still no deal. Finally, the devil offered the refreshing relief from thirst in exchange for the renunciation of Santiago. The walker still held to his faith, but he could feel himself weakening. Those hot days are rough. He beseeched heaven for help. And just like that, the devil went poof and Santiago appeared, leading the parched pilgrim to the Reniega Fountain. By the 16th century, though, the Basque name, "Perdonanza bidea," or "road to forgiveness," had taken hold here, speaking to what the pilgrim road to Santiago might offer to those heading westward.

Over time, too, the focus shifted from the fountain itself to that hilltop pass. A hospital was established there in the 15th century, along with a hermitage (last documented in 1816) and a sanctuary devoted to Santa María. A procession to honor the Virgen del Perdón still takes place annually on August 30. In the 1990s, though, the Sierra del Perdón garnered attention from Navarrese engineers when a "wind cannon" was discovered here, maintaining a steady, average speed of nearly 32km/hour. In the early days of harvesting wind energy with modern turbines, a belief persisted that such technology could only work on the coast. Here, though, was a chance to bring the green energy movement to the Navarrese interior. The first four turbines were installed in the Sierra del Perdón in 1994. Encouraged by the initial success, 36 more turbines were added by 1997. Each turbine stands 40 meters high; its blades reach forth an additional 20 meters. Each weighs 52.5 tons, a mix of steel and fiberglass. As an acknowledgement of the impact of this development on the Camino de Santiago, Energía Hidro- eléctrica de Navarra (EHN), the company responsible for the operation, collaborated with the local branch of the Amigos del Camino to commission the statues.

In the years that followed, Navarre became one of the leaders in wind energy, not only in Spain but globally, the "Silicon Valley of wind power." Navarre's initial successes and entrepreneurial environment triggered a proliferation of mutually beneficial industries. EHN, later acquired by Acciona, remains a prominent force in the wind power industry and is based outside Pamplona. Ingeteam, which specializes in electrical energy conversion, is located in the same area. Also nearby is the CENER Wind Turbine Testing Laboratory, where manufacturers are able to stress test their prototypes. With only five similar facilities worldwide, its presence is a huge boon to Navarre's related businesses. Gamesa, later acquired by Siemens and now based near Navarre, in Biscay, is the world's second largest wind turbine manufacturer. By 2008, more than 40,000 people in Navarre were employed in the wind energy sector.

What prompted this development? What made Navarre such a force in the field of wind energy? Javier Faulina and colleagues evaluated the region's remarkable progress over its first decade in 2005. First, they found that the Navarrese regional government, which enjoys a great deal of autonomy in Spain, eagerly embraced renewable energy sources. At the time, the region suffered from a major deficit in energy generation capacity, so the potential offered by wind and solar offered a way forward. Significant subsidies were offered throughout the decade. Those public funds were complemented by a robust private investing sector that displayed similarly enthusiasm about green energy potential. All of this resulted in the rise of the aforementioned enterprise sector in Navarre, which at the time included 54 companies all involved in the renewable field. The Navarrese people were also quick to support the initiative. An early public opinion survey highlighted widespread buy-in for green energy initiatives. Interestingly, and perhaps counter-intuitively, that survey also revealed the importance of establishing wind parks in highly visible areas, to build public recognition and reinforce that popular support.

While Navarre led the way, the rest of Spain followed, as is clear to any pilgrim who has followed different branches of the Caminos de Santiago. By 2011, Spain had one turbine for every 25km². Its wind power capacity jumped from just 2365 megawatts (MW) in 2000 to over 21,000 MW, accounting for over 16% of the country's total energy demand. Beyond the tangible economic and energy benefits, this wave of technological innovation has also been a symbolic boon to a country that has long carried a stigma of backwardness, beginning with its late arrival in the first industrial revolution. This time, Spain stood on the cutting edge.

In the years that followed, though, that enthusiasm ebbed. Despite that early popular support in Navarre, including belief in the value of prominent installations, the novelty soon wore off. As familiar landscapes were transformed by highly-concentrated sets of turbines, opposition grew, with some critics condemning the "crucified hills" and accompanying environmental consequences. This creates an awkward, uncomfortable situation, in which the cure for environmental degradation is itself perceived as part of the disease.

Beyond the environmental and aesthetic concerns, there are economic matters as well. While there are undeniable economic benefits to wind farms, those benefits are not distributed equally. Some lose far more than they gain. A recent *Wall Street Journal* story profiled María Martin and her husband who opened a lodging near the Basilica de San Martiño de Mondoñedo, on the Camiño del Mar. A proposed development would result in the installation of a cluster of 105m-tall turbines, which would serve to power the aluminum smelter in neighboring San Ciprian. The threat seemed existential to Martin; who would choose a turbine cluster as the site of their relaxing rural vacation? Regardless, after a short setback around 2013-16, the wind industry has proven that it's built to last in Spain.

As the technology develops, there is cause for hope that future wind farms won't require such conspicuous and naturally scenic locations. More recent installations have occurred deeper into the high plains of Castilla y León, Castilla-La Mancha, and the Ebro Valley, as newer turbines are able to function with lower wind speeds. These still have the potential to dramatically alter an environment; pilgrims on the Camino de Madrid near Peñaflor de Hornija can certainly attest to the impact of the massive wind farm interspersed among the fields. But if the economic benefits can infuse funds into more modest regions, while protecting more dramatic and vulnerable landscapes in service to preservation and tourism, it may prove to be a workable solution.

Can green energy installations and tourism coexist harmoniously? Again, I look back at my first visit to the Alto del Perdón and can't help but remember the enthusiasm I felt as I climbed towards the turbine, marveling at its towering form and its languorous blades. It didn't detract from the experience; on the contrary, it fed into the mythic feel. It's impossible to know how differently I might have felt if my first visit had preceded this installation; I suspect that I would have felt a sense of betrayal or bitterness at this sacred landscape being sullied.

The darker truth, though, is that the landscape had already been sullied, decades before. After you pass through the Alto del Perdón, pause before continuing onward. That won't be hard; it's an unpleasant thing to consider, making that jarring descent through the rocky stream bed. To your left, though, is something even more unpleasant to witness. It's a memorial, established in 2017 by Peio Iraizoz, that preserves the tragic story of what befell here during the Spanish Civil War. The NA-1110 road passes by, linking Estella and Pamplona, and in those years it often served as a conduit for the transport of political prisoners. For some, though, this marked the end of the line. At least 64 prisoners were executed here, at Alto del Perdón, while another 28 were killed elsewhere in the Sierra. The memorial features a set of 20 stones, organized in a spiral, to commemorate those 92 victims. Without question, there were others shot in this area. The problem is that the silence that pervaded the Franco years blocked any possibility of inquiry. The earliest exhumations occurred in the late 1970s, but they were far

from sufficient, and as the decades passed different construction projects transformed the land. We may never know
how many lives were taken here. Several months after the
memorial's inauguration, it suffered an act of vandalism.
A legendary fountain. A hermitage and sanctuary. A
road to forgiveness. A site of execution. A monument to a
millennium of pilgrimage and a transformative wind farm.
What might otherwise appear to be a quiet, lonely hilltop is
so much more than that.

Keep reading...

Guillermo Abril, "Por qué en Navarra triunfó la energía
    eólica," *El País*, 2017

Javier Faulin, et. al., "The outlook for renewable energy in
    Navarre: An economic profile," *Energy Policy*, 2006

José Javier Azanza López, "Peregrinos en piedra y bronce:
    El monumento conmemorativo jacobeo como
    patrimonio cultural y artístico del Camino," *Cuadernos
    de la Cátedra de Patrimonio*, 2011

Marina Frolova, et. al., "The Evolution of Renewable
    Landscapes in Sierra Nevada (Southern Spain): From
    Small Hydro- to a Wind-Power Landscape," *Renewable
    Energies and European Landscapes*, 2015

Matthew Dalton, "Tourism and Manufacturing Fight for the
    Future of Power in Europe," *Wall Street Journal*, 2023

P. Chias and T. Abad, "Impact Assessment of the Renewable Energies in the Cultural Heritage: The Case of the Way of St. James in Spain," *The International Archives of the Photogrammetry, Remote Sensing and Spatial Information Sciences*, 2014

Raquel Fernández-González, et. al., "The New Wind Energy Boom in Spain: Are Large Companies Once Again Dominating the Market?," *Energy Transition*, 2022

The Last Iberian Jews

Stage 5: Puente la Reina to Estella

First came England in 1290. France was next, originally in 1306 and then a second time in 1394, when Germany joined it. Not until 1492 did Spain follow suit, after the fall of Granada and the triumph of Ferdinand and Isabella. Portugal held out a bit longer, but in 1496 it finally yielded.

From one country after another, the Jewish populations were expelled, forced to pack up their belongings, sell what they could, and seek a port–any port–in the midst of the storm. It's not to say that life had been harmonious, that they had been treated well, or protected from abuse even, but it still must have been among the greatest tragedies of their lives.

While both Spain and Portugal had completed this process of ethnic cleansing by 1496, Jews remained on the Iberian peninsula, in one small corner. The Kingdom of Navarre, still independent, for a little longer yet, maintained its population, where Jews had found an oasis of stability for generations. It would only survive for two more years.

As discussed in Stage 3, Navarre has a distinct history within the Iberian peninsula, and while its geographic location has offered some economic advantages, this has also posed political challenges. The kingdom dates to the early 9th century, when the Basque population selected Iñigo Arista to rule as the first princeps. Its initial period of independence came to an end in 1054, when it fell under the sway of Aragón, but this was reversed with the ascension of King García Ramírez 'El Restaurador' in 1134. It took the papacy a while, but Pope Celestine III finally recognized Navarrese independence in 1196.

It was good while it lasted. In 1234, Sancho VII, King of Navarre, failed to produce an heir, and thus the crown passed onto Count Thibaut IV of Champagne. Not until 1328 would Navarre's monarch again reside in Navarre. Despite the musical monarchs, though, the region itself was relatively stable, and it featured a genuinely diverse population, including Aragones, Basques, Castilians, French, Gascons, Muslims, and, of course, Jews.

In fact, the Jewish community of Navarre was among the most significant in the Iberian peninsula. In the 12th century, Navarre's Jewish population clustered primarily in the towns of Estella, Pamplona, Sangüesa, and Tudela, and over the succeeding years the Jewish population grew. In the 13th and 14th centuries, estimates suggest that Jews comprised as much as 6% of the region's total population, with 300-400 families or 3000 people total. By their last century in Navarre, the region's Jewish population had dipped to 3.5% overall, but it's difficult to know how much of that is reflective of emigration and how much is a consequence of conversion.

But again, it was good while it lasted, even if it didn't start out well. When Alfonso I took Tudela in 1119, the Jewish population fled, though it was eventually enticed to return after royal assurances that it would carry the king's protection, and that religious freedom would be respected.

Within 50 years, another monarch, Sancho VI, gifted the fortified area overlooking Tudela to the Jewish community, a statement of its growing importance. That importance resulted in Navarre's Jews receiving a special status in the region, distinct from their peers in Spain and France. Even as Jews were expelled from the countries surrounding Navarre, they were welcomed here, and allowed to establish self-governing communities, *aljamas*, where they benefited from a number of privileges, and synagogues within which to practice their faith. The *aljamas* were empowered to organize their own taxes and invest the funds accordingly within their communities, while also being assured of the Crown's protection. It should be noted that at many points Navarre's Jews weren't actually required to live in an *aljama*, and a surprisingly significant number opted to live in predominantly Christian neighborhoods. The Jewish communities might have been exempt from taxes, but they still had financial obligations, in the form of the *pecha*, an annual contribution to the king, but in return they were allowed to own land and had free choice of occupations.

These policies weren't purely an act of goodness and decency by the Navarrese throne; on the contrary, it represented the economically prudent approach, adding significant wealth to the region. Jews were highly valued in public service. They served as royal ambassadors, secret agents, and intermediaries, but most important of all they were dependable tax farmers and indispensable money lenders, performing a pair of crucial, if sometimes unpopular, roles. (It's worth noting that what made tax collection especially labor-intensive is that there wasn't a single tax. In Tudela alone, there are records of Jews collecting *eleven* different taxes, including animal trading, fresh fish, salted fish, candles, fresh bacon, and salted goat meat.) Jewish physicians and surgeons were highly valued as well; as one example, the most famous Rabbi in Navarre, Juce Orabuena, served as the personal physician of King Charles II. They were also esteemed as craftsmen, and Jewish-made clothing, furs, and silverware were all well used at the court. Jews were also significant landowners, with a special emphasis on vineyards. Food was their primary focus as merchants, particularly fish, which held special importance during Lent. An important point to emphasize here is that the Jewish and Christian populations of Navarre, as well as the Muslim contingent, for that matter, were significantly integrated–socially and economically–even acknowledging the distinctly Jewish neighborhoods. They relied upon one another.

There is ample reason to believe that Jews stood on equal footing with Christians before the law. The Navarrese courts emphasized proper representation, oath-taking, and witnesses, with special sensitivity paid to inter-religious encounters. The laws of Estella, dating to 1164, offer an example of this: "If a Jew owed anything to a Christian neighbour of Estella, and the Jew denied the claim, the Christian will have to prove his case with two witnesses: one Christian neighbour of Estella, and one Jewish one. And if a Christian owed a Jew likewise." A Jew's oath in court carried every bit as much weight as a Christian's.

This is not to suggest that Jewish life in Navarre was perfect. There were ongoing efforts to push Jews towards conversion, as occurred throughout Spain, and these could generate tensely emotional encounters. The story of Samuel Ciriz, a Jew from Viana, stands out as an illustrative case. After originally declaring his intention to convert, he changed his mind. Given the abundance of stories of family members intervening in such situations, it's easy to imagine the significant pressure that he faced. When he backtracked, though, he incurred a 200-florin fine for making a "mockery" of Christianity. Problems also surfaced when sexual relations between Jews and Christians took place—or were merely rumored—and cases of conversion added further complications. For example, in 1373 a *conversa*, a Jewish woman who converted to Catholicism, had a Jewish lover from Tudela. She was condemned to burn for the act, while he was fined 100 florins. As Makoto Kato stresses, though, such stories are quite rare, and adultery with a Christian rarely resulted in this level of violence.

Similarly, there are broader instances of violence against Jews in Navarre, but they largely function as examples that prove the rule, highlighting the relatively unusual occurrence of these acts within the region. The short period of French rule, in particular, brought with it some of the discriminatory attitudes and practices that had contributed to Jewish expulsion north of the border, culminating in the destruction of Pamplona's *aljama* in 1276 and the confiscation of Jewish properties in other towns. An even more shameful chapter would unfold in Estella, a town where Jews had previously enjoyed a good deal of success. The community had thrived since settling here in the late 11th century, first establishing their *aljama* in the Elgacena neighborhood, before relocating it to the bailey of the castle of Belmecher in 1135. As David Gitlitz and Linda Davidson note, by 1264 the Jewish community had grown to 10% of the town's total population, with 110 families. Tragically, in 1328, in the midst of the Navarran civil war, a Franciscan friar stirred up a massacre of a significant portion of the town's Jewish population, while plundering multiple *aljamas*. The five leaders were subsequently hanged in Estella. And yet, Navarre escaped the anti-Jewish pogroms that scarred so many Iberian towns as the Black Death ravaged the peninsula in the mid-14th century. In addition, Navarre's Jews were quick to fight back and stand up for their rights at many other points, which perhaps underscores their sense of belonging and internalization of rights in the region.

Given all of that, why did this come to an end? Why did King Johan and Queen Catalina of Navarre ultimately turn their backs on their Jewish subjects? Once again, Navarre's geographical reality demands attention. By 1492, it was flanked by two burgeoning superpowers, with Spain having nearly completed its territorial expansion–just one Navarrese-shaped piece was absent from that puzzle–and France having finally extricated itself from the Hundred Years War, along with British occupation. And the century leading to that point had witnessed a deteriorating climate for Jews in Spain, culminating in the establishment of the Spanish Inquisition in 1478. As waves of violence crashed against Spain's Jewish communities in the wake of the Black Death, many finally gave in and opted to convert, at least publicly, to Catholicism. In the process, though, the "Jewish Problem" gave way to the "Converso Problem," as Church officials grew paranoid about insincere Conversos continuing to practice their faith in private and corrupt their more sincere peers, who were condemned as heretics.

The Inquisition lacked jurisdiction in Navarre, but its burgeoning presence near the border soon complicated matters. This came to a head in September 1485, when a group of Zaragozans rose up against the local Inquisitor, stabbing him to death in the cathedral. Several escaped into Navarre, hiding in Tudela. The Navarrese held firmly to their independence, prohibiting all inquisitorial edicts within their borders, and even chased a covert Inquisitorial agent back to Aragón.

Ferdinand and Isabella were not going to tolerate this. First, the king demanded that the murderers be handed over, threatening significant consequences for Tudela if they did not comply. Next, the monarchs turned to Pope Innocent VIII for support. He backed their play, issuing a Papal letter in April 1487 prohibiting any Christian ruler from admitting individuals fleeing the Inquisition, under penalty of excomm-unication. The Spanish monarchs only grew more belligerent from there, disrupting Navarrese commerce and establishing offices of the Inquisition along the border. However dis-tasteful, however unpleasant, Navarre finally had to yield, allowing Inquisitors into the country to investigate pending cases.

This marked the beginning of the end for Navarre's Jews.

For many years, historians argued that the expulsion of Navarre's Jews in 1498 was merely the final nail in the coffin. Salo Baron, for example, claimed that the community was "dying [...] even before it was struck down by formal decree of expulsion in 1498." In *The Last Jews on Iberian Soil: Navarrese Jewry 1479-1498*, though, Benjamin R. Gampel arrived at a starkly different conclusion. As he writes, "these Jews, though not scaling the political or economic heights attained by their predecessors, were demographically vital, economically vibrant, and communally capable of providing for the needs of their fellow Jews even as they maintained the welter of financial obligations to the Navarrese political entities to whom they were subject."

Perhaps they should have seen it coming. After all, in just the last six years, they had watched their Portuguese and Spanish peers' worlds tossed asunder; a not insignifi-cant number of those refugees had stumbled into Navarre, perhaps as many as 1,800. They have been accused of "ostrich-like behavior" for keeping things business as usual. And indeed, business-as-usual prevailed in Navarre in many ways; Gampel's meticulous surveying of the available evidence shows that no discernible shift occurred in the volume of property sales and debt liquidations in the years leading up to 1498, and Jews continued entering into long-term contracts during that same period. Those are not the actions of a people preparing for the worst, readying themselves to hit the road.

But when the expulsion order was issued as the calendar tipped to 1498, what could Navarre's Jews do? They had until March to either depart the region or convert to Catholicism. That makes it sound like they had two options. However, Navarre is a landlocked region, and it offered no viable evacuation route. Ferdinand and Isabella wouldn't permit passage, and the only country north of Navarre, France, had already been closed off to Jews for more than a century.

To remain a Jew required one to become a fugitive, in the hope that one might evade arrest long enough to reach a less hostile country. Gampel relates the story of Shemtov ben Shmuel Gamil, whose saga exemplifies the challenges involved. Gamil first headed towards Valencia, through Aragón, hoping to reach his children. He owned a business in Valencia, so it seemed like a safe bet. However, upon arrival he learned that his children had fled, while the business had been sacked. Gamil, meanwhile, was arrested, locked away for three weeks. After being saved by a young Muslim, he successfully reunited with his children, heading south with the goal of reaching Morocco. First, they had to reroute in order to avoid the Inquisition; then, in Almería, they were captured. Again, a Muslim assisted with their escape, and they proceeded to take up shelter in Granada, from where they planned to join a caravan to Morocco. Alas, they were ensnared once more, setting in motion their most prolonged stretch behind bars, nearly eight months in all, before finally making it onto a ship across the Mediterranean.

Such a gamble represented no choice at all for most Jews. So what could they do? They converted. Under coercion, with no viable alternative available, they abandoned their faith, their traditions, their identity. They became Catholics.

The expulsion of Navarre's Jews, in the words of Anna Katarzyna Dulska, "broke the thread" not only linking Jewish presence and activity there, but also of "the 'Jewishness' of Jewish quarters for over three centuries." In Estella, the *aljama* was completely abandoned following the expulsion order in the 16th century, and was soon overgrown with brush. It remained so, utterly forgotten, until some initial efforts were made to recover this area in the 1990s. Precious little progress has been made, beyond some small-scale archaeological efforts in 2017, but even those fleeting attempts were abandoned–for now, at least–due to property ownership issues.

One reminder, however modest, has made its mark on Estella. As a pilgrim, you're already used to keeping one eye on the road, watching for those bronze waymarks embedded in the pavement or cobblestones. In Estella, those have company. The Red de Juderías de España, or the Network of Jewish Quarters of Spain, has installed waymarks to call attention to these lost Jewish spaces, all across the country. Sadly, the original waymarks installed in Estella were promptly stolen. (The Camino markers were left untouched.) The replacements, though, have remained. They, at least, are still there.

Keep reading...

Alan D. Crown, "The last Jews on Iberian soil: Navarrese Jewry 1479-1498 (review)," *Parergon*, 1992

Anna Katarzyna Dulska, "Urban Jewish Heritage and its (in)visibility," *Journal of Heritage Tourism*, 2021

Benjamin R. Gampel, *The Last Jews on Iberian Soil: Navarrese Jewry 1479-1498*, 1989

David Gitlitz and Linda Davidson, *The Pilgrimage Road to Santiago: The Complete Cultural Handbook*, 2000

Lidia Becker, "Names of Jews in Medieval Navarre (13th–14th centuries)," *Names in a Multi-Lingual, Multi-Cultural and Multi-Ethnic World*, 2009

Makoto Kato, "Jews in Late Medieval Navarre," 2012

Rodrigo García-Velasco Bernal, "'Alā fūr Tutīla': Jews and Muslims in the Administrative Culture of Post-Conquest Tudela, c.1118–1220," *Al-Masaq*, 2017

Yom Tov Assis and Mark Meyerson, "The Iberian Peninsula," *The Cambridge History of Judaism: Part I, Jews in the Medieval Christian World*, 2018

All Hail the King

Stage 6: Estella to Torres del Río

In the English-speaking world, certain names feature most prominently when we start diving into the Camino de Santiago's 20th century resurgence. David Gitlitz and Linda Davidson stand at the forefront, and their masterpiece, *The Pilgrimage Road to Santiago: The Complete Cultural Handbook*, remains an essential resource for today's pilgrims. Jack Hitt, Laurie Dennett, and Edwin Mullins all hit the trail in the early stages of its return to glory, producing influential accounts of the walk, as did the more famous Shirley MacLaine and Paulo Coelho, though their books were, shall we say, more deeply embellished. Walter Starkie beat them all, and his *The Road to Santiago: Pilgrims of St. James* offers an invaluable perspective on the Camino in the 1950s.

Aside from Starkie, each of those authors remains in circulation, drawing varying degrees of attention from today's Camino-philes. And yet, lost in the wash, except to the most hardcore of contemporary pilgrims and academics, is perhaps the greatest of them all. Georgiana Goddard King represented a pioneer in several arenas. Born in West Virginia in 1871, she became a tremendously influential art historian, playing a key role in the first university department specializing in Spanish art at Bryn Mawr College.

Between 1913 and 1916, King made a series of trips to Spain, supported by the Hispanic Society of America and in the company of an accomplished photographer, with the goal of documenting medieval Spanish architecture and culture. This led her to the Camino de Santiago, which she traveled as a pilgrim, and culminated in her three-part tour de force, *The Way of Saint James*. Bringing together reflections from the road and her perceptive critical insights on the art and architecture of the way, this has held up remarkably well over the past century. Indeed, as Robin Haedong Kim has demonstrated, contemporary art historians would do well to begin their inquiry with King, who was ahead of the curve in so many ways.

We need look no further than Torres del Río for a perfect example of this. The small town, nestled in the crook of a hillside, features a tiny shrine, the *Iglesia del Santo Sepulcro*. For those who previously made the detour to Eunate–as you should, if at all possible–it seems like the matching pair to that site's *Iglesia de Santa María*. Both are compact, octagonal, and feature ribbed vaulting; they are also, it should be underscored, wonderfully evocative. That design has long tempted art historians to link these churches to the Holy Sepulcher of Jerusalem and the Knights Templar (see Stage 23 for more), originating with studies conducted by Pedro Emiliano Zorrilla and Julio Altadill y Torrontera de Sancho San Román in the 1910s. The connection, in their view, was straightforward enough: in order to evoke the great shrine of Jerusalem, the argument ran, Templars built replicas across Europe, borrowing the octagonal shape and "oriental"-style dome. Their theory took root and continued to shape the perception of both churches for the past century.

Around the same time, though, King paid her own visit to Torres del Río. She begins her account by describing the pilgrim's approach to the town:

> "At about the same distance from Estella in the opposite direction lies another example of the same rare type of church as Eunate, finer and more splendid, albeit unknown. El Sepulcro of Torres, octagonal, has dome and lantern, projecting apse, and separate staircase turret intact. The Logroño road curls around a hill-set city, and then in a wide curve sweeps down steeply to the shallow river valley: and thence you look across to Torres on the ascending hill, and catch the sun on lantern tower and arcaded sides."

Part of the joy of reading King's account, beyond her perceptive observations of the featured architecture, is the slice of life aspect, capturing a glimpse of village life in the years around World War I. For example, she affords us an opportunity to see a markedly different Torres del Río than we encounter today, one filled with children:

> "...a French ecclesiologist, it is said, driving through the country eight or ten years ago, before private motors had grown general, saw, and stopped to see more and to photograph, and was much molested by the crowding curious children. They are indeed tiresome as gnats, but not badhearted, except one boy, cross-eyed and cross-spirited; and their elders rebuked and dispersed them a dozen times, but always they gathered again, filling the open doorway of the empty church, and blotting out the patch of sunlight on the floor."

Even the dining experience carries unusual heft in King's narrative sweep:

> "Down at the inn on the post-road, friendly folk kept delicately out of the way, and the traveller lunched alone [...] with only a murmur of voices quiet as summer flies, reading and discussing the newspaper that she had brought down that morning by chance. Oh, the courtesy of these small Spanish places, so conscious yet so sure! Just because it is not spontaneous and necessary and personal, as in Tuscany, it tastes the sweeter. Here the landlord still feels himself the host, and the traveller the guest. The pretty daughter of the house, who served the table, was found in calico at the early arrival, and dressed herself in serge for dinner, and dressed her black hair, and craved pardon because the cares of house and kitchen prevented her sitting down to entertain."

But we're here to discuss the church, not King's lunch, and we thus turn to her descriptions of the place. It was invaluable, of course, to have a photographer along for the ride, and it's a pleasure to have the fruits of their labor included in the book, but King paints such a picture that her narrative could easily stand on its own. First, the exterior:

> "The wall arcade outside is pointed; noble columns run the full height at every angle; noble windows fill the centre of each bay in the stage above and admit light through pierced stone tracery into the interior; two windows under the wall ribs flank the apse. The door is a low round arch, a third of a circle, with the Patriarchal cross carved on the tympanum, with the

hood-moulding carved in dog-tooth, and a leaf on the abacus at the jamb. Shafts and capitals are lost. The corbels under the roof are fluted in four scallops, horizontally, the nearest thing to this being the supports of the cornice at Celanova, where the Mozarabic work goes back to the ninth or tenth century. The cornice is a shallow hollow in which lie balls, a Romanesque motive in Spain, already seen about Jaca and on the way to S. Juan de la Pena. The lantern, floored and blocked up, like that of S. Cruz de la Serós, has a small, round-headed window in each face and a column with blunt capital at each corner, a heavy cornice, and a door that opens on the western side, to which lead steps from the staircase tower. This lantern and the access to it resemble probably those originally at S. Martin of Fromista. The roof, like that of Eunate, consists of heavy slabs of stone, now well sunk in mortar. It carried once a stone cross over all, but that being destroyed not long since by a thunderstorm, a clock was set in, of which the face occupies the south wall, and the weights hang down, outside, in the north-west angle between church and tower."

One of King's greatest qualities as a scholar is her ability to draw connections between churches, approaching the architecture like a detective, seeking stylistic links across place and time. Above, we see her situating Torres del Río's *Iglesia del Santo Sepulcro* within the context of other churches along the Camino Francés and Camino Aragonés, but as her focus shifts to the church's interior, her aperture widens:

"Inside, a low stone bench runs all around, and the shafts of the lower range have disappeared, but their capitals, billet moulded, project from a string course of the same pattern, and on these descend the upper columns. Outside and inside, the church has a tripartite division marked by horizontal lines: without, one crosses at the springing of the wall arch, and the other at the sills of the windows: within, one at the point where the arch of the apse springs, and the other where the dome-ribs and the vault begin. The capitals of the upper range are varied: an oriental rosette of whorls, a centaur, a formal pattern based on the honeysuckle, pine cones, a leaf pattern based on the acanthus, network, leaf and pine cone, leaves in two rows forming a rich and broken pattern. It is vaulted with ribs that pass across and leave an open star at the centre: these come down on the shafts just named, at the corners, and on corbels fluted like those without, in the middle of each side. This sort of vault Street saw in a chapel of the cloister at Salamanca, and the present writer saw in one at Las Huelgas. It is Mudéjar: the workmen may have come from the Mozarabic quarter of Calatayud, or from elsewhere: in 1211, a certain Miguel de Burgana gave to the Prior and the Canons a Saracen slave that he had in Gotor. In the vault appear eight tiny windows of pierced stone, crowned with Mudéjar cusping like some at Toledo, and by tabernacles, 'heavenly Jerusalems' like those of the school of Chartres. The same sort of tabernacle reappears on a capital at Sangüesa, which belonged to S. John of the Hospital, at Villasirga, which was a Templar's church, at Carrión close by, and at Moarbes copied from Carrion, but these are not the only instances, even along the way. In the case of Sangüesa, Torres, and Villasirga, it may refer to the earthly Jerusalem, of which the lords in one sense all were knights. At the entrance to the sanctuary, where under a pointed arch a section of pointed barrel-vault precedes the semi-dome, stand two columns with well moulded bases and storied capitals: on the north, the Deposition in a form that seems copied from Master Benedetto's at Parma, on the south, the empty Sepulchre left after the Resurrection, as at Aries. The design on the abacus I do not understand, unless it was imitated from metal work. In the upper part of the two bays nearest the apse, windows open, their jamb shafts duly storied in the Romanesque vein.

"Here, then, is oddly assorted matter, gathered up by the side of the Way: capitals derived from Greek, from Roman, from Romanesque, and from Oriental sources, handiwork recalling Mudéjar, French, and Italian artizans."

Even an untrained eye, like mine, can quickly discern from King's account how nuanced her analysis is, particularly in comparison to a more simplistic approach that would equate an octagonal structure and a ribbed vault with a Templar homage. Still, an expert perspective can deepen our understanding of the matters at hand. In her insightful study, *The Santo Sepulcro in Torres del Río*, Robin Haedong Kim underscores the ahead-of-her-time nature of King's observations.

First, already in 1918 King called attention to the fact that in the Middle Ages Torres del Río had two religious structures, not one, and the conflation of these has continued to be a major source of confusion. Only six historical documents survive that speak to the town's churches, but fully half of them allude to an older church, the Santa María de la Redonda. It was first referenced in 1100, when funds were donated to the Monastery of Irache (famous for its wine fountain) to support the development of a monastery in Torres. A papal bull from 1172 reiterates the connection. King, though, recognized that the Santo Sepulcro is an entirely different church, while the Redonda is long gone.

This observation was crucial, because the second and more significant point flows naturally from there. The Templars, as King already recognized, had nothing to do with Torres del Río. On the contrary, we need only look at a different papal bull, dating to 1215, which outlined the possessions of the Order of the Holy Sepulchre in Iberia. That would be reinforced in the 14th century by a document naming Fray Pedro de Torres as the Knight Commander of the "house" of the "Santo Sepulcro de Torres."

Of the three military orders operating in the Iberian peninsula during the Spanish crusade–the Templars, the Hospitallers, and the Holy Sepulchre–the latter certainly holds a distant third place in public consciousness, and even that might be an overstatement. Like the Templars and Hospitallers, the Order of the Holy Sepulchre sought to protect pilgrims to the Holy Land, even if their operations in Iberia took a more classically monastic stance. Unlike the Templars, though, it survives, with some 30,000 knights continuing in service.

(Incidentally, given the similarities between the churches of Torres del Río and Eunate, it's worth noting that rumors of the latter's association with the Templars appear to be equ= ally spurious, as are the suggestions that it might include a pilgrim graveyard. On the contrary, credible evidence has been pushed forward by José María Jimeno Jurio to spotlight a connection between Eunate and an even more obscure order, the Brotherhood of Onat; the cemetery that exists outside the church would have served as a burial ground for the brothers. One takeaway from this discussion: while some art history questions are complex and require intense study, when we learn that the *Iglesia de Santo Sepulcro* belonged to the Holy Sepulchre, and the church of Eunate belonged to Onat, it's hard not to conclude that some scholars were vastly over-complicating matters. The answers were hiding in plain sight, right there in the names!)

King's most consequential observation was the connection she found between Santo Sepulcro and Mudéjar architecture. Instead of the direct link to the Holy Land offered by those asserting the Templar ties, King saw connections to the convent of Las Huelgas in Burgos and inferred that the architects may have come from Calatayud, near Zaragoza. The term Mudéjar applies to Muslims who remained in Iberia following the conclusion of the *Reconquista*, and the architectural style associated with this brings together Romanesque, Gothic, and Islamic elements. While Kim prefers the term Mozárabic, which refers to Christians who lived under Islamic rule during the centuries associated with the *Reconquista*, that distinction, while important in its own way, distracts from the larger point.

Navarre, Kim explains, has embraced the *Reconquista* narrative more, perhaps, than any other region in Spain. As Navarre rewrote its history in the 19th and early 20th centuries, it sought to ground its origins in the legends of indigenous Iberians, including the Cantabri people who were celebrated for their heroic resistance to all intruders. Within the narrower realm of art history, Kim claims, this has resulted in the erasure of Islamic influence from the region's architecture. Instead, the popular narrative asserts, Navarre's distinct style is the consequence of the Camino's influence, which brought an influx of foreigners, including many artists, along with monastic and military orders. And that is true, to a point; certainly, significant influences made their way southward into Navarre, but it would be foolish to ignore the north-bound movements as a consequence.

There's an important reminder to be found in all of this: Some would view art as separate from politics, appealing and satisfying in its own right, but perhaps less substantial than fields that appear to have a more direct, tangible impact on the world. However, even centuries after its construction, this small church in Torres del Río, seemingly so removed from the more bustling parts of contemporary Spain, remains a compelling piece of evidence in an ongoing debate about the story of medieval Iberia. Of course, if more of us would have listened to Georgiana Goddard King, we probably would have arrived at this point sooner.

Keep reading...

Georgiana Goddard King, *The Way of Saint James*, 1920

Javier Martínez de Aguirre, "Evocaciones de Jerusalén en la arquitectura del Camino de Santiago: el Santo Sepulcro y la Santa Cruz," *8th International Congress of Jacobean Studies*, 2012

Pedro Emiliano Zorrilla, "Otra iglesia de Templarios en Navarra. El Santo Sepulcro de la villa de Torres," *Boletín de la Comisión de Monumentos Históricos y Artísticos de Navarra*, 1914

Robin Haedong Kim, *The Santo Sepulcro in Torres del Río*, 2015

The Death of Cesare Borgia

Stage 7: Torres del Río to Logroño

While some chapters in this book focus on topics for which we suffer from an unfortunate dearth of credible information, this one seemed straightforward enough. For five hundred years, the Borgia family has been the subject of one book after another, and more recently one television series after another. It even inspired one of the Assassin's Creed video games. Even better, the obvious truth of the Borgias was salacious, titillating, and grizzly. What could be more fun to write about?

The problem, it turns out, is that a staggering portion of the Borgia story, or perhaps the Borgia legend would be a better way of framing it, has been built upon utterly spurious sources, including some of the most prominent satirists and gossips of the era, along with the family's most hated rivals in the aftermath of their fall. G.J. Meyer's work, *The Borgias: The Hidden History*, among other contemporary works, has helped to expose the deceits, along with the shoddy historiography, and forced a reckoning.

For our purposes, the most infamous Borgia, Cesare, stands at the center of this narrative, because when you visit Viana you might choose to stand on Cesare's remains. This is by design. While the man was originally buried within the town's *Iglesia de Santa María*, at some point between 1523 and 1549, perhaps at the instigation of a nearby bishop, he was kicked out of the club, his original tomb destroyed. He wasn't relocated to the cemetery; even that would have been too good for him. Instead, his remains were dumped in a hole at the base of the stairs leading to the main road, so that he would be "trampled on by man and beasts forever."

Truly, it seemed that no family had accrued comparable scorn, derision, or animosity to what the Borgias had achieved. Here is the legend as it fully metastasized, with special attention paid to the juiciest details. Gotta keep those pages turning...

The story begins with Alonso de Borja, who would become Alfonso de Borgia, and then eventually Pope Calixtus III. Even the greatest Borgia haters have a difficult time ascribing too much of his rise to nefarious affairs; instead, he benefited from good timing, better luck, the savvy choosing of sides, and maybe a wee bit of tactical violence on the side. He became the pope largely due to his innocuous nature and advanced age; he represented an inoffensive compromise, chosen by two hostile factions that couldn't push their preferred candidates over the finish line. His greatest passion in that role was to call for a crusade against the Seljuk Turks, responding to the growing threat that had just taken Constantinople a couple years prior. On the side, he elevated many of his family members to positions in Rome, but nepotism was hardly unheard of for church officials, and again, there's little indication that he ever exceeded the norms of the period. The greatest beneficiary of his familial largesse, Rodrigo, not only became a Cardinal, but also the Vice-Chancellor of the Holy Roman Church, a position in many regards akin to a modern chief executive officer.

With Calixtus's demise, Rodrigo and two younger Borgias, Cesare and Lucrezia, rose to prominence, and over time they comprised the heart of the dark legend. After decades of service as vice-chancellor, Rodrigo followed Alonso into the papacy, becoming Pope Alexander VI, and the accusations of scandal were hot on his heels. He sold cardinalates, critics claimed, to pad his pockets. Rumors circulated that he sought an alliance with the Muslim Turks against the Christian French. When the French swept through Italy in response, an invasion blamed in this account on Alexander's indiscretions, tongues wagged, that he dangled the heads of Peter and Paul over the ramparts, calling upon their power as relics to ward off the enemy.

Johann Burchard, a Renaissance chronicler whose account of the Borgia papacy has been at the heart of historical writing on the subject, summed up Alexander's reign with unflinching condemnation: "There is no longer any crime or shameful act that does not take place in public in Rome and in the home of the Pontiff. Who could fail to be horrified by the...terrible, monstrous acts of lechery that are committed openly in his home, with no respect for God or man? Rapes and acts of incest are countless...[and] great throngs of courtesans frequent Saint Peter's Palace, pimps, brothels, and whorehouses are to be found everywhere!"

While Cesare was fast-tracked into roles that were the envy of all in Europe—including bishop of Pamplona at 15, archbishop at 17, and cardinal at 18—he resented the limitations of a career in the Church. He grew so jealous of his brother Juan's wealth, it was claimed, and so embittered towards the young man's military incompetence, that Cesare arranged for Juan's murder. Cesare was also linked to plans for the murder of Lucrezia's first husband. While that marriage would be annulled—Cesare pressured her husband into admitting impotence in order to justify this—Lucrezia was pregnant, and rumors circulated that Cesare was the father, only to add that given her widely-discussed sluttishness, how could anyone be sure? When Lucrezia remarried, the husband was actually murdered, with Cesare once again receiving the credit. Other bodies were hitting the floor, including multiple Cardinals. Throughout this time, the Borgias became closely associated with rumors of poison, employed to eliminate rivals and steal their wealth. When Cesare finally gained release from his Church-bound life, the first man to ever resign a cardinalate, he transformed into a beacon of violence, sweeping across the Romagna without restraint, more force of nature than man.

The relationships between Alexander, Cesare, and Lucrezia consistently drew the most scurrilous rumors. These are most succinctly captured in a mock epitaph, written by the Italian poet Sannazaro, following Lucrezia's death: "Here rests Lucrezia by name [...] the daughter, wife and daughter-in-law of [Pope] Alexander." You might need to make a diagram.

Fun stuff, right? The Borgia legend has entertained generations of readers for half a millennium now, and with good reason. Perhaps it's unfortunate, then, that historians like Meyer have decided to let the facts (or the absence of them, at least) get in the way of a good story.

Let's begin with Pope Alexander's personal character. Meyer does some of his best work in this discussion, using the decades of Rodrigo's service as vice-chancellor to substantiate his claims. While Rodrigo certainly benefited from Calixtus's nepotism in his elevation to the role, his persistence in it as the papacy changed hands multiple times speaks to his efficacy and reliability. Pope Sixtus IV depended upon Rodrigo, not only for the execution of those core responsibilities, but also special assignments, like when he sent Rodrigo as a legate to Iberia to recruit support for a crusade and address some other local concerns. On that journey, Rodrigo was broadly empowered to "dispense papal indulgences in return for support of the crusade, pardon crimes other than murder, settle property disputes, impose a special tithe on the incomes of Spanish clerics, and even offer appointments to the College of Cardinals." He was even given the power to excommunicate. Rodrigo exceeded all expectations, going beyond his foundational task to resolve three key points of tension in the region. First, he helped to negotiate peace between the Catalans and Aragón. Next, he cleared the way for Ferdinand and Isabella to marry, despite being first cousins. Finally, he persuaded King Enrique IV of Castile to recognize Isabella as heir to that throne, meaning that the foundation had been laid for the unification of Castile and Aragón.

While that's just one story from Rodrigo's 35 years of service as vice-chancellor, again, his longevity in the role underscores his competence. Critics might acknowledge this, while still condemning him for padding his pockets in this role, an accusation that would follow all Borgias as they were elevated to positions of prominence. What is absent from these reasonable assumptions is an accurate under-standing of the expectations imposed on Church officials in these years. While each title and role brought with it increased wealth, the recipients were also expected to cover their expenses. Given the image and authority they were tasked with promoting, and the bribes that might be required to oil the machinery, many found themselves strapped for cash. To return to the example at hand, Rodrigo's elevation to legate was accompanied by the abbey of Subiaco near Tivoli and the bishopric of Albano, along with a special papal bull that released him from the obligation of yielding any of the benefices previously granted to him by earlier popes. And yet, within two months, he already lacked funds, seeking approval to mortgage or auction off future revenues to generate the money necessary for his immediate responsibilities. Certainly, Rodrigo was hardly a pauper, but far from cynically enriching himself at the expense of the Church, an argument can be made that he maximized his available resources to ensure the effective discharging of his duties.

For all the condemnation that had already been and would continue to be lavished upon the Borgias for nepotism, it's worth pausing at this point to recognize that Sixtus was utterly shameless on this front. Among all the beneficiaries of his shamelessness, Sixtus's favorite, Pietro Riario, was rumored by many to be the pope's son (another Borgia parallel, given the stories that would circulate around Rodrigo and Cesare). As Meyer puts it, Pietro enjoyed "an avalanche of nepotistic largesse. He was archbishop of Florence as well as bishop of a handful of cities and head of the great abbey of Saint Ambrose in Milan, and he bore the honorary title of patriarch of Constantinople. His income was stupendous [...] but so inadequate to his way of life that he was piling up debts at a rate that should have alarmed Sixtus." It wasn't enough for Pietro; nothing could be enough. Instead, he plotted with Milan's Duke Galeazzo Maria Sforza to have the duke elevated to King of Lombardy, after which he would march on Rome and establish Pietro as the pope. Before he could hatch the plan, though, Pietro was struck down by fever. There are two points to emphasize here. First, many of the behaviors attributed to the Borgias with accompanying shocked outrage were commonplace at the time. And second, in many regards, the Borgias—Alonso, Rodrigo, and Lucrezia first and foremost—seem to have held themselves to a higher standard than many of their peers.

Let's talk about Lucrezia. More than any other Borgia, the historical scorn affixed to her badly-damaged reputation is unjust, inaccurate, and indefensible. Her third marriage to Alfonso d'Este offers the most compelling example to illustrate this. Initially, the Este clan was not only disinterested in the proposed union, they were appalled at the concept. Ultimately, due to pressure from France and an unprecedentedly exorbitant dowry from Alexander, the Estes came around, but only on the condition that a close examination would reveal that Lucrezia's behavior to that point would not bring shame to the Este name. The rumors circulating about Lucrezia at this time were the most tawdry of her life; if there were any fire lurking beneath that smoke, one has to imagine that the Estes—equally humorless and sincere in their defense of their reputation—would have sniffed it out and broken the arrangement. One of Duke Ercole d'Este's closest and long-standing agents, Gian Luca Castellini da Pontremoli wrote to him that, "Your Highness and Lord Don Alfonso will be well satisfied because, quite apart from her perfect grace in all things, her modesty, affability, and propriety, she is a Catholic and shows that she fears God." As Meyer concludes, Castellini's presence in Rome positioned him close enough to see the activities of the Borgia circle firsthand, and he had zero incentive to deceive the Estes.

While that was sufficient to seal the deal on the marriage, Lucrezia soon found herself in an unenviable situation, living under "the cold gaze of a hardheaded father-in-law, a distinctly infatuated husband, a hostile sister-in-law, and platoons of other in-laws and courtiers all looking for reasons to find fault. Nonetheless, as the years passed, she gradually won everyone over, "becoming a revered figure in Ferrara, loved for her kindness [...] and admired for her piety." When she died at the age of 39, the Estes and the city of Ferrara went into mourning. She deserved far, far better than history would bestow upon her.

To the extent that criticism of the Borgias is fair, it is mostly attributable to Cesare's actions, along with Alex= ander's ever-increasing indulgence of the man as he moved into his last decade of life. While gossip certainly circulated during all of the Borgias' lives, only after the fall of Cesare did the dark legend take firm hold, thanks to the concerted efforts of his rivals. At the front of that list was Pope Julian II, whose ambitions as Cardinal Giuliano della Rovere were thwarted for decades by the Borgias. After his election to the papacy, he proceeded to torture many of Cesare's minions to generate damning details, real or not, to indict the family.

Once freed from his red robes, Cesare took to the field, eager to make his mark upon the secular world. First in line with Alexander's goals, but eventually pushing well beyond them, he set out to recover lands in the Papal States and Romagna that in many cases had been established as the pope's rightful worldly domains, only to be lost over the centuries. As a military leader, Cesare was willing to be as brutal as necessary to achieve his goals, but in time he made even better use of the terror generated by the stories that arose from this, taking many fortified towns without a fight. Most noteworthy about his approach, though, was his focus on effective leadership once in power. In many places, Cesare displaced warlords and self-serving nobles, who had few concerns beyond personal enrichment. By contrast, as Meyer puts it, Cesare delivered "governmental machinery that functioned fairly and efficiently and delivered real justice." The effectiveness of this emerged soon enough, when a wave of rebellion threatened Cesare's rise, only to find no traction in his newly-seized towns in the Romagna, where the residents were content with the new administration.

Even the notoriously cynical Machiavelli, who repeatedly found himself in Cesare's company, found much to admire.

In *The Prince*, he would later write, "Cesare Borgia, called Duke Valentino by the common people, acquired his state through the fortune of his father and lost it in the same manner, and that despite the fact that he did everything that a prudent and capable man should do to put his roots down in those states that the arms and fortune of others had granted him [...] if he did not profit from what he established, it was not his fault but resulted from the extraordinary and extreme malice of Fortune."

Without question, bad luck played a critical part in Cesare's eventual downfall. Both Cesare and Alexander fell ill at a dinner party on the Tiber, likely infected by an insect bite. Alexander died and Cesare was enfeebled for an extended period of time. All around, his enemies were sharpening their knives; when he needed to be at his best, Cesare could barely move. Even when he initially enjoyed a fortunate break with the selection of the next pope, Pope Pius III, a man who would have kept the Borgias in his good graces, this only played prelude to a crueler twist of fate. 18 days later, Pius was dead, and that notorious Borgia-hater, Giuliano della Rovere, took his place as Pope Julius II.

Julius's elevation was only made possible with Cesare's support, and Machiavelli was horrified to learn that Cesare had taken certain assurances from the man at face value. By this point, though, the impact of having the rug pulled out from under him twice in quick succession, combined with the lingering effects of a life-threatening illness, had robbed Cesare of many of the qualities that so impressed Machiavelli. The man who had once shaped Italy with the power of his own will now stood at the mercy of others.

Most of his final days were spent incarcerated, first in Rome, then in Ostia, and finally, after a fateful decision by Cesare to choose Naples over France in his lone chance at freedom, Spain. Even then, he still had one last chance. In a flicker of his once bold and outrageous self, Cesare orchestrated the first successful prison break from the fortress of La Mota in Medina del Campo. Eventually, he found himself in Navarre, where his brother-in-law Juan, or King John III, held power. It was a tenuous power, though, as Spain, France, and the Holy Roman Emperor all had designs on the region, and were contributing to the fomentation of internal revolt.

A man of Cesare's military expertise was thus quite welcome, and he was placed in charge of the siege of Viana, where upstarts under the Count of Lerín had thrown in with Aragón. Early on the morning of March 12, 1507, the story goes, a storm raged over Viana. While the surrounding lands would be drained over the years and made more amenable to agriculture, in those days the terrain was swampy, made all the more so by the downpour. The rebels sought to capitalize on the nasty weather by slipping a relief team through the Navarrese forces. Alerted to this fact, Cesare surged to life, leading a party to chase down the rebels. For a man of Cesare's experience, it's difficult to believe what happened next. Caught up in the hunt, he charged into a gulch, only to find himself without backup, surrounded by the enemy. Was it heroism? Was it foolhardiness? Regardless, it was a death sentence. Later, well after his body had been stripped and abandoned to the elements, a lance thrust to the side would be identified as the killing blow.

Allyson L. Mizumoto-Gitter has recently offered a look at the lasting impact of Cesare Borgia upon Viana, and also the transformation of how he has been remembered within the town. The initial placement of his tomb within the church reflected what was initially a heroic portrayal, as displayed in the accompanying inscription: "Here lies in a little earth he who everyone feared, he who held peace and war in his hand. Oh, you who go in search of worthy things to praise, if you would praise the worthiest then your path stops here and you do not need to go any farther." That shifted to scorn and condemnation between 1523 and 1549, when his afore-mentioned ejection occurred. Interestingly, Mizumoto-Gitter argues that this may have been to the benefit of the memory of Cesare; after all, how many of the dead lining the churches and cathedrals of the Camino can you identify today? Most have been long abandoned to history. By contrast, accurately or not, complimentary or not, Cesare's tomb became invested with the most enduring thing of all–a compelling story.

Over the course of the 20th century, Cesare Borgia continued to take new forms, changing alternately into a good neighbor, a martyr for Viana, and a symbol of Navarran patriotism. Once Franco's fall reopened the region in earnest to tourism, Cesare was reincarnated yet again, into a marvelous marketing gimmick.

Cesare Borgia was no saint. (Though a later Borgia, Saint Francis Borgia, would in fact be canonized.) In many ways, he was a product of his times. His shortcomings, in particular, were shared by many of his peers. His qualities, though, were distinct, and Meyer rightly wonders at the end of his account if the Italians under his sway would have been better off in the long run if he had enjoyed more years in power. Regardless, for all his faults, and the faults of his family members, it seems indisputable that the Borgias have fallen prey to some shoddy historical work.

There's a persistent belief, quaint in its own way, that the truth will win out, that the narrative arc of the universe is long, but it bends towards accuracy. It took half a millennium, but maybe, if we're willing to let go of a much more entertaining story, that will be the case for the Borgias.

Keep reading...

Allyson L. Mizumoto-Gitter, *Cesar Borgia in Viana - Historical Memory in Navarra*, 2014

Christopher Hibbert, *The Borgias and Their Enemies*, 2006

G.J. Meyer, *The Borgias: The Hidden History*, 2013

Ivan Cloulas, *The Borgias*, 1987

Johann Burchard, *At the Court of the Borgia, Being an Account of the Reign of Pope Alexander VI*, 1506

A Mother's Tomb

Stage 8: Logroño to Nájera

Grief is somehow intensely personal and universal. To love and to lose is a tragedy, a life-altering tribulation that feels unique and unknowable, carrying a profound sadness that remains with us to our final days. At the same time, though, to be human is to understand, on a visceral level, our undeniable vulnerability, our existential fragility, and we are thus shaken by the grief of total strangers. In striving to convey our sense of loss, the sheer magnitude of the loss involved, we shift the smallest share of that burden of grief onto others, and in so doing we perpetuate, in the most modest manner, but the only one available to us, our departed beloved.

Modest as that gesture may be, it can echo across centuries.

Despite initial appearances to the contrary, the town of Nájera is a welcoming place, one that benefits from a marvelous location, wedged as it is between the Río Najerillo and the stunning red cliffs. Its story originates with García Sánchez III, son of King Sancho III of Pamplona, who succeeded his father to the throne in 1034. His early years in power were extremely lucrative, and he channeled some of those funds into the creation of the monastic complex of Santa María la Real in Nájera in 1044. There are significant parallels between Santa María and another medieval monastery, San Juan de la Peña (a must-visit spot on the Camino Aragonés), including their positioning up against a cave on a cliffside, and an accompanying legend that served as each site's origin story.

Santa María la Real's legend goes that García was hunting in the area when his falcon suddenly bolted after a dove. The king followed the bird's trajectory into a grove of trees, and soon discovered a hidden cave, light emanating from within. A statue of the Virgin sat inside, flanked by the falcon and dove, each resting meekly, with a vase of lilies and a bell before them. García immediately ordered the creation of a chapel on the spot.

As is so often the case, what survives today is a mix of different pieces from the monastery's evolution over the years. The 11th-century church still technically survives, though with significant modifications applied over the years. The 16th-century cloister is delightful. Far more striking than the built environment, perhaps, is the cave, still inhabited by the Virgin, which is claimed to be the very same one discovered by García.

For our purposes, though, the most noteworthy sight can be found on the way to the cave–the Pantheon of the Navarran Kings. While the overarching structure came later, many of the tombs date from the 10th through 13th centuries, and as the name implies it contains the final remains of many royals, including García. And yet, all of their tombs are outshined by one other, the tomb of a young mother-to-be, who died tragically in childbirth.

Blanca, daughter of King García Ramírez of Navarre and his first wife, Margaret of L'Aigle, was born around 1135, and as the daughter of royalty she was, in the words of

David Gitlitz and Linda Davidson, "destined to live as a pawn in the dynastic politics of the age." Engaged to one prince at age 5, then to a king at 14, she finally married Sancho III of Castile at 16. Her primary responsibility at that point, of course, was to produce an heir, and four years later she accomplished that task, bringing the future Alfonso VIII, one of the greatest medieval kings of Spain, into the world in November 1155. The historian Diego de Yepes wrote that Blanca "was so fortunate in her [single] offspring... that from her descend a number of kings whom we see today in Europe." Alas, she would not be around to see his rise. She died on August 12, 1156, after a prolonged illness attributed to complications resulting from childbirth.

Attraction was not a requirement of royal marriages; love represented a genuine rarity. In the case of Sancho and Blanca, though, it seems Cupid had aimed well and true. We are told that the young couple were unusually devoted to one another, excited about growing their family and the future that lay ahead. And suddenly, at what should have been the happiest moment of their lives to that point, they were robbed of that future.

The depth of Sancho's grief is on display in what art historians agree is the most noteworthy work of funerary architecture in the region, the tomb of Doña Blanca. It's worth taking a step back for a moment and setting the table here. Iberian aristocracy in the medieval years commonly repurposed old Roman sarcophagi for their own tombs. (Fun fact: sarcophagus literally means "man-eating.") There was a cynical reason for this; Iberian royalty could link themselves to the Roman political tradition this way, suggesting a direct line of legitimacy between the two. It also, perhaps, and more generously, speaks to a shared humanity; times may change, but we all eventually face the same conclusion. Regardless, the ancient tombs were complemented with new lids, and those were the primary place where a lasting statement could be made about the person enclosed within.

As Elizabeth Valdez del Alamo has written, Blanca's sarcophagus was designed–with extensive input from her grieving husband–with an emphasis on maternity, martyrdom, and salvation. It was quite unusual to see a feminized approach to funerary sculpture, but in Blanca's case it was explicit and comprehensive. The tomb features allusions to numerous Biblical stories, as was customary. However, each of those stories–the Adoration of the Magi, the Judgment of Solomon, and the Massacre of the Innocents–center on women, featuring mothers and wives. At the center is the representation of Blanca's death, easy to miss for a modern audience, given that it features an infant being lifted to the heavens by angels. The primary symbolic intent of that infant, though, is to portray Blanca's soul; it's difficult to separate that, though, from the circumstances of her death following childbirth. As del Alamo perceptively observes, this is simultaneously a scene of birth, a scene of death, *and* a scene of rebirth.

How can we ever process such grief? The earliest surviving written story, *Gilgamesh*, centers on the titular character's inability to come to terms with the loss of his best friend Enkidu. So many of the ancient classics explore similar ground, like Achilles in *The Iliad*. Within Iberia, the great writer Isidore of Seville in 589 explored the practice of Spanish funerary lamentation, connecting it back to the Biblical lament of Jeremiah, related to the loss of Judah and Jerusalem, and the Greek lyric poet Simonedes's *threnoi*, or songs of lamentation written for funerals. In medieval Iberia, the custom became known as "faciendo el llanto," or making lament, which had a distinctly performative quality. For example, at the funeral of Alfonso VI of León and Castile in 1109, the men in attendance tore their hair from their heads and ripped apart their clothes, while the women clawed at their faces and screamed in anguish.

Doña Blanca's tomb is a manifestation of "faciendo el llanto" in its own right, underscoring the intensity of Sancho's grief. On one side, we see Sancho himself, surrounded by his court, in the midst of their agony, preserved in perpetuity. What is most unusual in this rare portrayal, as del Alamo spotlights, is the appearance of Sancho himself–eyes shut, arms spread wide, cape flung back. The man is fainting, a distinctly unmasculine act, but a painfully sincere and genuine one.

Because everything can be criticized, of course there are people out there who claim to know the proper–and improper–ways to grieve. There's a long tradition of such pomposity. Within the Church, excessive grief could be viewed as a lack of faith in the divine plan, and undue attachment to worldly affairs. John Chrysostom, one of the most influential early Christian theologians, explored this topic in his discussion of Jesus's raising of Lazarus, and specifically the moment at which Jesus wept prior to the resurrection (John 11:35). There's a model here worth emulating, Chrysostom emphasizes, but it demands closer scrutiny. Jesus's "weeping is not an ordinance prescribing lamentation, but is a most fitting measure and an exact standard whereby we may, with proper dignity and decorum, endure sorrows while remaining within the limits of our nature. Thus, neither women nor men are permitted to ind-ulge in mourning and excessive weeping, but only to the extent that it is fitting to grieve over sorrows; they are permitted to shed a few tears, but this must be done calmly, without bellowing or wailing, without rending one's tunic or sprinkling oneself with dust, or committing any of the other improprieties that are typical of those who are ignorant of heavenly things. For one who has been purified by Divine doctrine must be fenced around by right reason, as by a strong wall, and must manfully and strenuously ward off the onslaughts of such emotions; he must not accept any crowd of emotions that flows in, as it were, to some low-lying place, with a submissive and compliant soul."

A few tears! Done calmly!

Saint Ambrose, writing around the same time as John Chrysostom, began his discussion of this topic from a similar vantage point. In *On the Death of Satyrus,* he notes, "Let us then begin at this point, that we show that the departure of our loved ones should not be mourned by us. For what is more absurd than to deplore as though it were a special misfortune, what one knows is appointed unto all?" While some grief might be appropriate, he adds, an excessive display is not only unnatural, it's far more concerning: "Let, then, grief be patient, let there be that moderation in adversity which is required in prosperity. If it be not seemly to rejoice immoderately, is it seemly so to mourn? For want of moderation in grief or fear of death is no small evil." For all of that, though, Ambrose would then narrate the story of Tabitha in Acts 9:36-42, in which the devoted follower of Jesus was raised from the dead by Peter following the tearful appeals of her friends and family. Ambrose reflects that, "If the tears of a few widows could obtain for Tabitha the return to life, the tears of an entire city could certainly touch the heart of Christ for the salvation of our departed loved one and acquire for him the patronage of the Apostles." For all the hazards associated with grief, it has its uses!

Even today, we struggle to come to terms with grief. When formal recognition of clinical depression finally arrived in the United States with its inclusion in the Diagnostic and Statistical Manual (DSM), it posed some surprising challenges. First and foremost, pretty much anyone grieving the loss of a loved one would tick all the boxes to merit a

depression diagnosis. As a consequence, DSM-III introduced what became known as the "grief exception" or the
"bereavement exclusion." The manual indicated that the
persistence of depressive symptoms could continue up to a
year in the aftermath of the loss of a loved one, but if they
persisted beyond those 365 days, they would cross the line
into mental illness. But then, the timeline accelerated in
DSM-IV, downsizing the acceptable grieving window to just
two months. By DSM-5, the exception was eliminated
altogether. This generated ample controversy, with some
claiming that the change would "medicalize" grief and others
asserting that the risks of unrecognized, severe depression
merit the alteration.

And perhaps Sancho fell victim to this, never recovering
from the loss of his beloved Blanca. He died suddenly, a
mere two years later, from "unspecified causes." What lived
on, though, was that eternal wail captured in Blanca's tomb,
a husband held perpetually in the throes of despair.

Keep reading...

David Gitlitz and Linda Davidson, *The Pilgrimage Road to Santiago: The Complete Cultural Handbook*, 2000

Elizabeth Valdez del Alamo, "Lament for a lost queen: the sarcophagus of Doña Blanca in Nájera," *Memory and the Medieval Tomb*, 2019

Elisabeth Van-Houts, *Medieval Memories*, 2001

Peter N. Stearns & Mark Knapp, *The Emotions: Social, Cultural and Biological Dimensions*, 1996

Ronald Pies, "The Bereavement Exclusion and DSM-5: An Update and Commentary," *Innovations in Clinical Neuroscience*, 2014

Saint Ambrose, *On the Death of Satyrus*, 379

The Evolution of the Hanged Innocent

Stage 9: Nájera to Santo Domingo de la Calzada

A great story demands to be retold, and by this point you've almost certainly already encountered the defining legend of Santo Domingo de la Calzada, the miracle of the hanged innocent. But here it is one more time, for good measure:

In 1130, a young German pilgrim named Hugonel was traveling with his parents to Santiago de Compostela, and they decided to spend the night in Santo Domingo. As they settled in at their inn, the serving girl made a pass at Hugonel, but the lad, being a good pilgrim, demurred. Alas, the servant girl took rejection poorly, and instead of nurturing a healthy grudge, like a normal person, she decided to frame Hugonel, slipping the inn's silver into his pack. As the family prepared to continue on their journey the following morning, the girl accused him of theft, and when the bags were inspected, sure enough, the boy was guilty as charged. It didn't take long before the gallows were strung, the boy hung, and the parents–bereft, one imagines–back on the road to Compostela.

One can't imagine what went through their minds as they later worked their way back to Santo Domingo, still early in their long journey home, and approached the gallows. They certainly couldn't have been prepared for what happened–their son calling to them, as alive as ever, thanks to the support of Santiago, or, in the Cathedral of Santo Domingo's semi-official retelling, the beloved local saint Domingo. They ran immediately to the local magistrate, finding him at lunch, dining on roasted chicken. Scoffing at such nonsense, he declared that their son was "no more alive than the chickens on my dish." And, of course, at that exact moment, the rooster and the hen–no worse for the roasting–sprang to life, strutting and crowing across the table. Their son was saved. In some cases, the story concludes there; in others, the young girl takes his place on the gallows. The hen and the rooster, meanwhile, were given pride of place in the cathedral, with claims that their distant descendants continue to hold that spot today. In Spanish, this is known as the leyenda del gallo (rooster) y la gallina (hen).

So essential is this story to the pilgrimage that it features in the Codex Calixtinus itself, the original Camino guidebook published in the 12th century. (No annual updates available for that one, alas.) Upon closer inspection, though... the story, while similar, has some important differences!

Most fundamentally, instead of being set in Santo Domingo, the story centers on pilgrims arriving in Toulouse, France, which is situated on the Via Tolosana, one of the four traditional branches of the Camino through that country. In place of a family, we see just a father and son, though still German. The timeline has shifted back 40 years, to 1090. And this time, an embittered girl isn't thrown under the bus; the innkeeper himself bears responsibility for callously getting the father drunk and then slipping a silver cup into the man's luggage. Why? The miracle story attributes it to "blind avarice," as he aspired to steal the wealth the pilgrims carried, still so early in their long journey to Compostela.

Regardless, the innkeeper put on a show the following morning, storming after the pair of pilgrims in high dudgeon and exposing the "theft." After they were dragged through the streets to the local judge, he quickly ruled that their goods would be forfeited to the host and that–in a remarkably cruel twist, though the story suggests it was an act of mercy–one of them must be hanged as punishment. The father wanted to be hanged to save his son; the son wanted to be hanged to save the father. For whatever reason, we learn that the son paid the price, while the father carried on to Compostela. 26 days later, the father returned to Compostela–I sure hope he traveled on horseback and not on foot, to cover some 2400 kilometers in that time span–and we see him burst into tears at the sight of his son's body. At this point, his son, still very much alive, declares: "Do not grieve, most loving father, about my pain, but rather rejoice. For it is sweeter for me now than it had ever been before in all my former life. For the Most Blessed James, holding me up with his hands, revived me with all manner of sweetness." No chicken dinners were disrupted in the making of this story; on the contrary, the son's survival, while dangling from the gibbet, was proof enough of his innocence. The innkeeper took his place. In French, this is referred to as the miracle du pendu-dépendu, or the hanged innocent.

But wait, we're not done! Portugal has its own famous take on this miracle story, set in the town of Barcelos, on the Camino Portugués. And this time, instead of a cynical innkeeper or an aggrieved teen, we have a case of wrong-place, wrong-time. A Galician pilgrim happened to be passing through Barcelos immediately after a robbery occurred–note that in this retelling there was an actual crime committed, by *someone*–and the townspeople were disturbed by their inability to find the culprit. At the inn that night, one suspicious Barcelos resident pointed the finger at the pilgrim. The Galician declared his innocence and explained his devotional pilgrimage to honor James, Paul, and Our Lady of Fatima, but the authorities were unmoved and sentenced him to hanging.

Just before his date with the gallows, the pilgrim was allowed, as his last wish, to speak with the judge. He once again reiterated his innocence; the judge once again scoffed at such a notion. In this version of the story, though, we cut to the chase. No month of pointless dangling required. Instead, the pilgrim pointed to the roasted rooster (no hen involved; perhaps the judge was dieting) on the table before the judge and declared, "It is as certain I am innocent as that rooster crows when they hang me!" Everyone laughed and the poor pilgrim was dragged off. Before long, though, that rooster sprang to life, and the authorities dashed to the gallows to prevent the ultimate act of injustice from occurring. In the pilgrim's view, according to one version of the story, he was saved through the interventions of Santiago and the Virgin Mary. In Portugal, this is known as the "lenda do Galo" (legend of the Rooster).

How about one more for good measure? The Spanish poet Gonzalo de Berceo, born near the monastery of San Millán de la Cogolla, was a remarkably influential theological writer in the 13th century, and his Milagros de Nuestra Señora offers one of our best examples of miracle stories from this time period. His take on this particular legend occurs in "Miracle 8" and is titled "The Pilgrim Deceived by the Devil." He credits it to the great abbot, Hugh of Cluny.

A Cluniac friar named Guiralt (so we've switched from German to French), Berceo begins, was not always so wise. As a young man, he engaged in promiscuous behavior and other sinful acts. And then, as a spur of the moment act, he decided to go on pilgrimage to Compostela. The problem, though, was that instead of spending the night prior to his departure in prayer, he spent it in bed with his mistress. He would pay the price for this indiscretion.

Three days or so into his journey, he encountered an angel. "Welcome, my friend," the angel said to the pilgrim, "you seem to me a little thing, innocent like a lamb." If that sounds like an awfully creepy way for an angel to introduce itself, your Creepy Radar is appropriately dialed in, for in fact this was the Devil, disguised as an angel. He continued to feign concern for the pilgrim, noting that because of his decision to embark on pilgrimage without first making penance, "Holy Mary will not reward you for this!" At this point, the Devil pretended to reveal his "true" self to the pilgrim, that of Saint James. Guiralt immediately acknowledged his failings–"I see that I have committed great iniquities"–and beseeched the saint for help. Brace yourself. This is about to get ugly. The saint declared: "This is my judgment: / that you cut off the parts of your body that commit fornication; / then cut your throat: thus will you do service to God, / for you will make sacrifice to him of your very flesh." Entirely credulous, Guiralt did as commanded: "the poor crazy wretch cut off his genitals; / then he slit his own throat and died excommunicated."

When Guiralt's friends discovered his body, they panicked and ran off, worried that they would be blamed for the act if caught nearby. The Devil and his minions, meanwhile, carried off the poor pilgrim's soul "to the fire," during which they happened across the real Santiago. The saint was outraged: "Treacherous tongue wagger," he said to the Devil, "your speech cannot be worth a bogus coin; / using my voice, as a false advocate / you gave bad advice, you killed my pilgrim!" Without that deception, Guiralt never would have harmed himself: "you killed my pilgrim with a skillful lie." In lieu of Judge Judy, the Devil and Santiago opted instead to bring their dispute before the Virgin Mary, and she ruled in Guiralt's favor: "the soul over which you have the dispute / shall return to its body and do penance."

Guiralt's soul returned to its body thusly, though not without repercussions: "Guiralt of the slit throat cleaned his face / and stood there a short while like someone bewildered, / like a man who is sleeping and awakens annoyed." The scar barely remained visible upon his throat; many of his other injuries were healed completely. His genitals, though, were lost for good. (Berceo helpfully informs the curious that "for passing water, the hole remained.") The story quickly spread along the Camino; we learn that all the townsfolk in Compostela came out to witness Guiralt's arrival, and that upon his return home he was celebrated as a new Lazarus. In recognition of his salvation, he decided to join the Order of Cluny.

In each of these retellings, we see the power of miracle stories in the Middle Ages lay in part in their adaptability. A great story is a relevant one, and while the broad brushstrokes of the plot remained somewhat consistent across all four versions, each permutation offered something distinct and important that reflected its particular context. As Matthew Carey Greenhalgh explains in *The Pilgrimage to Meaning Along the Camino de Santiago*, miracle stories often originated locally, through oral transmission, and thus spoke directly to the people in that area, perhaps featuring saints of special adoration. The genre spread quickly in the Middle Ages, replacing the theologically-heavy discourse of the early Church with more digestible Gospel lessons, "emphasiz[ing] dramatized action over complex argument."

From the miracle's relatively stripped down and straightforward first version in Toulouse, it was thus modified to respond to local needs and interests. This is most evident in the heroes featured in each retelling. Berceo subordinates Santiago to the Virgin Mary, while in Santo Domingo de la Calzada, the local saint gradually took center stage. Interestingly, we can see this process play out in real time, thanks to Greenhalgh's survey. A 16th-century writer, Andrew Borde, focuses on God and Santiago as the saviors; not long after, Fray Luis de la Vega credited the Virgin Mary and Santo Domingo. But then, starting around 1702, in the account of José González Tejada, we see the erasure of the Virgin Mary and Santiago from the narrative. Tejada, it has to be noted, served as the cathedral's canónigo, and thus had a vested interest in how the story was told. In both the Santo Domingo and Barcelos versions, it must be noted, as well, that the poultry also functioned as heroic figures, and this linked the narratives with Matthew 26:34, in which the rooster emerges as a symbol of the resurrection.

The rooster emerged early on as a key figure in both versions. For example, in Santo Domingo de la Calzada, a papal bull issued by Pope Clement VI in 1350 authorized the integration of a chicken coop into the cathedral. The pilgrim Hermann Künig von Vach, passing through more than a century later, made a reference to the chickens, as did Dominico Laffi in the 17th century. Meanwhile, in Barcelos, the Cruzeiro do Senhor do Galo, a stone crucifix near the Paço dos Condes, features a hanged man and a rooster. It dates to the 14th century.

Walter Starkie, who rambled along the Camino Francés in the mid-20th century, underscored how important this miracle story was to Santo Domingo de la Calzada: "The cock and the hen miracle was a godsend to the town, for it led to a revival of pilgrim interest in the Saint's old road from Nájera to Burgos on which traffic had diminished in the fourteenth century, when many of the foreign Jacobeans followed other routes, and certain skeptical historians attribute the spate of miracles that took place at the tomb of Saint Dominic in the fifteenth century, especially that of the white cock and hen, to the propaganda campaign of the innkeepers on the road who needed more rich pilgrims to fleece."

If that smacks of cynicism to contemporary pilgrims, it has to be acknowledged instead as a more realistic accounting of the medieval Camino, which far from an established, singular track, was protean and in constant flux. Towns had to fight to maintain their relevance, and a colorful, evocative story worked as well then as it does now to appeal to travelers. Pilgrims departing Santo Domingo would customarily wear a chicken feather in their cap, while Barcelos pilgrims would leave with a rooster image; in both cases, they helped to embellish the reputation of the towns left behind.

The miracles included in the Codex Calixtinus were intended to aggrandize the cult of Santiago; the retellings in Santo Domingo de la Calzada and Barcelos served, at least in part, to elevate those towns. But what about Gonzalo de Berceo's R-rated version? Instead of the absolute innocence of the victims featured in each of the first three narratives, in Guiralt we have a man whose guilt is indisputable, and the punishment he incurs is far more disturbing. Berceo, it has to be noted, was a poet and a performer, and in Greenhalgh's estimation his retelling was "ingenious for its ability to attract audiences by portraying a character as imperfect as someone from the congregation." If the dancing chickens struck some as a bit cartoonish, Berceo's smacked of a grizzlier reality, a fate to be avoided. At the same time, though, he strived–once his audience's attention had been well and truly secured–to impact a message of grace and forgiveness, an uplifting end to an uncomfortable story.

The miracle story's journey doesn't end there, however. Greenhalgh extends this discussion even further, spotlighting Tirso de Molina's 17th-century retelling of the "hanged innocent" legend, *La Romera de Santiago*. Taking Berceo a step further, not only is the central figure–Count Lisuardo–indisputably guilty, but he is guilty of one of the most heinous acts possible, forcible rape. And instead of Lisuardo being the pilgrim, in this version it's his victim, Doña Sol, who is on the Camino. When King Ordoño sentences Lisuardo to death by hanging, it stands in contrast to our previous victims given its very legitimacy.

In this retelling, though, which shifts from the hanged innocent to the not-hanged guilty, Lisuardo is saved by a distinctly different sort of miracle. Admittedly, it doesn't hold up well to modern sensibilities. Lisuardo's betrothed, the king's sister Linda, devises a scheme by which Lisuardo might marry Doña Sol instead, a move that would, as Greenhalgh puts it, "accommodate both her and Sol's honor." This is framed as a profound act of forgiveness and reconciliation, with the two women serving as Lisuardo's deliverance. Instead of the Virgin Mary acting directly upon this narrative, Juan Luis Vives argues, she is represented by two who emulate her example.

A great story demands to be retold, and it has, time and time again. One is left to wonder, though: how should the hanged innocent be reimagined for the 21st century?

Keep reading…

Francisco Gonçalves and Carlos Costa, "Galo de Barcelos: Património e destino turístico," *Revista Turismo & Desenvolvimento*, 2016

Gonzalo de Berceo, *Miracles of Our Lady*, translated by Richard Terry Mount and Annette Grant Cash, 1997

Matthew Carey Greenhalgh, *The Pilgrimage to Meaning Along the Camino de Santiago*, 2016

Patricio Urquizu, "Le miracle V du Codex Calixtinus (Le Pendu dépendu) dans la pastorale basque de saint Jacques et autres pièces de langues néolatines," *Littératures Classiques*, 2018

Thomas Coffey and Maryjane Dunn, *The Miracles and Translatio of Saint James: Books Two and Three of the Liber Sancti Jacobi*, 2017

Tirso de Molina, *La Romera de Santiago*, 1670

Toasting La Rioja Goodbye

Stage 10: Santo Domingo de la Calzada to Belorado

Your time in La Rioja has been all too brief, just two full stages and a short stint this morning. What La Rioja might lack in geographical heft, though, is more than offset by an oversized reputation. Its name is a global brand today, thanks to the vinicultural industry, but that is a relatively recent phenomenon. Even this political region didn't originally carry the Rioja name; only in 1980 was the Logroño province reestablished as the Autonomous Community of La Rioja, a move made deliberately to better leverage that link to the wine. While that represented a savvy tourism move, it doesn't accurately reflect the boundaries of Rioja red, which spreads well beyond this political area. Nearly one-third of it, in truth, belongs to the Basque Country and Navarre.

What is indisputable, though, is the sterling reputation of Rioja wine. In the early 2020s, it was already long-established as a fixture atop international listings, including prominent placement on Wine Spectator's Top 100 and James Suckling's Top 100, but it reasserted its dominance in 2024 by placing six different wineries in William Reed Business Media magazine's World's Best Vineyards, including the top ranked Bodegas de los Herederos del Marqués de Riscal. Its economic importance to the region is nearly absolute. In comparison to California, another celebrated wine region, Rioja has dedicated 36 times as much land to cultivation, while 24 times as many Riojans (and their neighbors) are employed in the wine cluster–the thousands of different enterprises associated with the growth, production, packaging, and marketing of wine.

The story behind the rise of Rioja is one worth toasting, as its emergence as one of the world's finest red wines was far from inevitable two centuries ago. Instead, it required bold leadership and courageous innovation, along with an ample measure of resilience, in order to reach this point.

The story begins, as Mikel Larreina and colleagues detail, quite a long time ago. Evidence has been found to suggest the presence of viniculture in this area as far back as 6000 BC, but grapes have grown here even longer, and they were part of human diets 30,000 years ago. Roman rule brought this to a new level, and while that ebbed under Moorish occupation, we can still find references to small vineyards here throughout the Middle Ages.

By the 18th century, though, significant problems were emerging related to Riojan viniculture. First and foremost, a growing trend towards monoculture already existed in some parts of the region. Instability in the wheat market persuaded many to opt for turning to vineyards instead. Even more consequential were the *desamortizaciones*, in which lands were seized from the Church and other religious orders, and then auctioned off. Much of that freshly privatized land was converted to viniculture. On one hand, then, when bad harvests struck the area over successive years, villages starved, unable to afford the food necessary for survival. On the other, though, a different sort of problem took shape around good harvests. Overproduction became the bane of

Rioja in this era. Indeed, so much wine was sloshing around that it often ended up being distributed for free, poured out into the street, or mixed into mortar for construction.

It should be noted, as Ludger Mees explains in his book, *The History of Rioja Wine: Tradition and Invention*, that the wine industry also suffered from some old-fashioned or ill-conceived methods. Most alarming was the one-size-fits-all approach to the harvest, which took place by decree between mid-October and mid-November. It didn't matter if the grapes were ripe. (And some of them certainly weren't.) They were all tossed into the same batch, poured together without distinction into barrels, regardless of how uneven the fermentation process was. To round things out, the wine-makers mixed the other assorted remains from the pressing into the final product, to add more "flavor" and "color" to the wine. This Rioja wine had a particular application in those days, adding vital calories to the diets of manual laborers, and they expected their wine to be "coarse and earthy" and "full of sediment."

As such, the Rioja wine industry in the early 19th century demonstrated some potential, especially given its geographical virtues, but it hardly stood out within the Spanish wine market, never mind the French juggernaut to the north. Even when the first feeble attempts at trans-formation were made in 1787, when a Riojan priest sought to bring Bordeaux methods to bear in the region, they were dashed as Spain struggled through decades of political instability and military conflict, no thanks to Napoleon.

Only in 1860 would the glorious transformation finally begin in earnest. Instead of innovation being the purview of a singular priest, at this point a larger coalition took shape, including the provincial government of Álava, a group of wealthy winegrowers, and a newly developed circle of ex-perts in the field, who collectively brought a new technical orientation to the work. The most critical step in all of this was the decision to recruit a ringer, bringing in Jean "Cadiche" Pineau from Bordeaux to serve as the enologist-in-chief for the region. At the same time, they agreed to import 9,000 vines of nine different varieties to employ in an experimental fashion, to elevate the quality of the product throughout the region. The most remarkable aspect of this innovative process was the level of optimistic buy-in from all different constituents. By the end of the first year, the Deputy General stated that, "we have taken a great step forward in the improvement of winemaking," while Pineau declared that "next year almost all the owners will make Bordeaux style wine." They were both correct.

Of course, if those were the singular changes, Rioja wine would have improved in quality, but it's difficult to claim with any confidence that the industry would have boomed. On the contrary, this required ample amounts of techno-logical development across the larger region, some luck, and a profound cultural shift.

First, the technological developments. As the Industrial Revolution swept across Northern Spain, one of the earliest impacts of that transformation came in the realm of rail transport. A new railway line, established in 1864, linked Bilbao with Tudela, while another spur line connected Miranda del Ebro with the Madrid-Irún route. As a consequence, Rioja's wine-producing regions suddenly had easy access to a major port and the French border, significantly expanding its reach.

The rise of industries throughout the province of Biscay, and within Bilbao in particular, had many consequences for the region, but the most direct impact for the Rioja wine industry was the accompanying emergence of large banks and other investment agencies. Suddenly, deeper pockets were available to support the kinds of technological innovations necessary to bring Rioja viniculture into the 20th century.

The shrinking of the world, caused by improved transportation, brought with it some unanticipated challenges. Among them, it facilitated the spread of insects and disease, and the most relevant manifestation of this in viniculture was the phylloxera outbreak in France in the late 19th century. When samples of American vines were brought to Europe in the 1850s, a tiny freeloader came along for the ride. And since that freeloader, the grape phylloxera, native to North America, was previously unknown to Europe, this new world of vineyards was entirely at its mercy. The first vines in the Rhône valley began to deteriorate in 1863; by the century's end, as much as 90% of Europe's vineyards were destroyed. The impact on the French economy was utterly devastating.

While La Rioja would certainly not escape the epidemic unscathed, the timing of its rampage through Europe proved beneficial to the region. The French market, bereft of its traditional wine supply, was forced to open itself up to Spanish producers, and in 1885 more than 70% of the province of Logroño's wine output ended up abroad. That wouldn't last, of course; the French vineyards bounced back within a decade. In the meantime, though, this provided many Rioja growers with a dramatic infusion of capital.

The most surprising requirement for Rioja wine to flourish was a cultural shift, which Mees refers to as the "invention of gourmet." The problem that the region's wine producers faced as they cultivated a higher quality vintage was their market's lack of readiness for it. Again, wine primarily functioned in those days to keep peasants and laborers on their feet. As the bourgeoisie developed, though, new appetites and tastes emerged, along with the social desire to differentiate in ever more nuanced ways between the elite and the common. It was in Paris, of course, where the modern restaurant first appeared, allowing for an individualized dining experience. With that came the art of gastronomy, which found increasingly sophisticated applications for wine. As Cyrus Redding wrote in the 19th century, "The true enjoyer of wine finds it exhilarate the spirits, increase the memory, promote cheerfulness; if he be something of a wit, it draws out his hoarded stores of good sayings and lively repartees, during the moment of relaxation from thought, at the hour when it is good to sit a while. This cheerful glass calls into action his better natural qualities, as with the ruby liquid he swallows 'a sunbeam of the sky.'" This emerging market also incentivized wine producers to favor quality over quantity, a transition made possible by a more careful study of which lands yielded the best product. While Spain lagged behind France in this area, by the late 19th century the new middle and upper classes in the provinces of Biscay and Gipuzkoa began bringing these cultural affectations to Iberia.

La Rioja was ready to capitalize upon those opportunities as they arose, thanks to a successful marketing push, beginning with the promotion of the Medoc Alavés branding in the 1860s. Later years would bring the Spanish government's distinction of Denominación de Origen Rioja and the Rioja region's Wine Control Board, which would serve to protect the integrity of the product and maintain high standards, both of which have bolstered the reputation and reliability of the wine.

The 20th century certainly didn't bring smooth sailing to the Rioja wine industry. While World War I brought boom times, the global economic crisis of the 1930s, the Spanish Civil War, and the subsequent decades of economic isolation all brought great difficulty to the region. After Franco's fall, though, the rise of La Rioja has been the envy of the industry. Thanks to the high standard of quality established in the preceding century, the low value of the Spanish peseta, and the surging worldwide demand for wine in the 1980s and 1990s, La Rioja became highly desirable. From 42,000 hectares of vineyards in the 1990s, La Rioja jumped to 61,000 in 2008; grape production more than doubled, from 220 million kilograms to 470 million within that same timeframe.

Given its remarkable success, one wonders what might be next for La Rioja's wine industry. Intriguingly, the wine experts assembled by Mees–but certainly not pilgrims on the Camino–suggest that its biggest problem is that it's too cheap. For example, he quotes Sarah Jane Evans, who observes that, "Given the strength of the brand Rioja, it should not be available in the UK for £5 or less. And indeed, many very fine Riojas also sell themselves too cheap. As consumers we may enjoy the fact that fine Rioja wine is good value, but frankly it's not good business, is it?"

It's at moments like this that I realize I would make a terrible businessman. From my vantage point, Rioja wine currently offers the best of all worlds. Its growers and producers are making a solid living, at worst. The most prestigious among them are absolutely raking it in; just check out the Gehry-built "City of Wine" at Bodegas de los Herederos del Marqués de Riscal. The best vintages of Rioja rank among the world's finest, and yet its more run-of-the-mill products offer a high standard of quality to people on humble budgets. This seems like an accomplishment to be celebrated!

While you depart La Rioja today, never fear. Thanks to the efforts of those bold innovators, you can grab a Rioja red all along the Camino. And for now, at least, it won't break the bank.

Keep reading…

Barbara Hendry, "The Power of Names: Place-Making and People-Making in the Riojan Wine Region," *Names*, 2006

Ludger Mees, *The History of Rioja Wine: Tradition and Invention*, 2022

Mikel Larreina, et. al., "Development Rooted on Riojan Soil: The Wine Cluster and Beyond," *The Open Geography Journal*, 2011

Our Cannibal Origins

Stage 11: Belorado to Atapuerca

There are several chapters in this book that contest the 'timeless' quality that contemporary pilgrims often ascribe to the landscape, outlining how the Spain we encounter on the Camino is, in many regards, a product of recent centuries and decades, one that would be unrecognizable to its medieval denizens.

In this stage, though, pilgrims pass through terrain that was indelibly marked so long ago that we have to change the scale of our discussion. "Old" in this case, no longer means medieval or even classical; those are passing fancies in comparison to the secrets long stashed within the Sierra de Atapuerca. This hilly region, spanning perhaps twelve square kilometers, climbing over 1000 meters in elevation at its peak, is riddled with cavities in the limestone, carved out over the millennia by subterranean water flow. Time passed, the hills filled in, and those pockets were lost. Until, that is, a mining company at the turn of the 20th century had aspirations to build a railroad line through the region to expedite the transport of minerals. While those plans were scuttled, that didn't happen until the company had already hacked a trench through the Sierra, exposing a series of caverns that contained animal and human remains.

Excavations didn't begin until the 1970s, but once they did, they shook up everything we thought we knew about the earliest humans. Many of the most dramatic discoveries have been made in the Gran Dolina cave site, plunging 27 meters deep but never spanning wider than 17 meters. In 1994-95, archaeologists found almost 90 human fossil remains, along with 150 artifacts in this space. Over the subsequent 18 years, 60 more human fossils were uncovered. In another cave, the Sima del Elefante, or Elephant Pit, an even more remarkable discovery occurred in 2007-08, when the fossilized lower jaw and teeth of a human were found that are roughly 1.2 million years old.

Old bones are exciting enough, but only after the archaeologists inspected those bones more closely did they realize the most noteworthy aspect of this treasure trove. It was the faces. The hominins of the Sierra display modern, sapiens-like, human faces, something entirely unexpected given where they fit in the timeline. And behind those faces lurked significantly greater cranial capacity. As a consequence, the team behind the discovery, led by Bermúdez de Castro, argued that this represented an entirely new species, Homo antecessor.

The dominant paradigm for the earliest days of humanity is that we originated in Africa and then spread into Eurasia. For a long time, the anagenetic evolutionary model held sway in explaining how this unfolded, proposing a linear progression through three distinct evolutionary phases: Homo habilis, Homo erectus, and Homo sapiens. The Atapuerca discoveries, though, tipped the balance towards the cladogenetic model of speciation, which replaces the clean, linear framing of the former with a series of different speciation events. Given that the early humans coming out of Africa would have migrated in different waves across many years, and that they would have faced prolonged periods of reproductive isolation due to changes in climate and environment, it stands to reason that we might see different cladogenetic events, or evolutionary splits, across Eurasia. Bermúdez de Castro and colleagues theorize that Homo antecessor might represent one of those successive waves of migrants, signifying a speciation event that distinguished this population from Homo ergaster / Homo erectus.

Elsewhere in the Sierra, excavations in a different cave, the Sima de los Huesos, revealed the remains of 28 individuals, roughly 400,000 years old. The most exciting aspect of this discovery, though, is that these turned out to be Neanderthals, the earliest found anywhere in Europe. The timing and location of Neanderthal divergence from modern humans has long been a source of debate, with many speculating that this occurred before their migration out of Africa, and others suggesting that it took place after they arrived in Europe.

Bermúdez de Castro and colleagues have determined that Homo antecessor shares "three derived traits with modern humans, Neanderthals, and African and European Middle Pleistocene populations," including the "convex superior border of the temporal squama, an anterior position of the incisive canal, and a marked nasal prominence." Given that, they suggest, Homo antecessor "appears to be the common ancestor of all of them." Has Atapuerca connected the dots between humans and Neanderthals? It's far from a done deal, but the evidence is intriguing.

Also intriguing, or maybe disturbing, is the evidence related to these early humans' diets. The archaeologists have been able to determine, through pollen analysis, that the climate during the years when these early humans lived was slightly warmer than Burgos today. Meanwhile, dental analysis performed by Alejandro Pérez-Pérez and his team has revealed "dietary habits that include significant amounts of abrasive plant foods that cause highly abrasive loads on enamel surfaces." While the environmental conditions faced by the different eras of humans in Atapuerca changed across the millennia, sometimes becoming quite harsh, the available evidence indicates that they often had access to a varied diet, combining meats and plants.

Alas, that varied diet also included human flesh.

Let's go back to the Gran Dolina dig. Among those many human fossil fragments, researchers have been able to identify eleven distinct individuals: six young children, three adolescents, and a pair of young adults. As Isabel Cáceres and colleagues explain, the most damaged human remains are skulls, mandibles, maxillae, a femur fragment, and vertebrae, which happen to be the most nutrient-rich bones. By contrast, the bones with the most limited marrow content are largely unbroken. As Palmira Saladié and Antonio Rodríguez-Hidalgo put it, with perhaps a little too much gusto: "The bodies were scalped, skinned, disarticulated, eviscerated and defleshed." Stone tool cut marks are particularly commonplace on the parts of the body featuring the strongest muscle attachment, including along facial bones. A major goal of such efforts would be to gain access to the sweet, sweet brains.

It wasn't that long ago that cannibalism was denied as a human practice, not the stuff of credible anthropology. In 1979, William Arens authored *The Man-Eating Myth: Anthropology and Anthropophagy,* in which he rejected all claims to cannibalism, across the world and all of human history, with the rare exception of extreme cases of survival. It was as bold a claim as it was untenable, and while it generated ample attention, it was soon discredited within the field. The

600,000-year-old Bodo skull, found in Ethiopia, appears to be the oldest example of cannibalism, but there are many others. Our most extensive evidence of the practice comes from the Americas, where indigenous practices persisted in some cases to within the past few decades. Some disputes persist; both Fontbrégoua in France and Krapina in Croatia have proponents arguing that these sites offer evidence of cannibalism or ritual burial. Overall, though, Saladié and Rodríguez-Hidalgo note that "In the European prehistory, there are 17 confirmed assemblages where human cannibalism has been recorded."

A similarly contentious debate centers on the "why" behind cannibalism. Setting aside those more explicable, if horrifying, situations where survival is on the line, like the Donner Party, what drove humans in so many places to feed upon their fellows? And my goodness, it seems like everyone has their own theoretical framework to explain this. One centers on social divisions, thinking about cannibalism as aggressive (eating enemies) vs. affectionate (friends and family), or endocannibalism (eating in-group members) vs. exo-cannibalism (outsiders). Fernández-Jalvo and colleagues focus on functional aspects, breaking cannibalism down into nutritional, gastronomic, ritual/magical/funerary, and pathological. Boulestin keeps it simplest, favoring just two categories: exceptional and socially instituted. Saladié and Rodríguez-Hidalgo, meanwhile, propose three: survival cannibalism, aggressive cannibalism and funerary cannibalism. (This would make an excellent dinner topic in the albergue; impress all of your new friends!)

As for Atapuerca, Isabel Cáceres and colleagues first asserted that this functioned as a case of gastronomic cannibalism. As noted, the climate during the period under examination was mild and accommodating, and the species diversity recorded in this specific part of the excavation site distinguished itself as the richest encountered at any level of the site. Given that high level of flora and fauna available, no argument can be made that this was a survival situation. On the contrary, this was a lifestyle. Saladié and Rodríguez-Hidalgo, meanwhile, propose a different explanation. What we're seeing here, they suggest, "was an accumulation of episodes of intergroup violence in which the individuals who were attacked were those who represented a smaller threat to the attackers." This is aggressive exocannibalism, "related to the protection and expansion of a catchment area," or, as Keith F. Otterbein has labeled it in *How War Began*, "the first war."

While those debates are likely to continue for a while, so too do the excavations. In 2022-23, another site in the Sierra, the Sima del Elefante, yielded the remains of another human (named "Pink") and lithic tools. A much more press-worthy discovery was made back in Gran Dolina in 2024: the remains of an 850,000-year-old Homo antecessor. How many more clues to our collective past are lurking beneath the surface in the Atapuerca hills? It's something to chew on.

Keep reading...

Alejandro Pérez-Pérez, et. al., "The diet of the first
   Europeans from Atapuerca," *Scientific Reports*, 2017

Isabel Cáceres, "Human cannibalism in the Early
   Pleistocene of Europe (Gran Dolina, Sierra de
   Atapuerca, Burgos, Spain)," *Journal of Human
   Evolution*, 1999

José María Bermúdez de Castro, et. al., "The Atapuerca Sites and Their Contribution to the Knowledge of Human Evolution in Europe," *Evolutionary Anthropology*, 2004

José María Bermúdez de Castro, et. al., "Homo antecessor: The state of the art eighteen years later," *Quaternary International*, 2017

Marta Yustos and José Yravedra Sainz de los Terreros, "Cannibalism in the Neanderthal World: An Exhaustive Revision," *Journal of Taphonomy*, 2015

Palmira Saladié and Antonio Rodríguez-Hidalgo, "Archaeological Evidence for Cannibalism in Prehistoric Western Europe: from Homo antecessor to the Bronze Age," *Journal of Archaeological Method and Theory*, 2017

El Cid and El Generalísimo

Stage 12: Atapuerca to Burgos

He stands just south of the Camino as it proceeds into the center of Burgos, poised as ever–astride his warhorse Babieca, sword pointing forward, his majestic beard and cape flowing in the breeze–to strike out in defense of Christianity. The statue of El Cid in the city of El Cid. A fiction within a fiction.

The statue dates to 1947, and as Nora Berend explains, the timing was hardly accidental. For years by this point, Burgos had been asserting its deep ties to the medieval warlord, Rodrigo Díaz, otherwise known as El Cid, Campeador. In truth, the city had few links to the man during his life, despite what the medieval classic *The Poem of the Cid* might assert. The first initiative in support of this came in 1531, when the city built a series of statues atop the Puerta de Santa María, a medieval gate that pilgrims still pass through today. While primarily intended to win over King Carlos I, one of the featured figures in the display was El Cid, identified on the work as "the strongest citizen, fright and terror of the Moors." In 1593, the local authorities took another step forward in securing the link between man and city, establishing a memorial at some houses said to have belonged to El Cid. As the years passed, the buildings crumbled and the first memorial fell into disrepair, but in 1784 the city installed a new plaque, claiming that "In this place stood the house where in the year 1026 Rodrigo Díaz de Vivar, called the Cid Campeador, was born." Other Cid-related objects–of dubious provenance–one might call them relics at this point, also hold places of prominence in Burgos, including his sword La Tizón, Bishop Jerome's crucifix, and one of the two chests used by El Cid to dupe Jewish money lenders, which is oddly displayed in the Burgos cathedral.

Of course, that's not the only link to El Cid in the cathedral. The man and his wife, Doña Jimena, were interred in the heart of the holy building, at the intersection of the nave and transept, in 1921, as part of the cathedral's 700th anniversary celebration. The perfect place to honor a great Christian warrior.

The raising of a statue of El Cid in 1947, then, was very much in keeping with this long-established connection. However, much had changed elsewhere in Spain in the meantime. The Spanish Civil War had concluded, with General Francisco Franco assuming dictatorial control in 1939. Even before the war had broken out, the Nationalists had been framing their struggle as a "reconquest," invoking that medieval language to convey a religious battle to save Christian civilization. The archbishops of Santiago de Compostela and Zaragoza reinforced this narrative in 1936, when they "declared the Nationalist cause a religious crusade." You could draw a straight line from Santiago Matamoros to El Cid Campeador to El Generalísimo.

In this way, Berend writes, "The Cid was thus appropriated by a murderous regime, used to justify both mass killing and foisting a Christian nationalist Castilian identity on Spain." The city of Burgos was thus well positioned to cash in on its centuries of manufactured ties to El Cid, and for a time it earned distinction as the "capital of the crusade," serving as the first seat of Franco's government. Beyond the primary statue of the Campeador, then, the local authorities also organized the establishment of a series of statues on the bridge crossing the Arlanzón River south of it. The elevation of El Cid was hardly limited to cut stone, however. His legend became foundational to the Spanish national story under Franco, and textbooks extolled his importance as "a first leader of the Reconquest."

On its surface, the *Poem of the Cid* affirms such a heroic portrayal of the man, the Spanish equivalent of the French Roland. The great epic poem, likely dating to the 12th century, opens with El Cid already established as an outstanding warrior. The initial drama, though, derives from his having run afoul of King Alfonso VI. Rivals, jealous of El Campeador, convinced the king–who already "nursed an ancient rancor against him"–that his vassal had stolen money from the throne, culminating in El Cid being sent into exile. Right from the start, the narrator makes it clear that such claims were spurious. "The Cid," after reading the letters ordering his exile, "was much grieved, and yet he did not wish to disobey, although he was allowed only nine days' grace in which to leave the kingdom." Even in the face of a capricious, unfair monarch, El Cid's loyalty is unswerving. He will do his duty.

And so, El Cid sets forth to win back Alfonso's favor, in the only way he knows how–by defeating a whole bunch of Moorish armies. Ultimately, this builds to his conquest of Valencia, a defining triumph. Throughout the poem, we are reminded time and again of El Cid's Christian virtues. When he first departs Burgos, he turns to the cathedral, raises his right hand, crosses himself, and declares: "Praise be to Thee, O God, / Who guide earth and sky; / thy grace be with

113

me, / glorious Santa María [...] and if fortune bear with me, / fine gifts on thy altar, / rich offerings I shall lay, / and a thousand Masses / have sung in thy chantry." On his last night in Castile, pondering when he might next return to his home, he was visited in his sleep by the angel Gabriel, who exhorted him forward: "Ride forward, Cid, / good Campeador, / for no man ever rode forth / at so propitious a moment; / as long as you live / that which is yours will prosper." Heartened by the visitation, he thanked God and rode confidently into exile.

His merits as a warrior are beyond dispute; even the historical record will find no fault on that front. We are informed in the poem, though, that each military engagement was steeped in religiosity. During a battle in Alcocer, for example, "The Moors call on Mohammed / and the Christians on Saint James." As the Campeador and his men push onward, the narrator asserts that, "My Cid knew well / that God was his strength." When his forces finally prepare to take Valencia, El Cid declares, "In the name of the Creator / and of Saint James the apostle, / attack them knights, / heartily, with a will." When victory is won, "It is a great day / for Christendom."

Throughout the narrative, El Cid's honor is beyond dispute. His paramount goal is to display his fervent loyalty to King Alfonso VI. At the same time, though, he fulfills his promises to the Church, sending back Minaya Alvar Fáñez with enough gold and silver to fund those thousand masses. Following his victory in Valencia, El Cid states that "when God would give us aid / let us heartily thank Him for it; I would ordain a bishopric / in the lands of Valencia." Equally important, El Cid's men, who model the same loyalty and devotion as the lord, benefit mightily from their service. "His men are so rich," the First Cantar ends, "they cannot count all they have." Ultimately, Alfonso is persuaded of the folly of his error, drawing back into the fold his loyalest of servants: "with all my heart and soul; / I hereby pardon you / and grant you my favor; / be welcome from this hour / in all my kingdom."

The historical record surrounding El Cid, however, paints a distinctly different picture. In the opening to his classic, *The Quest for El Cid,* Richard Fletcher writes that "In Rodrigo's day there was little if any sense of nationhood, crusade, or reconquest in the Christian kingdoms of Spain. Rodrigo, himself, as we shall see, was as ready to fight alongside Muslims against Christians as vice versa. He was his own man and fought for his own profit."

A young Rodrigo Díaz served in the household of Sancho, son of King Fernando I, at some point in the late 1050s. Following Fernando's death, he divided his kingdom among his three sons, with Castile going to Sancho, León to Alfonso, and Galicia to García. Soon after, Rodrigo rose to a position overseeing Sancho's household militia. After Fernando's widow—and the boys' mother—died in 1067, all hell broke loose. Sancho won a partial victory over Alfonso, then Alfonso and Sancho aligned to knock out García with a (doomed) vision of ruling Galicia jointly, and soon after Sancho defeated Alfonso again. The latter, though, would have the last laugh, following Sancho's death—orchestrated, perhaps, by his brother—in 1072. Having reunified the three kingdoms, Sancho only got to enjoy his efforts for nine months. Alfonso VI, meanwhile, would have 44 years on the throne.

While the loss of his liege lord represented a setback for El Cid, he bounced back. A capable field commander would always find patronage, and he soon gained a position under Alfonso. That wouldn't last, though. For reasons that remain somewhat murky, he managed to fall out with Alfonso in the early 1080s, possibly following an aggressive—and unsanctioned—move executed by El Cid against Moorish holdings near Toledo. In any case, Alfonso banished Rodrigo from the kingdom soon after. While that detail aligns with the poem, what happened next stands in stark contrast. Far from striving with absolute devotion to win back the king's good graces, El Cid found employment under Ahmad ibn Sulayman al-Muqtadir, ruler of the Zaragoza *taifa*. Over the next five years, he led the man's armies, often in direct conflict with Christian forces. In 1084, he went on the offensive, ravaging southern Aragón and Catalonia.

Just as El Cid and Alfonso were on the verge of open conflict, when the latter besieged Zaragoza, the tide turned precipitously for the Christian king. Word arrived that Almoravides forces, led by Yusuf ibn Tashufīn, had crossed into Iberia from North Africa. Alfonso rallied his forces in an attempt to fend off Yusuf's advances in Sagrajas, but suffered a decisive defeat. On the heels of that setback, Alfonso quickly reconciled with El Cid, a pragmatic move if ever there was one. Despite those years in Zaragoza, it would be easy to still cling to a traditional *Reconquista*-themed narrative here, arguing that when it mattered most, when the future of Christian Spain stood imperiled, El Cid came through and saved the day. On the contrary, though, multiple rounds of exile and reconciliation would follow over the succeeding years, during which time the Campeador stole tribute from Alfonso, captured the Christian count of Barcelona, and ultimately invaded Alfonso's kingdom by laying waste to La Rioja. In the midst of this, in an act that underscores the messiness of the era, Yusuf turned on the Muslim *taifa* leaders, who he found lax in their religious practices, and conniving in their backstabbing ways. Indeed, some of them, realizing that they had swallowed a spider to capture the fly, were already exploring a new alliance with Alfonso.

Far from a loyal Christian vassal, then, Rodrigo Díaz embodied the values of his time, a mercenary in the eyes of some, a warlord according to others, but certainly not the epic figure portrayed in the *Poem* or in Francoist retellings. It didn't take long following his death in 1099, though, for the narrative surrounding the man to transform. The First Crusade launched in his final years; the religious struggle was formally extended to Iberia in 1123. Over those same years, the Camino moved into its peak era, under the leadership of Archbishop Gelmírez (see Stage 32). A need existed for heroes to exemplify the values central to this new conflict, and evidence to the contrary be damned, the bones of El Cid's life were sufficient material from which to build a compelling story.

While the medieval troubadours and the folk historians did their work, the persistent glorification of the El Cid narrative would likely have diminished over the centuries, if not for his modern biographer, Ramón Menéndez Pidal, whose *La España del Cid*, first published in 1929, changed everything. As Fletcher summarizes Pidal and his book, "A patriot whose native land was going through troubled times, he presented his countrymen with a national hero in whom they could rejoice and to whose virtues they should aspire. For Menéndez Pidal there was no disjunction between history and legend. The Cid of history was as flawless in his character and deeds as the Cid of legend." Berend underscores the important motives driving the historian's work: "He was not merely looking to study the past; he fervently wanted to help his compatriots, providing a moral compass based on history."

Had Menéndez Pidal instead sought to present history unvarnished, not only would El Cid's story have appeared quite different, but so too would have the entire medieval era. The very word, *Reconquista* doesn't appear in any written source until the 18th century, just as nationalist ideologies were beginning to percolate around continental Europe. On the contrary, as Maria Rosa Menocal has displayed in her revisionist work, *The Ornament of the World: How Muslims, Jews and Christians Created a Culture of Tolerance in Medieval Spain*, most of medieval Iberian, or Andalusian, history featured a substantial degree of multi-cultural harmony. Even though it all fell apart in the end, Menocal writes, that period "reveals the inevitable tensions between our desire for cultural coherence, on the one hand, and the excitement and vitality of contradictions in ourselves and in our midst, on the other."

Her work asserts an alternative view of the *Reconquista*, instead embodying the idea of *Convivencia*, first coined by Américo Castro, which characterizes this time period as one of harmonious, peaceful coexistence for the Muslims, Christians, and Jews all living side by side. It's a beautiful vision, and Menocal's account is rife with compelling examples of the cultural dynamism of the era. For Berend, though, this alternative framing is a bridge too far; the "myth of *convivencia* [...] may be opposed to that of the *Reconquista*, but it is just as much a myth." It's a fair warning, one we should heed. As tempting as it is to repurpose history in service to prosocial goals in the present, the consequences of such applications all too often prove to be dire. One needs look no further than how the Francoist regime, building on Menéndez Pidal's work–almost certainly to his horror– "turned the alleged Reconquest into a common past for Spaniards, through which they constructed their identity, the very essence of the Spanish nation." Berend continues, stressing how the "indiscriminate use of terror, coupled with the lofty rhetoric of crusade and *Reconquista* made the Cid particularly relevant as a heroic precursor of Franco."

Towards the end of *Ornament*, Menocal cites a famous quote from the novelist F. Scott Fitzgerald: "The test of a first-rate intelligence is the ability to hold two opposed ideas in the mind at the same time, and still retain the ability to function." In El Cid, the man and the legends, we see the multiplicity of identity, and the political applications of those historical manipulations. The same is true for medieval Spain, the era at the core of the mythical construction we so love to inhabit when walking the Camino. The challenge becomes one of holding these competing narratives–the *Reconquista* and the *Convivencia*–in each hand, while grappling with how each offers a deliberate distortion of the historical record.

Keep reading...

Maria Rosa Menocal, *The Ornament of the World: How Muslims, Jews and Christians Created a Culture of Tolerance in Medieval Spain*, 2002

Nora Berend, *El Cid: The Life and Afterlife of a Medieval Mercenary*, 2024

Richard Fletcher, *The Quest for El Cid*, 1989

W.S. Merwin (trans.), *The Poem of the Cid*, 1975

Our Daily Bread

Stage 13: Burgos to Hontanas

In 2013, Gregorio Varela-Moreiras and his colleagues shared the results of Spain's Food Consumption Survey, which measured national consumption data from 2000 to 2012. If you had to guess–no cheating!–which of the following food groups comprised the largest share of the Spanish diet: cereals, eggs, fish, fruits, legumes, meat, milk/dairy, oils and fats, sugar and derivatives, or vegetables?

The answer might surprise you. Based on weight, the winner's podium has fruits in third place, vegetables in second, and milk/dairy securing the gold. One of the most common pilgrim complaints about the Camino is the prominence of greasy meat and fries in the *menú del peregrino*, while many others bemoan the dearth of vegetables on offer. As for me, between the morning *tostada*, the lunch-time *bocadillo*, and the bottomless bowl of bread at dinner, I quickly found myself overdosing on baguettes on my first couple Caminos.

Perhaps that theme is reinforced by our formal arrival today in the *meseta*. This is the bread-basket of Spain– Castilla y León is responsible for generating 43% of Spain's bread wheat–a role it has filled ever since Roman rule.

Indeed, the roots of wheat in the *meseta* go back even further. As Conxita Royo and Guillermo Briceño-Félix have documented, the earliest evidence of wheat cultivation in Spain dates to the Neolithic period, around 5500 BC, during which time it functioned as a trade crop. Wheat has been a defining part of the *meseta* for millennia now.

With the arrival of first the Greeks and then the Romans between the 4th and 2nd centuries BC, the wheat industry expanded across the peninsula, and "cereal production reached unprecedented levels." This was driven to a significant degree by the introduction of a complex irrigation system that substantially expanded the amount of arable land on the peninsula. Arab rule benefited wheat production in the region as well, given their greater appreciation for scientific research, which offered insights into advanced agricultural techniques. Around 1800, wheat grew on 2.9 million hectares in Spain, a figure that climbed dramatically over the next 30 years to reach 5.1 million hectares in 1830. And yet, this subsequently declined even more sharply, first to 4.2 million hectares in 1934 and then all the way down to 2.1 million hectares in 2006.

What happened? Bread remains critically important to the human diet. Miguel Sanchez-Garcia and colleagues have shown that bread wheat was the second most consumed staple crop in the world in 2011, responsible for "18% of the daily calorie intake worldwide," while Alecia Kiszonas and Craig Morris note that 770 million metric tons of wheat are produced annually.

There are three main factors driving the decline. The most straightforward, which might feel more like a matter of semantics than substance, is a shift in some areas from bread wheat to durum wheat, which is mostly used in Spain for pasta and semolina production. Royo and Briceño-Félix note that in the 1990s, European Union subsidies encouraged many farmers to make the switch, so those incentives certainly contributed to the larger trend. That wasn't the lone cereal shake-up, though; many farmers also abandoned wheat entirely, in favor of barley, which traditionally offered higher, more consistent yields and stable pricing.

The second factor in the decline in bread wheat production in Spain is the parallel drop in bread consumption. In 1964, the average Spaniard consumed 134 kilograms (kg) of bread per year—nearly 300 pounds. That decreased significantly throughout the 1970s, and it has only continued to fall ever since, plummeting all the way to 27 kg in 2023. This has raised alarms in some circles; the Spanish journalist Ibán Yarza, who the Diario de Sevilla dubbed the "guru of artisanal bread," bemoaned the fact that bread "has been desacralized" in Spain. Part of this is driven by dietary fads and a belief that bread is unhealthy and contributes to weight gain. At the same time, though, the timing of the initial decline corresponds to the end of Franco's rule, the reopening of the country, and the arrival of an ever-growing abundance of outside foods. Greater choice, in conjunction with growing resources, resulted in a more diverse diet.

From an agricultural perspective, though, the most important part of the story is the third factor. Far from a declensionist narrative, this turns our attention to the triumph of the past two centuries, as the scientific revolution transformed farms around the world. The forefathers of crop improvement, as told by Kiszonas and Morris, were the German botanists Rudolph Jakob Camerius (1694) and Joseph Gottlieb Kölreuter (1761-66), who respectively pioneered the study of plant reproductive organs and plant fertilization. Between the development of botany in the 19th century and genetics at the turn of the century, new insights and practices emerged to support wheat hybridization. It's important to underscore how long it took for this process to play out; as late as 1949, Kiszonas and Morris note, more than a third of the wheat crop in the Eastern United States was composed of landraces–that is to say, locally adapted, domesticated crops that developed over time.

Royo and Briceño-Félix explain how the wheat breeding revolution unfolded in Spain. The first big push took place in the 1920s, with research efforts benefiting from collaboration across Europe. Of course, conditions on the continent deteriorated over the following two decades, with the Spanish Civil War and World War II disrupting experiments and the flow of information. By the 1950s, though, conditions had stabilized in the country, relatively speaking, and agricultural experts were steered towards one overriding priority: yield increase, with special attention paid to drought-resistant genotypes. The success of those efforts (in conjunction with the use of modern herbicides and fungicides) is indisputable; the Spanish Ministry of Agriculture, Fisheries and Food has determined that bread wheat yields in the country have essentially doubled since the 1970s. This is important to keep in mind when evaluating the substantial decline in hectares devoted to growing wheat bread; it doesn't require a mathematical genius to understand what's happening if the land is halved but the yield doubled.

The downside of that growth in quantity is the neglect of quality. As Kiszonas and Morris explain, throughout the last quarter of the 20th century, in Spain and elsewhere, "wheat breeding efforts concentrated on yield increases, with grain quality improvement being a secondary breeding objective." There's reason to think that Spain was particularly lagging on the quality front, as the country's first bread wheat quality classification system failed to include many of the elements already long employed in other European countries. Kiszonas and Morris speculate that this "lack of regulation may have contributed to traditionally large imports of bread wheat grain," which accounted for more than half of all wheat consumed in the country in 2012. One of the major problems was the negative relationship between yield and protein content; as the breeding modifications resulted in rising yields, this coincided with declining protein levels, which Sanchez-García and colleagues explain occurred as a consequence of the "dilution of nitrogen compounds when carbohydrate deposition increases during photosynthesis." I'll take their word for it.

Nonetheless, despite the slow start, wheat quality has experienced a resurgence over the last few decades. The introduction of modern varieties of bread wheat, imported from outside of Spain, has corrected the protein problems, while also allowing Spanish bread wheat to "meet industrial requirements in terms of fermentation tolerance and stability."

It's quite understandable, of course, that as Kiszonas and Morris put it, "Wheat quality has historically been the last to utilize new technology for breeding." After all, for most of human history the far greater concern has been achieving sufficient supply to meet the ravenous demand. As far back as Ancient Rome, Evans informs us, the unreliability of the wheat harvest meant that "the spectre of starvation haunted the imperium Romanum, an imminent and frequently deadly pestilence." And because nearly all the wheat-growing areas in Spain are located in rainfed environments, the annual variance in rainfall means that wheat yields can vary drama-tically from year to year. At long last, though, Spain has achieved a higher standard of financial stability, and it has gained access to a much wider diversity of foodstuffs. For bread to remain a prominent part of the Spanish diet, and to sustain the cultural prominence it has long enjoyed, the agronomists of today will need to devote ever greater attention to elevating the quality of the available breeds.

Keep reading...

Alecia M. Kiszonas and Craig F. Morris, "Wheat breeding for quality: A historical review," *Cereal Chemistry*, 2018

Bob Belderok, et. al., *Bread-Making Quality of Wheat: A Century of Breeding in Europe*, 2000

Conxita Royo and Guillermo Briceño-Félix, "Wheat breeding in Spain," *Institute for Food and Agricultural Research and Technology*, 2011

Gregorio Varela-Moreiras, et. al., "The Spanish diet: an update," *Nutrición Hospitalaria*, 2013

J. K. Evans, "Wheat Production and Its Social Consequences in the Roman World," *The Classical Quarterly*, 1981

Miguel Sanchez-Garcia, et. al., "Changes in bread-making quality attributes of bread wheat varieties cultivated in Spain during the 20th century," *European Journal of Agronomy*, 2015

We're All Wrong About Saint Anthony's Fire

Stage 14: Hontanas to Boadilla

It stops you dead in your tracks. After a quiet walk from Hontanas along a single-lane road, dotted with trees, it gradually takes shape, the old ruins jutting forth from the golden fields. Despite its centuries of decline, the old Monastery of San Antón remains an evocative fixture on the Camino, and the pilgrims passing beneath its archway crossing the road can't help but pause and imagine what once existed here. The answer to that, though, will require a 2000-year journey linking legend and epidemiology.

Saint Anthony just wanted to get away from it all, in order to get closer to God. And thanks to his friend, Saint Athanasius, we know a great deal about his journey, even if the line between truth and embellishment is often difficult to parse. Born into a rich family in Egypt in 250, Anthony lost both of his parents at 18. When he walked into his church, his ears suddenly rang with the words of Matthew 19:21: "If thou wilt be perfect, go sell all that thou hast and give to the poor, come and follow me, and thou shalt have treasure in heaven." Without hesitation, Anthony gave his family's extensive properties to his fellow villagers and prepared for his next step.

The devil, however, could not tolerate such resolution, and besieged Anthony with a cloud of arguments against such a dramatic move. Undeterred, Anthony fended off the devil, who fled to lick his wounds, before resuming his assault. In the meantime, Anthony decided to harden his body to better withstand such ravages, limiting his sleep and diet, distancing himself from such base human needs. He took to the tombs, isolating himself from society, and at this point a pack of devils assaulted him without restraint. Sounding a little like an action hero defying his enemies with a brash "bring it on," Anthony declared, "Here am I, Antony; I do not run away from your blows!" The devils charged him in a twisted menagerie of different forms—lions and serpents and scorpions and bears. None of them could touch Anthony. He dismissed them all: "If you had any power in you, it would have been enough that just one of you should come." Finally, the devils dispersed, and a light shined brightly in the tombs, accompanied by a resonant voice: "I was here, Antony, but I waited to see thy resistance. Therefore, since thou hast endured and not yielded, I will always be thy helper, and I will make thee renowned everywhere."

With that, Anthony set forth for the desert, settling into the abandoned fort which would become his home for decades. Removed from temptation and distraction, he aspired to live an unblemished life, engaged in fasting and prayer. As word spread of his efforts, Anthony became a model, inspiring generations of hermits to seek isolation and alienation in a strange land and an austere life.

Eventually, his friends coaxed him back from the desert, and he earned a reputation as a healer par excellence, as through his presence and prayer many saw illnesses cured, injuries mended, and evil spirits expelled. Anthony distanced himself from the miracles, asserting that healing comes only from God, and on God's schedule. Nonetheless, the connection between Anthony and healing would persist across the ages.

Not everyone could endure the life of a hermit; the solitude, in particular, could wear on a person. But certainly many found the appeal in austerity, asceticism, and prayer, and as a consequence Anthony's life also served to inspire the idea of monasteries, functioning first as a sort of ad hoc association of desert hermits, and eventually coalescing into a more formal structure.

After Anthony died in 356–at the age of 105, incidentally–his bones were destined to embark upon a journey that exceeded his own travels. Initially, his burial place remained secret, until he was re-interred in Alexandria, Egypt in the 6th century, in a tomb marked with a tau, the Egyptian cross that would become the symbol of his order. (The tau, incidentally, has a fascinating history of its own, appearing on Egyptian temples during the era of pharaohs, in the books of Ezekiel and Revelation as a sign of redemption, and in the signature of Saint Francis's letters.) When Saracen forces conquered Egypt in 635, the relics were translated to Constantinople for safe keeping. The story becomes much more complicated and divisive from there. Indeed, by the time all the machinations were com- plete, no less than three Saint Anthonies were claimed to be interred at different sites in Europe. Most important for our purposes, though, were the relics in La Motte St. Didier, near Vienne, France, as that became the birthplace of the Hospital Brothers of Saint Anthony in 1095. While another two centuries would pass before Pope Boniface VIII granted formal recognition to them as canons regular in 1297, the brothers were already well established across Europe within decades, serving their dual medical and military purposes.

The brothers came to Castrojeriz in the 12th century, after Alfonso VI donated the land for a new monastic complex in 1146. What happened next is known to us in large part thanks to Robert Mullen and Rebekah Scott, who compiled the aptly named, *San Antón A Little History*. And unfortunately, the "little" part of that wasn't merely an editorial choice; instead, it's reflective of how little information has survived the centuries, as the monastery's records were destroyed by fire following its closure in 1789. Nonetheless, we know that the monks here were originally tasked with a tripartite mission, devoted to protecting the Camino, caring for pilgrims, and offering medical services. Over time, the military responsibilities would ebb, but the medical function would only rise in importance. On one hand, the monastery never grew beyond a modest size, at no point exceeding 12 brothers and a superior, with an equivalent number of house servants. On the other, though, the monastery was none-theless a bustling operation, complete with a bakery, a smith, a winery, and, most amusingly, a thriving pack of pigs that were free to roam the streets and fields of Castrojeriz, fattening themselves on the public dime. Before anything else, though, it was as a hospital, as a place of healing, that San Antón made its mark.

But what were those monks treating? On the surface, the answer couldn't be more obvious: Saint Anthony's Fire. That condition has the saint's name written all over it, after all. And yet... what, exactly, is Saint Anthony's Fire? Consult almost any source you like—your favorite Camino guidebook, the Gitlitz and Davidson masterpiece, even the Wikipedia entry—and you will find the same answer: ergotism. In the Middle Ages, we learn, Europe periodically suffered from instances of mass poisoning, caused by a fungus, Claviceps purpurea, which sometimes grew on grain, and particularly on rye. That fungus generated ergot, an alkaloid-containing product which is quite harmful to humans. As Gianfranco Cervellin and colleagues explain, ergotism has two main clinical manifestations: gangrene, or chronic ergotism, and convulsions, or acute ergotism. As such, the most common physical consequences of ergotism were the drying and blackening of affected tissues, leading in extreme cases to "mummified limbs" dropping from the body. There were psychological impacts as well, including hallucinations and depressive conditions, causing some to view the afflicted as having a "diabolic nature." This led to one intriguing theory linking the Salem Witch Trials to an ergotism outbreak, however that is by no means the prevailing understanding.

By contrast, the idea that Saint Anthony's Fire is a synonym for ergotism certainly has become a consensus view. As Alessandra Foscati explains in her exhaustive study, *Saint Anthony's Fire from Antiquity to the Eighteenth Century*, though, instead of a conflagration we're looking at a conflation here, one that has muddied the epidemiological waters of at least a millennium's worth of history.

The problem has its roots in the term *ignis sacer*, or Holy Fire. Lucretius first referenced *ignis sacer* in an epidemiological context, in his 1st-century BC work, *De Rerum Natura*. He writes, "man is at the mercy of a wide range of ailments and it can even happen that the foot suddenly swells, sharp pain often seizes the teeth, or else attacks the eyes; the holy fire breaks out and creeping over the body burns whatever part it has seized upon." Later, he also links *ignis sacer* to the Plague of Athens. Right from its earliest uses, then, we see the term being applied to a broad range of ailments. Two centuries later, Columella employed *ignis sacer* in an entirely different way, noting that shepherds typically used it to describe a "pustule." The great natural scientist Pliny, meanwhile, linked this to a skin ailment caused by contact with thapsia root, a plant in the carrot family. The most fully-formed description of *ignis sacer* in the classical era comes from Celsus. As Foscati summarizes, Celsus wrote that it "can manifest itself in two different ways, either through the presence of red spots and burning pustules that spread over the body and primarily attack the chest, hips, extremities and soles of the feet or through dark red ulceration of the surface of the skin that mostly affects the elderly." The key point here is the sheer elasticity of the term; over these years, it described mild-to-serious skin conditions as well as an autonomous disease.

The use of *ignis sacer* did not become any more precise in the Middle Ages, or even the early modern era. As Cervellin and colleagues note, the "combination of poor hygienic conditions, infrequent changes of clothing, rare hand-washing, and overcrowded living facilities contributed to make skin affections commonplace in previous centuries." And *ignis sacer* was the perfect moniker to encompass those burning, unpleasant sensations. As such, in the words of Foscati, it has been linked to "too many diseases to attempt to provide a complete list: we will just mention that it has been plausibly related to anthrax, malignant pustules, certain forms of herpes, eruptive fevers (especially smallpox) and scurvy." It quite commonly became used to explain individual cases of gangrene, disconnected entirely from any sort of epidemic connection.

It should be noted that the "holy" part of Holy Fire is a matter of great consequence. Disease in the superstitious medieval world rarely functioned as a neutral force. On the contrary, it often offered a mark of divine judgement–a punishment imposed on sinners and a promise to the faithful that justice would be done, sooner or later. The most punitive sorts of diseases often disfigured the afflicted, especially in "less noble" parts of the body like the stomach and groin. One particularly vivid example of this, which shouldn't be read while eating, comes from Lactantius's *On the Deaths of the Persecutors.* He describes how God struck Galerius, infamous for his persecution of Christians, "with an incurable plague. A malignant ulcer formed itself low down in his secret parts, and spread by degrees." While doctors were initially able to halt its progression, "the sore, after having been skinned over, broke out again; a vein burst, and the blood flowed in such quantity as to endanger his life." After another intervention bought Galerius a spell of peace, "the blood streamed more abundantly than before. He grew emaciated, pallid, and feeble, and the bleeding then stanched. The ulcer began to be insensible to the remedies applied, and a gangrene seized all the neighbouring parts. It diffused itself the wider the more the corrupted flesh was cut away, and everything employed as the means of cure served but to aggravate the disease." The finest physicians in the land were brought to Galerius, but the patient only deteriorated further: "his bowels came out, and his whole seat putrefied." It got worse. Good lord, it got worse: "the distemper attacked his intestines, and worms were generated in his body. The stench was so foul as to pervade not only the palace, but even the whole city; and no wonder, for by that time the passages from his bladder and bowels, having been devoured by the worms, became indiscriminate, and his body, with intolerable anguish, was dissolved into one mass of corruption." Galerius survived, but his body was a statement of his sin: "the different parts of his body had lost their natural form: the superior part was dry, meagre, and haggard, and his ghastly-looking skin had settled itself deep among his bones while the inferior, distended like bladders, retained no appearance of joints."

It makes sense, then, that Saint Anthony, among others, would be called upon to bring relief. A divine punishment requires divine intercession, and Anthony fit the bill. Not only was he associated with healing, but his connection to the desert and devilish assaults linked him to fire and burning as well. Those pigs of Castrojeriz come into play here as well, because the story ran that the brotherhood treated skin diseases in part with pig fat. The critical point to emphasize, though, is that even as *ignis Sancti Anthoni* began to appear in references in the Middle Ages, there is not a single medieval source that applies the term to an epidemic. Foscati has the receipts. When Saint Anthony's Fire was referenced, it solely occurred in the context of an individual disease. As far late as the 16th century, Foscati continued to fail to identify a single case of an epidemic linked to Saint Anthony's Fire or ergotism.

So what happened? How did these become synonyms? The discovery of the food-borne nature of epidemics is often attributed to physicians at the University of Marburg in 1597. Even that, though, fails to explore ergotism. Better to turn instead to Denis Dodart in 1676, who observed the appearance of contaminated rye and speculated on connections between that and an ongoing epidemic in the Sologne region. By the 18th century, physicians would finally pin down ergotism. Even at this point, though, there was no link being asserted between ergotism and Saint Anthony's Fire.

Not until 1767 would François Raymond crack that door open. But then, just a few years later, a French physician named Read barreled through the opening, writing in his *Traité du Siegle ergoté* that, "The different diseases that afflicted France in the 10th, 11th, 12th, 13th and 16th centuries which were variously called sacred fire, burning disease, hell fire and Saint Anthony's disease owe their origin to the use of rye ergot." Other physicians would quickly follow Read's lead, and before long the narrative gained precedence, carrying on largely undisputed to this day.

Foscati sums this process up succinctly: each of these physicians "subjected various past sources to retrospective diagnosis based on their pre-established idea of the disease rather than striving to understand which disease (or diseases) the term Saint Anthony's Fire actually referred to in these sources with philological criteria that were still alien to them," and as a consequence they "ended up simply likening Saint Anthony's Fire to gangrene of any type and aetiology just as their predecessors had done."

There's a powerful lesson to be found in their error, one that moves us far beyond epidemiology or nosography. It's hardly uncommon, upon the discovery of new information, or the acquisition of deeper insights, to reevaluate prior learning or experiences. Sometimes, this can be instructive; only once we see the full shape of things can we retro- actively connect the dots or understand the causal links. All too often, though, our reinterpretation of the past falls prey to our desire for narrative simplicity. Just because there are dots to be connected, after all, doesn't mean they should be.

This is not to suggest that ergotism wasn't a legitimate concern in medieval Europe. At least 83 ergotism epidemics have been documented, and they continued to wreak havoc as late as 1951, when an outbreak in France killed nearly 250 people. It's also not to assert that the Hospital Brothers of Saint Anthony never treated victims of ergotism; they absolutely must have. That was just one of a wider set of ailments, though, that they faced in their good works.

In time, though, medical care shifted from the realm of faith to science, improved hygiene reduced some of the issues with skin inflammation, and changes in agriculture reduced the prevalence of ergotism. And, of course, pilgrim traffic on the Camino declined. What purpose remained for the monks of San Antón? Finally, Pope Pius VI declared the Order of San Antón extinct in Spain in 1787, turning all of its properties over to the Crown. A small cohort of monks stuck around to tend to the remaining patients, but within 20 years it was all over. Some of the property was repurposed; other parts were left to the elements.

Ever so slowly, though, the old Monastery of San Antón has been saved, at least in part. In May 2001, a pilgrim, Ovidio Campo Fernandez, and the property owner, Eliecer Diez Temino, made a deal, resulting in the creation of the Albergue de San Antón, a donation-based pilgrim refuge that, by design, has no electricity, no phone, no wifi, no hot water. What it offers in abundance, though, is hospitality and care. And in that regard, it sustains a nearly millennium-old tradition. That particular flame, at least, still burns.

Keep reading...

Alessandra Foscati, *Saint Anthony's Fire from Antiquity to the Eighteenth Century*, 2019

Gianfranco Cervellin, et. al., "One holy man, one eponym, three distinct diseases. Saint Anthony's fire revisited," *Acta Biomed*, 2020

Robert Mullen and Rebekah Scott, *San Antón A Little History*, 2016

Saint Athanasius, JB McLaughlin (trans.), *Saint Antony of the Desert*, 2010

The Restoration of *Iglesia de San Martín*

Stage 15: Boadilla to Carrión de los Condes

The first time I walked through the Roman Forum, I was, of course, overwhelmed by the scope of the place. The sheer antiquity of the Forum defies easy interpretation. It has to be said as well, though, that the absolute degradation of the site plays its own part in the interpretive challenges. What would it be like, I wondered, if instead of leaving this in ruins, with old rocks piled haphazardly around the crumbling foundations, our greatest archaeologists and engineers collaborated to rebuild the forum, to restore its lost glory? How could we be satisfied with the ruined reality, when an alternative is possible?

But then I learned about Knossos, the one-time center of Minoan civilization on the island of Crete, linked indelibly to the myth of the minotaur in its labyrinth and his unfortunate run-in with Theseus. Like millions of other wide-eyed tourists, I visited Knossos, and in the moment I was quite taken with the palace complex. Here was a place I could visualize, a site whose history offered vivid glimpses of what once stood so proudly, as opposed to merely preserving all that we have lost.

The truth, though, is more complicated. These days, the story of Knossos is tied as closely to Arthur Evans as Theseus or the minotaur. The one-time curator of Oxford's Ashmolean Museum developed a passion, or maybe an obsession, with the Cretan ruins. When he first set foot on Crete in 1894, the site of Knossos hadn't yet been recovered, but he had studied the matter deeply, and he put his money where his mind was, purchasing a land covered in olive groves and then conducting a mostly self-financed excavation. While he had no experience with such endeavors, he enjoyed support from two of the brightest minds in the field at the time, including the director of the British School of Archaeology at Athens. Duncan Mackenzie, another archaeologist who played a key part in the dig, deserves credit for his meticulous diary entries, along with extensive sketches and photographs, which allows us to recreate Evans's process. And Evans as well did a meritorious job of carefully documenting each layer of earth as the excavation unfolded, taking note of the precise depth of each object discovered. Given the criticism to follow, it's only fair to acknowledge that Evans made some commendable moves.

He was also immediately confronted with a significant challenge. Almost as soon as he revealed these ancient structures to the world, he realized that their preservation required bold intervention. The Minoans built their palace with a combination of limestone, sandstone, and gypsum, and exposure to the elements would quickly wear away those vulnerable materials. Evans took quick action, installing a roof over the throne room complex in 1901. Unfortunately, heavy rains wiped out the second landing of the Grand Staircase in 1905, further underscoring the urgency involved. Again, Evans demonstrated credible responsive-ness in his treatment of this.

Here is where matters become much more complicated: As his biographer, Sandy MacGillivray explains, "It was a time of reconstruction. The First World War was so horrible. Architects wanted to build a new world, and Knossos became part of that." While Evans began with wood, brick, and steel bars to reinforce structures at the site, following World War I he embraced concrete, and while that was lar-gely unprecedented in Greece, it was largely in keeping with broader trends in architecture. Instead of merely preserving, Evans proceeded to rebuild. Alexandra Karetsou writes that he "restored entire stories of the palace," and after initially trying to employ the materials used by Minoans, "he now started to imitate ancient materials by modern means, painting them accordingly." Karetsou politely evaluates these choices, noting that Evans was "realising an architectural vision that arose from a lengthy (nearly 20 years) study of the archaeological data but was also the product of a creative imagination." Greek archaeologist Stylianos Alexiou criticizes Evans for operating "without an adequate sense of the original, thus altering the character of the ruins and bringing about its disunity." The barbs grow only more pointed from there. The French scholar René Dussaud marvels at "the brazenness of Evans's actions," accusing him of "completely rebuilding the palace of Minos from scratch" and creating the "unpleasant impression of entering a completely redecorated apartment."

Potentially more concerning, as laid out by Spencer P.M. Harrington, is the lasting impact of these fanciful recon-structions on our understanding of Minoan civilization. He spotlights the architect Clairy Palyvou, who asserts that, "This has completely changed the feeling of Minoan archi-tecture." It's interesting, though, that Palyvou subsequently adds that, while he and his contemporary colleagues wouldn't have followed Evans's approach, "deep inside, most of us are not that upset with what he did." This speaks to my initial ambivalence; while something is most certainly lost in such reconstructions, there is something potentially profound to be gained for modern audiences.

Is there a point, though, at which the restorations and reconstructions proceed so far beyond the original that the connection between the two, growing all the more tenuous and feeble over the centuries, finally snaps?

Thanks for your forbearance. We come, at last, back to the Camino, and specifically to the town of Frómista. In her highly regarded (and rightly so!) Moon guidebook to the Camino de Santiago, anthropologist Beebe Bahrami writes that "the reason why people visit Frómista" is "the *Iglesia de San Martín*, one of the jewels of medieval Iberia, built in the 11th century. San Martín is worth all the time you can offer it, both to take in all the stone images engraved in the corbels and capitals inside and out, and also to enjoy the visceral feeling of being in a sacred space built to perfect proportions for the human form." I can't take issue with any of that; I was astonished by the space in my first visit, and eagerly anticipated my return on each subsequent pilgrimage. However, it also has to be noted that any proper evaluation of the church leads us back into the same labyrinthine twists and turns as Knossos, grappling with the authenticity and integrity of the space.

By the 19th century, the *Iglesia de San Martín* had fallen on hard times. Founded in 1066 (or perhaps 1090, as recent historians suggest), and once part of a thriving monastic complex, over the course of the 18th and 19th centuries it was stripped of its incomes, had its properties confiscated, and gradually deteriorated until alarms were raised that one of the region's architectural masterpieces might be lost. José

Luis Senra and Laura García Blas have mapped out what unfolded next in great detail. In 1850, the Spanish politician Pascual Madoz warned that the vaults were on verge of collapse; a decade later, the scholar and painter Valentín Carderera y Solano expressed his fondness for the church and declared that "it is worthy of careful preservation." The cleric D. Segundo González, a decade later, rang alarm bells more vigorously, writing to the bishop of Palencia that the church was, "in a state of imminent ruin and requires prompt repair." The problems went far beyond the vault by this point, as the excessive weight bearing down upon the transept generated cracks in supporting pillars throughout the structure. When the secretary of the Provincial Commission of Monuments of Palencia finally paid a visit here in 1894, he effectively threaded the needle between despair and optimism, comparing the church to a patient facing death, whose cure was "not only possible, but easy."

At long last, restoration efforts were set in motion in 1895, under the guidance of Manuel Aníbal Álvarez. While Álvarez had received no formal training in restoration practices, he spent 1875 in Italy, during which time he participated in restoration projects on Rome's Pantheon of Agrippa and Venice's Doge's Palace. Joaquin de Ciria praised the selection, noting that if Álvarez "has any defect, it is his excessive modesty, well known and celebrated by all," adding that he conducted the restoration of San Martín "with that affection of the artist at heart who puts all his senses into what he executes."

It wasn't the affection that troubled the many critics of Álvarez's work. Rather, critics—including many contemporary art historians—claim that the church's "historical importance was destroyed by over-restoration." Álvarez didn't merely shore up foundations and reinforce the roof; he utterly eliminated large parts of the original structure. As much as

20% of the original materials were removed, an act that Senra has condemned as an "archaeological crime." To make matters worse, documentation of these efforts, in contrast to Knossos, are almost non-existent. There is no record at all of what was effectively swept into the dustbin of history.

Álvarez insisted that the restoration efforts would be conducted with "the same existing stones and placed in the same places [...] and that if some ornamented ones were missing (which would be very few) [...] they would be placed with old stone, so that the color does not clash, and without ornamentation so that there is never confusion between the old and the modern." However, his actions ran afoul of these promises time and time again. The southern part of the church was completely destroyed and removed. A new foundation laid in response to this also necessitated the dismantling of the central and southern naves, along with the transept and the southern apse. Meanwhile, the church's much-admired ornamentation faced equally dramatic changes; Manuel Gómez-Moreno has reported that this included a wave of newly-sculpted features, including 11 capitals, 86 modillions, 46 bases, and 12 cymatia. The original altarpiece was also scrapped, as were the secondary altarpieces and part of the choir. Even the tombs, located both inside and outside the church, were exhumed and moved elsewhere.

Miguel Ángel García Guinea writes that, "After its restoration at the beginning of the century, it constitutes an example of Romanesque architectural art so complete, defined and clean of other styles, as no other is seen along the entire route." And of course that's true. How many other Romanesque churches were built, almost in their entirety, in the 20th century? While Álvarez's rebuilt *Iglesia de San Martín* preserves the broad lines of the original structure, he deserves equal billing as the church's restorer and architect-in-chief.

In the end, though, this brings me back to where I began, grappling with ambivalence and no closer to an answer. Is this–the dramatic reimaginings of San Martín and Knossos–a bad thing? From their very beginning, churches and cathedrals were works in progress, evolving over time as revenues grew, architectural styles shifted, and urban populations rose or fell. These were literally etched in stone, but not figuratively so; they could and would be transformed or replaced. They were also, it should be noted, covered in vibrant color, vivid and alive. So many of the structures that we protect so fiercely today–as we should!–are ruined and gray, fading reminders of what they once were. Could we be managing this better?

Keep reading...

Alexandra Karetsou, "Knossos after Evans: past interventions, present state and future solutions," *British School at Athens Studies*, 2004

José Luis Senra, "La realidad material de la iglesia de San Martín de Frómista en el siglo XII: de 1066 a 1904," *San Martín de Frómista, ¿Paradigma o Historicismo?*, 2005

José Luis Senra, "Rebellion, Reconciliation, and a Romanesque Church in León-Castile (c.1109–1120)," *Speculum*, 2012

Laura García Blas, "San Martín de Frómista. Revisión historiográfica de su construcción y restauraciones," *De Medio Aevo*, 2013

Spencer P.M. Harrington, "Saving Knossos," *Archaeology*, 1999

The Long Reach of Rome

Stage 16: Carrión de los Condes to Terradillos de los Templarios

The walk from Carrión de los Condes dominates pilgrim conversations for days prior to its encounter. The longest stretch of open space on the Camino, with no villages, services, or even people–aside, these days, from a seasonal food truck–this can be a bogeyman of sorts, causing many to worry about their capacity to make it through. The terrain is easy enough, but the lack of shade can make hot summer days oppressive, and the flatness of the earth conveys a sense of barrenness and endlessness. Even when the Camino finally delivers pilgrims into Calzadilla de la Cueza, it's easy to feel like civilization is holding on for dear life. Certainly that was the case when David Gitlitz and Linda Davidson passed through. They note that in 1974, "no roads to the town were paved; perhaps a third of the houses were inhabited, and the rest were falling apart. Adobe was the only material in use." From the earth, to the walls, and back to the earth again.

And yet, within this unforgiving landscape, the past persists, sometimes spectacularly so. A Roman highway, linking Bordeaux and Astorga, passed through here, and its remains are still walkable at different points in the *meseta*. Logically enough, then, that also brought Romans to the region, and they left their mark as well. Just 3.5km south of Calzadilla de la Cueza sits one such example, the villa of La Tejada, located near Quintanilla de la Cueza.

The Roman conquest of Iberia originated in its long, turbulent conflict with Carthage, and Rome's ultimate success in the Second Punic War in 206 BC brought with it the southern and eastern coasts of the peninsula. The complete subjugation of what would become known as Roman Hispania would take time, including a series of brutal battles between 159 and 133 BC, followed by another set of conflicts led by Julius Caesar (61-59 BC), and a final push by Octavian into Galicia in 19 BC. The Romans, of course, were always eager to expand their agricultural base, and Hispania offered significant potential as a source for wheat, olive oil, and wine, especially after large-scale irrigation projects transformed the land.

Like Calzadilla, so too would many of those civilizing efforts fall prey, over time, to the ravages of the land. Indeed, the entire story of the late Roman Empire has been framed as a declensionist narrative, shaped by the powerful legacy of Edward Gibbon's *The History of the Decline and Fall of the Roman Empire*. However, more recent scholarship has called that framing into question. As Alexandra Chavarría Arnau explains, the "extraordinary development" in rural residential architecture in the *meseta* in the 4th century, long explained "in terms of 'crisis and decline', connecting it with the conflicts of the 3rd century, a flight of the aristocracy from the cities, and a generalised ruralisation of society," now merits reconsideration. No such urban decline was at work in Hispania during those years; on the contrary, the cities continued to flourish throughout the 4th century.

Hispania discovered a newfound relevance to the wider Roman realm in those years. Around 375, a young man settled in his family's ancestral home in Cauca, near present-day Segovia. His journey there from the Danube must have been a fraught one, triggered as it was by the sudden execution of his father, a high-ranking general, whose fall remains a mystery to this day. Absence makes the heart grow fonder, and before long the young man was recalled to service, though that process is equally murky. What is clear, regardless, is that a meteoric rise followed. By 379, the young man, Theodosius, became emperor of the Eastern Roman Empire, and in 394 he secured control of the empire in its entirety–the very last to do so.

Over time, a story took shape around the centrality of Hispania to Theodosius's story. Born and raised in Iberia, and then subsequently sheltered there, the land was viewed as integral to his identity, and as he rose in power critics claimed that he filled the eastern court with westerners. Neil McLynn has resoundingly challenged such notions. It's unlikely that Theodosius spent much time at all in Iberia as a child; it would have been expected that the child, possibly even the newborn, would have accompanied his military father in the field. And precious few of his early officials, it turns out, had Iberian roots.

Nonetheless, his resurgence illustrates a Roman world that, despite its sprawling size, was smaller than ever, with this young man traveling from the Danube to Cauca and back again to Constantinople, and if Hispania didn't become the new emperor's administrative base, it certainly was no backwater. Wealth and influence were well established there, and one couldn't be a wealthy, influential Roman without a country villa.

The explosion of monumental villas in the Roman *meseta* in the 4th century was unparalleled in Hispania's history. Country villas had long been in place, of course, but this period saw their transformation into what Fernando Regueras and Caridad San José characterize as an "arrogant architecture" with "luxurious ornamentation." While much has been lost, one key component of that ornamentation survives: the mosaics. All told, some 400 mosaics have been recovered in the region to this point, the overwhelming majority of them being located in rural areas. While an earlier wave of mosaic development occurred more prominently in urban areas, like Astorga, those primarily date to the 1st through 3rd centuries. The rural realm then took precedence, thriving in the 4th and 5th.

Geometric designs were most commonplace among these mosaics. Some frame this as an economic matter; certainly, such designs would have been easier to produce and require less skill. Others attributed it to the rise of Neopythagorean thought or the resurgence of aniconic beliefs; while I'll avoid a deep dive into those rabbit holes, suffice it to say that they favored a shift away from idols and towards deeper learning, often with an esoteric bent. Nonetheless, the mosaics weren't exclusively geometrical. Most popular were hunting scenes, which also aligned with one of the most common activities among the residents. In other cases, the mosaic content aligned with the function of the room. For example, baths were often adorned with pelagic- or ocean-themed scenes. These are particularly prominent in La Tejada, where scenes include the Titan Oceanus, surrounded by four dolphins and other fish, Neptune and Amphitrite (the Roman god of the sea and his wife), and the Mosaic of the Fishes. Of special interest is the "oriental" nature of some of the designs, which in this context refers to the Eastern Roman or Byzantine influence.

The reality is that we know precious little about what happened at La Tejada. For a time, it was regarded as just another of the monumental villas in this area, revealing the same kind of expansive *pars urbana*, or public area, as many of its peers. The prominent bathing areas, though, have led to some speculation that it could have functioned as a roadside spa for travelers navigating that long Roman road.

A great deal remains to be discovered. Part of the challenge, Chavarria Arnau explains, is that "archaeological work in Spain focused until the 1980s almost exclusively on the discovery and conservation of the decorative elements of the residences, especially the mosaics." As a consequence, they tended to ignore more functional spaces, or the less prestigious houses owned by farmers and other rural workers. Some of that has been lost, but much of it is still there, waiting to be explored.

It's impossible to see the world without narratives, but it's fascinating to consider the many ways that our sense of Rome has been shaped by erroneous framings. The declensionist story has been debunked; even as the "barbarians" swept Iberia over the succeeding centuries, they were overwhelmingly "romanized" peoples who largely maintained what had been built. The dominant impact of Theodosius on Hispania–and Hispania upon Theodosius–doesn't withstand scrutiny. And our perception of rural Roman architecture has been shaped in part by a selection bias that favors the most beautiful and intricate structures at the cost of more mundane ones.

To what degree, one wonders, are erroneous or limiting narratives shaping our views of our Camino, of the landscapes and towns we're passing through. Any critical reflection on that, I would suggest, should start with notions of barrenness in this area.

Keep reading…

Alexandra Chavarría Arnau, "Interpreting the Transformation of Late Roman Villas: The Case of Hispania," *Landscapes of Change*, 2004

Alexandra Chavarría Arnau, "Villas in Hispania during the Fourth and Fifth Centuries," *Hispania in Late Antiquity: Current Perspectives*, 2005

Fernando Regueras and Caridad San José, "Mosaics of the Hispanic Meseta Norte: Phases, Officinae, Artistic Taste," *Journal of Mosaic Research*, 2017

Luis C. Juan Tovar, "La Terra Sigillata de Quintanilla de la Cueza," *Serie Arqueología*, 2000

Neil McLynn, "'Genere Hispanus': Theodosius, Spain and Nicene Orthodoxy," *Hispania in Late Antiquity: Current Perspectives*, 2005

Fray Bernardino de Sahagún and the Other Santiagos

Stage 17: Terradillos de los Templarios to Calzadilla de los Hermanillos

Most pilgrims miss him. The Camino arcs through Sahagún, winding in from the southeast and passing out through the southwest, following Calle Antonio Nicolás for a good chunk of that, and many of the pilgrim-focused services thus cluster in those areas. Travel a little north, though, and you can find Bernardino in the middle of an odd block, an island of sorts situated alongside Avenida de la Constitución. Sahagún's most famous son, history's first anthropologist, departed Spain for the New World and never returned. With a cross in one hand and a book clasped tightly in the other, his statue serves as a reminder that, even in the worst of times, and the most conflicted of situations, an individual is capable of transcending their own ingrained prejudices and becoming a force for good.

Bernardino de Sahagún was born in 1499. We know little of his origins, but given his education, he must have been born into the minor nobility, or at least a family of some means. The Sahagún of his youth was well past its peak. Just a few years earlier, the Benedictine monastery, once a powerhouse under Cluny, had fallen under control of the monastery in Valladolid, further reducing its economic and political power. Nonetheless, one has to imagine that even past its prime, its rich heritage–even today, the Romanesque, Gothic, and Mudéjar remains are still evident–would have captured the imagination of the young Bernardino. He pursued higher education in Salamanca, and during those years he decided to become a Franciscan.

As Miguel León-Portilla outlines in his biography of Bernardino, these were dramatic, often turbulent, years for Spain and the Church. The unification of Spain was finally completed, with the integration of Granada and Navarre. Alongside that, the Spanish Inquisition grew into its fullest form, striving ever more aggressively to root out false conversos and moriscos, Jews and Muslims who had claimed conversion to Christianity but maintained their old beliefs and practices. Reports from overseas also brought dramatic news, as Columbus, Cortés, and da Gama reshaped the world map. And in 1517, Martin Luther set the Christian world ablaze, igniting the Protestant Reformation. Alongside the fear of heretics, then, there would follow paranoia involving the creeping influence of Luther and his ilk, undermining the faith from within. Bernardino, facing all of this, found purpose in his Franciscan vows, believing that poverty and charity offered the cure for the corruption plaguing the Church and the world.

In the wake of Cortés's conquest of Mexico in 1521, plans quickly took shape for the Bible to follow the Sword. Fray Bernardino would be recruited to join the second wave of Franciscans to cross the Atlantic, part of a group of twenty missionaries that arrived in 1529. In the process, he managed to find a vastly more unstable and chaotic environment than the one he had just left. Fray Toribio de Benavente, one of the original cohort of fourteen Franciscans, laid out just how disastrous conquest had been for the indigenous populations, as epidemics and famines ravaged the people. And those were likely less brutal still than the Spanish oppressors who "rankle and corrupt, with a stench like that of fly-bitten carrion." He added that, "with the great fear that [the Indians] acquired for the Spaniards from the time of war, they would give whatever they had; but because the levies were so constant, they would sell their children and lands to the merchants in order to satisfy them." Entire towns had been emptied, due to the combined impact of slavery, tribute, plague, and starvation.

In the midst of all of that, though, the Franciscans had reason for optimism. As Bernardino would later write, "we were told that [the Indians] had come to the Faith so completely, and were almost all baptized and so wholly in the Catholic Faith of the Roman Church, that there was no need to preach against idolatry because they had truly abandoned it." One would imagine that a people who had so recently been confronted with the challenges emerging from the forced conversion of Jews and Muslims might be more skeptical about the same process unfolding so smoothly in the New World, but never underestimate our remarkable capacity for self-deception.

Bernardino was not so easily convinced. He threw himself into this profoundly different environment, visiting towns, climbing volcanoes, and laboring to learn the Nahuatl language. And he quickly discovered that reports of widespread conversion had vastly overstated the reality on the ground. The problem as he diagnosed it was the blindness of his fellow Franciscans to native thought and practices. In order to purge the idolatrous beliefs from the people, and thus save their immortal souls, Bernardino and his colleagues first needed to understand them. He compared their situation to that of a physician, who would struggle, as León-Portilla paraphrased it, with "effectively prescribing the medications for the patient without first knowing from which humor or from which cause the illness stems." Critics of Bernardino will emphasize this starting point–that his initial focus on learning served the goal of eradicating indigenous culture, in order to excel in his missionary ambitions. That's an entirely fair position to take. But it's not the whole story.

A key development in the life of Bernardino de Sahagún occurred in 1536, when he transitioned from direct missionary work to a teaching role at the College of Santa Cruz in Tlatelolco. There were two significant consequences that flowed from this. First, Bernardino's work as a teacher provided him with an opportunity to build extended relationships with young indigenous minds, some of whom would become invaluable assistants, before developing into credible scholars in their own right. He was impressed by what he learned about them: "they are quick to learn and employ the mechanical arts. [...] Also in trades such as tailor, shoemaker, silkmaker, printer, scribe, reader, accountant, singer of plainsong and with organ accompaniment, flute player, pipe player, sackbut player, trumpeter, organist; he knows grammar, logic, rhetoric, astrology, and theology; all of this we know from experience, that they have talent for it and learn it and know it, and they teach it, and that there is no art for which they do not have the talent to learn and use it."

Second, Bernardino's position at the college also empowered him to dedicate an ever-growing part of his life to research, diving into Mesoamerican culture. And on the road to conversion, a funny thing happened. He found a great deal to admire, and felt a palpable urgency to preserve what could be saved, before it disappeared forever. There was no time to waste. Just two years before he began his research in earnest in 1547, the first round of the terrible cocoliztli epidemics swept through Mexico, killing somewhere between five and fifteen million people. Bernardino had to face this firsthand: "I was in Tlatelolco and buried more than ten thousand corpses; at the end of the pestilence, I caught the disease and was close to my end."

Finally recovered, he studied the Huehuetlahtoili, the ancient wisdom ascribed to Aztec elders, and found them every bit on par with the writings that have survived from classical antiquity. Across the fields of rhetoric, moral philosophy, and theology, they more than held their own, and he discovered that "the wise, eloquent, virtuous, and courageous" scholars behind such work were "held in high esteem." He was so struck by advice offered by Mexican parents to their children that he wrote that, "because of the language and style in which they are expressed, [the advice] would be of greater profit spoken from the pulpit than many a sermon preached to the boys and girls." As corrupted as their practices were by idolatry, Bernardino admired their deep-seated spirituality, observing at one point that "The language and affection [employed] as they prayed to their principal god" made use of "beautiful metaphors and figures of speech." There was much to appreciate about the political system as well. It doesn't quite rise to the level of "and other than that, Mrs. Lincoln, how was the play?", but his observation about their government echoes the sentiment: "And if that manner of governing had not been so infested with idolatrous rites and superstitions, it seems to me that it was quite good."

The most profound, lasting consequence of Fray Bernardino's efforts in these years was his compilation of the *Historia General de Las Cosas de la Nueva España*, a twelve-volume masterpiece that is responsible for saving much of what we know today about Aztec culture. The work is bilingual, in Spanish and Nahuatl, and also includes a substantial number of illustrations. Despite the missionaries' stated goal of eradicating indigenous religious practices, the *Historia General* preserves that worldview in remarkable detail. The section on "divine things" spans 112 pages, including a breakdown of the priesthood, a survey of all rituals practiced, and a description of every feast day, complete with a color painting for each one. Bernardino lauded their medical knowledge in particular, and years later, in the aftermath of another shattering epidemic, he bemoaned the loss: "It is to our great shame that the native Indians, rational and prudent, knew how to remedy the harm that this land imposes on those who live in it, obviating the things of nature with contrary exercises; yet we sink to the bottom with our evil inclinations." Had such expertise still been around, he suspected, the indigenous practitioners would have been able to mitigate the damage and save lives.

Fray Bernardino benefited from steadfast support at many points in his work. Two of the Franciscan leaders in the New World, Provincial Fray Miguel Navarro and Father Diego de Mendoza, sang his praises, writing that Bernardino and his colleague Fray Alonso de Molina "are the ones who can turn anything into the Mexican language and write in it, as they have been doing for many years hence and continue to do it today without tiring. It would be a great service to God and to Your Majesty and for the good of the natives to order the Viceroy and the prelates of the Order, while these two religious are still alive because they are now rather aged, that they should furnish them with all possible favor and warmth so that they can occupy themselves in writing in the Mexican language."

As the years passed, though, and Bernardino increasingly showed signs of "going native," some within the Church turned on him. There's a thin line, after all, between preserving and promoting, and if some could see the merit behind his claim that understanding was the first step towards elimination, it was equally easy to argue that Bernardino's succeeding steps had led him towards a very different destination. His writings were declared to be dangerous and denounced before the Council of Indies. Then, they were confiscated under royal order in 1577, following an edict by the Spanish Inquisition prohibiting the dissemination of sacred scripture in indigenous languages. Whether through genuine misunderstanding, willful obtuseness, or outright resistance, Fray Bernardino avoided the complete loss of his manuscript, and we are fortunate that it survives to this day.

Over the course of Spanish conquest and colonial rule, Fray Bernardino was just one of nearly two million Spaniards who crossed the Atlantic. They didn't just bring aspirations of easy wealth and spiritual glory with them, though. They also brought Santiago.

By the 16th century, the transformation of Saint James into Matamoros, the Moor-Slayer, was already well established. His first artistic appearance in that form, the Tympanum of Clavijo in the south transept of the Santiago Cathedral, dates to the mid-13th century. Don't be deceived by stories of Santiago Matamoros riding to the salvation of Christian soldiers in the Battle of Clavijo in 834; there is zero evidence to support such a thing. The myth took shape centuries later, around the time that Castilian soldiers began shouting Santiago's name as they rode into battle. By 1492, the link had solidified. As Ferdinand and Isabella rode into Granada, securing their final conquest, the heralds shouted, "Santiago! Santiago! Santiago!" Also by that point, the

Santiago shown in art took a more direct role, no longer just appearing as a beacon of hope to rally Christian forces, but rather wielding a sword with gusto, severing Moorish heads from their bodies.

Perhaps it was natural, then, that as the battlefield shifted from Iberia to the New World, it took on a similar guise. As Heather Dalton explains, Hieronymite friars referred to Indians as "Moors," while Cortés described indigenous temples in Veracruz as "mosques." The colony of Havana's coat of arms featured Santiago on horseback, sword raised overhead, and Antigua, Guatemala replicated that.

In the years that followed, a series of fascinating developments unfolded. Before long, Santiagos Peregrino and Matamoros were joined by a third incarnation, Santiago Mataindios. In a carved altarpiece recovered from Aztec ruins, dating to the early 1600s, we can see this taking shape—the man is half-gladiator and half-Conquistador, the shell on his familiar hat having been replaced with a sun, the Moors underfoot swapped out for dismembered Aztecs.

Santiago's impact was felt even more keenly further south, in the Incan Empire's final days. In the limited descriptions we find of James in the Bible, we learn that he and his brother John were referred to by Jesus as the "Boanerges," or sons of thunder, because of their temper. That reference would carry special weight in the New World. In the Siege of Cusco in 1536-37, the Christian forces, led by Hernando Pizarro, were surrounded by an Incan army. As Felipe Guaman Poma de Ayala relates, "at that moment when the Christians were completely under siege, [Santiago] made another miracle in the city of Cuzco. Those who witnessed the event say they saw Santiago come down from the sky [...] preceded by an enormous clap of thunder, followed by lightning that fell on the Inca fortress of

Sacahuaman [...] Santiago came down to earth in this way to defend the Spanish."

There were lasting consequences to this appearance. Poma de Ayala adds that, from that moment, the Incans referred to lightning as "Santiago." As it happened, the Incans had already worshipped a God of Thunder, by the name of Illapa, who was also associated with forces of power and domination throughout the region. As time passed, a syncretic process unfolded, with Santiago and Illapa being viewed in the highlands, in particular, as one and the same. The Spanish Christians came to be horrified by this usurping of their patron saint, ultimately prohibiting indigenous children from being called Illapa or Santiago.

That, however, didn't mark the end of the story. In the 19th century, when indigenous Peruvians rose up in revolt against the Spanish, they rallied behind a divine force of their own. His name? Santiago Mataespañois.

Fray Bernardino de Sahagún and Santiago Mataespañois together offer us an invaluable reminder. Cross-cultural contact isn't a one-way street. The worldviews, value systems, and practices—not to mention the blade itself—cut both ways.

Keep reading...

Bernardino de Sahagún, Arthur J. O. Anderson (trans.),
   *Florentine Codex: General History of the Things of New
   Spain*, 2012

Heather Dalton, "Santiago Matamoros/Mataindios: Adopting
   an Old World Battlefield Apparition as a New World
   Representation of Triumph," *Matters of Engagement:*

Emotions, Identity, and Cultural Contact in the Premodern World, 2021

Irene Silverblatt, "Political Memories and Colonizing Symbols: Santiago and the Mountain Gods of Peru," *Rethinking History and Myth: Indigenous South American Perspectives on the Past*, 1988

Miguel León-Portilla, *Bernardino de Sahagun: First Anthropologist*, 2002

Storks on Steeples

Stage 18: Calzadilla de los Hermanillos to Mansilla de las Mulas

When I was a kid, I learned about storks from a most reputable source: cartoons. I was led to believe that these majestic birds were responsible for delivering babies to awaiting parents. As an adult, I discovered that this connection wasn't just a comedic gimmick, but rather the persistence of a Greek myth–and a decidedly dark one at that. As Isabelle Gerretsen explains, the story there centers on cranes, which became conflated with storks over time (something that makes me feel better about my inability to distinguish between cranes and herons). Hera, awkwardly the wife and sister of Zeus, was among other things the goddess of childbirth. When she caught Gerana, the queen of the Pygmy folk, having an affair with Zeus, Hera transformed her into a crane. Gerana, however, had just given birth to a baby, and she was loath to lose her child, so she wrapped it in a blanket, picked up the package with her beak, and flew off.

In the 19th century, Hans Christian Andersen repackaged this mythic narrative as folktale in his story "The Storks." The mechanics here are much more straightforward. Andersen writes that there is a "pond in which all the little children lie, waiting till the storks come to take them to their parents." Lest this sound like a lovely vision, it must be added that the storks in the story conspire to wreak vengeance on a naughty little boy who had sung about hanging, frying, and shooting them. "There lies in the pond a little dead baby who has dreamed itself to death," notes the mother stork to her aggrieved children. "We will take it to the naughty boy, and he will cry because we have brought him a little dead brother." Folks, don't mess with storks.

In a more figurative sense, storks are also lifebringers, as they play a crucial role in dispersing seeds. Researchers found nearly 10,000 seedlings within close proximity to each white stork nest, mobilized by the storks' transport of weeds and animal dung as nesting materials. Czarnecka and Kitowski have dubbed white storks "ecosystem engineers," explaining that they "affect energy and matter flows in an ecosystem by creating or destroying living space, and thereby altering environments of other organisms." As one example of that, white stork nests are cohabited by house sparrows, tree sparrows, starlings, kestrels, and grey wagtails. They also assist with human agriculture, as they prey upon species that cause significant damage to crops, including brown locusts, caterpillars, and the common vole.

The European white stork originates in the north, with many hailing from the Elbe River Biosphere Reserve near Brandenburg, Germany. Traditionally, these storks have wintered in Africa, enjoying the warmer climate in places like Ethiopia, Senegal, and Nigeria. In between, they've followed one of two migratory trajectories, either heading southeastward through Turkey, or southwestward through France and Spain. To the joy of many pilgrims, including this one, this brings many storks to the Camino de Santiago, and their presence is felt most keenly in the *meseta*. It's rare indeed to come across a church in these small towns without a long-established stork nest on its bell tower.

It could have been very different. The European Union categorized the white stork as an Annex I species in 2009, which meant that it was "in danger of extinction, vulnerable, rare, or requiring particular attention." Despite that, today it has been labeled a "species of Least Concern." It's not that the officials decided to simply be unconcerned about the stork's extermination. On the contrary, thank goodness, it's because the bird has bounced back to a remarkable degree. Alejandro López-García and José Aguirre found that the 215 occupied nests in greater Madrid in 1984 had surged to 2,327 in 2021. Barbarin and colleagues found a similar story in Navarre, where their 2021 study documented 739 pairs, the highest number ever recorded in the region. A country-wide 2020 census found 36,217 storks in Spain overall, giving it the largest population in Europe, outside of Poland.

Two key changes drove this dramatic transformation. The first involves the placement of stork nests. Storks have long taken advantage of the built environment; there's some indication that this originated as far back as the Neolithic era. It's not that they won't make use of trees or cliffs; the study conducted by Barbarin and colleagues in 2021 found that nearly half still established their nests in trees, and most notably the holm oak, cedar, ash, and fir. Rather, human structures, like churches, electrical pylons, chimneys, antenna towers, and street poles seemed equally acceptable, and in places they were rising in popularity. Two different studies, conducted by Tryjanowski et. al. and Vaitkuviene & Dagys found the same trend, with traditional structures abandoned in favor of manmade options.

One of the biggest advantages for storks and other birds living in urban environments is the "scarecrow effect," which refers to the common phenomenon of nest predators being scared away by human activity in the area. The birds are impressively strategic, though, in how they approach these spaces, as Cem S. Kayatekin and colleagues have demonstrated in their study of Segovia, Spain. Nest placement isn't random. First, stork nests avoid busy bus routes and major arterials. Second, they prioritize a more elevated position, relative to the surrounding area. It's not about absolute height, but instead the adjacent buildings; on average, the researchers found that storks settled in nesting locations that were 12 meters higher than their surroundings. While this obviously allowed for improved surveillance, it also provided for an easy departure, no aggressive flapping required. Third, the structures need to be flat, or shallow-sloped, for reasons that are obvious enough–it makes the nest-building process much more straightforward. Finally, proximity to food matters. Interestingly, though, it's less about distance and more about visual exposure; every stork nest in Segovia has unobstructed sight lines, linking them to nearby meadows or wetlands.

This leads quite naturally into the second change that has supported the stork resurgence. Recent decades have brought, in Barbarin's words, "new, superabundant feeding sources" to storks in Spain. This includes the red swamp crayfish and an American crab species, which sounds pretty good. It also includes, possibly even more consequentially, landfills. Which… well, maybe that robs storks of some of their charm.

The importance of landfills to storks, though, can't be overstated. In the Madrid area, storks were first documented to be engaging in dumpster-diving in the 1980s. Over the course of the next two decades, the birds committed to the lifestyle, abandoning traditional nesting sites in superior habitats in order to live closer to the dumps. The advantages of this were obvious. First and foremost, matters of taste aside, landfills guaranteed a consistent and predictable source of organic material. Not only did this result in better fed storks, it also had a direct, positive impact on breeding. Foraging at landfills contributed to increases in the number of eggs laid by a bird in a single nesting, along with the size of those eggs. It also improved the odds of survival for those offspring.

For all that, though, the urbanization of Spain's storks has its downsides. First, about those landfills. It turns out–and you might be surprised to learn this–that a diet of garbage has its nutritional hazards. Studies are revealing increased rates of E. coli and higher levels of antibiotic resistant bacteria, not to mention heavy metal concentration, raising concerns about potential public health consequences of this arrangement. Furthermore, while the trash buffet certainly facilitates higher growth rates, it also creates greater risk of juvenile storks consuming indigestible or otherwise hazardous items.

In addition, while there are fewer predators around man-built structures, there are plenty of human-related hazards. The use of pylons for nesting, in particular, has resulted in thousands of white storks being killed annually through collision with and electrocution by power lines–likely approaching a tenth of the total population. Along with that, the stork's thin skull leaves its brain more vulnerable to radiation and microwaves. Balmori found that storks nesting within 200 meters of a cell phone station in Spain had lower levels of reproductive success than their peers.

A less life-and-death issue, but one that has special relevance to pilgrims, is that stork nests are heavy, and special effort has been made in recent years to remove stork nests from Spain's older churches, especially when they are undergoing restoration. While these changes are offset with the introduction of artificial pole nests situated more closely to stork-friendly feeding areas, they come at the cost, of course, of a visual cherished by many on the Camino.

When I was a kid, the storks brought new life to humans. Today, humans have returned the favor, offering storks a new life of their own: sedentary, settling permanently atop man-built structures, with an all-they-can-eat smorgasbord in close proximity. What will happen next? The European Landfill Directive has called for the gradual reduction of all open-air landfills within the EU. There are excellent environmental reasons to make this change, but the consequences for Spain's burgeoning stork population will require further adaptation and accommodation.

Keep reading...

Alejandro López-García and José I. Aguirre, "White Storks nest at high densities near landfills changing stork nesting distributions in the last four decades in Central Spain," *Ornithological Applications*, 2023

Alfonso Balmori, "Possible effects of electromagnetic fields from phone masts on a population of white stork," *Electromagnetic Biology and Medicine*, 2005

Isabelle Gerretsen, "How an ancient Greek myth still shapes our minds," *BBC*, 2023

Cem S. Kayatekin, et. al., "The Relationship between the Built World and the Nesting Habits of the European White Stork: A Case Study of Segovia, Spain," *Athens Journal of Mediterranean Studies*, 2024

Joanna Czarnecka and Ignacy Kitowski, "The White Stork as an Engineering Species and Seed Dispersal Vector when Nesting in Poland," *Annales Botanici Fennici*, 2013

Juan M. Barbarin, et. al., "Breeding population trends and recent changes in the nesting behaviour of the White Stork Ciconia ciconia L., 1758 in Navarre, north of Spain," *Munibe Ciencias Naturales*, 2021

Mark C. Mainwaring, "The use of man-made structures as nesting sites by birds: A review of the costs and benefits," *Journal for Nature Conservation*, 2015

The Church that Outshined the Cathedral

Stage 19: Mansilla de las Mulas to León

If you happen to arrive in León on a sunny day, don't dawdle. Get thee immediately to the cathedral. There's never a bad time to visit the lovely monument, but when the light comes blazing through the towering stained glass windows, the interior erupts in color. Burgos may have the most impressive sculptural work, and Santiago... well, it's Santiago. But the cathedral of León was made for a gentle stroll, letting the magic of the place wash over you, one pane at a time.

If you had visited León in the Middle Ages, though, your priorities may well have been different. The cathedral certainly would have demanded your attention, but the visit would have varied based on your timing, given that four different structures existed on the site, ranging from a Visigothic church in 924 to the Gothic cathedral, which originated in 1205. The awe you feel today might not be too dissimilar to the medieval pilgrims here in the 1300s, when the Gothic structure was first completed.

There's a good chance, though, especially if you visited León a century or two earlier, that your top priority might have been a different church, located northwest of here. Because the Basilica of San Isidoro housed some of the most important relics of the Camino, and the story behind it speaks to the powerful forces behind the pilgrimage's rise to prominence. Book V of the Codex Calixtinus, the original guide to the pilgrim road, underscored the compulsory nature of the visit: "in the city of León, one must visit the venerable body of St Isidore, bishop, confessor and doctor, who instituted a most pious rule for the church clergy and imbued the Spanish people with his teachings, and graced the entire sacred church with the flower of his writings." The cathedral, meanwhile, didn't merit a reference.

Admittedly, if you had visited León *too* early in the Middle Ages, you wouldn't have been able to visit the basilica at all. San Isidro, originally dedicated to San Juan Bautista, initially served as the Leonese royal family's private chapel under the rule of Fernando I and Sancha (1037-65). Even the translation of San Isidoro's relics to León in 1063 didn't alter that dynamic. Though the daughter of Fernando and Sancha, the infanta Urraca, proceeded to rebuild the church following their deaths, bringing the latest in Romanesque style to the city, her vision remained aligned with that earlier function, keeping it very much in the family. (As an aside, since it certainly confused me when I first encountered it, *infante/infanta* in this context generally means prince/ princess, and applies to the children of royalty who were not immediate heirs to the throne.)

Even before the translation of relics, León had already established itself as a must-visit stop on the Camino, with the Codex referring to it as the "capital city of king and court, full of all good things." Its lineage was indisputable, originating with the Asturian resistance in Covadonga that has historically symbolized the beginning of the so-called *Reconquista*, and the capital transferred here from Oviedo in 910. While Ferdinand I split his kingdom among his sons upon his death (did this strategy ever work, at any point, for any monarch?), Alfonso VI, initially just the King of León, knocked out his brothers and then proceeded to expand beyond his father's accomplishments. Most consequential, for good and bad, was his decision to conquer Toledo in 1085. While it's easy to view that as a positive step, reclaiming a historic city for God and Kingdom, historians underscore that through this act Alfonso essentially killed the goose that laid the golden eggs. For years by this point, Alfonso and other Christian Kings had made a fortune by running a protection racket of sorts, offering military support to the splintered, Muslim *taifa* kingdoms throughout the peninsula. By taking this step, Alfonso shattered the status quo, losing access to most of that easy money, and setting the stage for the Almoravid incursion that would soon follow.

If Ferdinand had too many sons, Alfonso suffered from just the opposite problem. When his only son, Sancho Alfónsez, died in battle in 1108, he was left with no male heirs. And thus, upon his own death a year later, the crown of León and Castile passed to his daughter, Queen Urraca (not to be confused with the infanta Urraca).

Queen Urraca is, in many ways, a remarkable figure—the first queen to rule entirely on her own, as opposed to as a consort, in not just Spanish history, but across all of Europe. Despite that, though, she has suffered from exceptionally bad press. Our best source for her years in power, the *Historia Compostelana*, was initiated by Diego Gelmírez (much more to come on him in Stage 32), and Diego and Urraca can be most generously characterized as "frenemies." Of the three canons responsible for the authorship of the *Historia*, one, a Frenchman named Giraldo, bore unconcealed animus for Urraca, and his efforts shaped the dark legend that would dictate the perception of her for centuries to come. One quickly discovers, when reading Giraldo's work, that the mere notion of a queen in power was abhorrent to the man, as exemplified in his observation that, the "spirit of a woman is weak and unstable and it rapidly loses control." He attributed to Gelmírez a similar observation that Diego "knew that she easily paid attention to gossips and his detractors, and he knew her spirit to be too weak and womanly to govern in peace and justice the kingdom of Spain." As the years followed, the stories of her deplorable behavior only grew more vivid. Most infamous, perhaps, is the apocryphal story of her death. When leaving the basilica of San Isidoro, the story goes, having spent years enriching herself at its expense, she was caught mid stride–one foot in the church, one foot out–when she collapsed to the floor and was crushed to death.

While that particular story is nonsense, and the harshest criticism of Urraca overblown, there is no question that she faced unprecedented challenges as she took the throne. Surely, Giraldo wasn't the only man casting doubt on the capacity of a woman to rule. Potentially more damaging, though, were the repercussions of Alfonso's conquest of Toledo, as Urraca's years in power were shaped by what Richard Fletcher has referred to as an "endemic fiscal crisis." Ongoing challenges to her rule–in Galicia, Portugal, and Aragón–following a failed marriage to Alfonso 'El Batallador,' combined with the looming threat of the Almoravids, only stretched her capacity even thinner. (Surely, this is the only time in history when a woman bore responsibility for men's poor choices, financial irresponsibility, and belligerence.)

And despite all of that–or, perhaps, as Therese Martin argues, entirely *because of* that–her attention turned to pilgrimage. The aggrandizement of the cult of San Isidoro could serve to enrich León, elevating the saint and the city side by side, and in the process solidify Urraca's base of power. The primary focus of these efforts was the transformation of the private church of her grandparents into a pilgrimage church, catering to the needs of the faithful.

Urraca knew firsthand the power of pilgrimage, as she had ruled over Galicia with her first husband, Raymond of Burgundy, before her ascension in León, and her years in Santiago de Compostela coincided with the early construction work on the Romanesque cathedral. Urraca and Raymond embraced their role as patrons, making two donations to the cathedral during his lifetime, and then Urraca continued this with seven more donations after his death. She even chose to inter Raymond in the cathedral, earning him the distinction of being the first royal figure to be buried there. Their focus wasn't limited to the cathedral itself, though; in 1095, she and Raymond granted safe-conduct to merchants en route to Compostela, highlighting her recognition of the broader economic ecosystem within which pilgrimage functioned. (Not all of Urraca's experiences in Santiago were positive, though. Not by a long shot. More on that, as well, in Stage 32.)

Urraca's efforts with the Basilica of San Isidoro must be understood within that larger context. Instead of allowing her aunt's plans for the church's redesign to proceed, she spearheaded some dramatic changes. Her decision to add a projecting transept, the cross section cutting across the nave, stands out as the most important innovation. This required the tearing down of some parts of the new construction that had just been completed, a move that must have thrilled the architects. It's quite unusual to have a transept of this sort without a dome, but the late change necessitated the decision to go with barrel vaulting through the crossing instead; a dome would have required an entirely new support system. The transept was crucial for the church's reimagining as a pilgrimage shrine. While ambulatories–the aisled walkway that passes around the nave and apse, allowing for easier access to chapels and their relics–are often highlighted as the key architectural innovation to facilitate pilgrim traffic, the transept proved even more essential. Among all the Romanesque churches in Spain, only Santiago's had a transept before San Isidoro–and in that case, Urraca happily exchanged preeminence for continuity, forging a connection between the two shrines.

As Martin explains, beyond the immediate needs of acc-ommodating pilgrims, Urraca also cleverly designed the new church to reflect her link to her predecessors, underscoring the legitimacy of her reign. For example, she opted to keep the original Roman walls on its western edge, maintaining a link to her grandparents. Meanwhile, the doorway linking the west end of the church to the pantheon is horseshoe-shaped with polylobed arches. While horseshoe-shaped doors had been relatively commonplace in earlier architecture on the peninsula, they had largely disappeared by the 11th century, but their presence here connected the church with Seville (the original site of San Isidoro) and her father's conquest of Toledo. Meanwhile, thanks to Martin's exhaustive study, we know that this was the first appearance of polylobes in a Christian setting. The most striking design choice made by Urraca, though, at least in the view of this humble scribe, was her transformation of the pantheon. In place of what had been a rather austere, simple space, solely adorned with a simple pattern of red lines, she arranged for the addition of elaborate frescoes. Not only did this serve to commemorate her ancestors, it also integrated some wonderfully creative representations of New Testament scenes, the signs of the Zodiac, and even some apocalyptic imagery. Be sure to make time to visit this when you're in León.

The expansion of the Basilica of San Isidoro and its opening to the public as a shrine represented just one part of Urraca's larger plan for the transformation of León into a pilgrimage center. Alongside the church, she also founded a pilgrim hospital next to San Isidoro, and made donations to other pilgrim-related sites. She also became a patron of the Military Orders of Jerusalem, with an eye towards making the pilgrim roads safer for travel. Her successors would carry this work forward, highlighting the lessons they learned from Urraca. In 1152, her daughter donated the land upon which the Hospital of San Marcos would be built, though you might better recognize it today as the Parador luxury hotel. Oriented towards more humble travelers back in the Middle Ages, it also became the headquarters for the Order of the Knights of Santiago. Urraca's grandson, meanwhile, changed the course of the Camino through León, in order to ensure that it passed directly by San Isidoro.

The success of their collective efforts is best reflected in the wealth of miracle stories that began circulating around León and San Isidoro as early as 1118. We have Lucas of Tuy, a canon at San Isidoro, to thank for his compilation of these miracles, *Los Miraglos de San Isidoro*. Writing a century or so after Urraca's death, as discussed by Michael Hollas, Lucas had sufficient distance from her efforts to be able to fully appreciate their fruitfulness, but he also was proximate to some worrying trends, for León at least, as the center of secular power had shifted by this point to Seville, while Santiago de Compostela and Oviedo had both surpassed León as pilgrimage destinations. It fell to Lucas to reinvigorate the city and the saint, through his own written endeavors. And while he would fail in that larger goal, his impact as a historian is essential to our understanding of this time period, and particularly to a proper appreciation of the cult of San Isidoro.

Of all the saints, it's difficult at first to understand the appeal of Isidoro. Neither martyr nor great Christian warrior, Isidoro of Seville was instead a bishop and a scholar in the 6th and 7th centuries. His historical significance is largely attributed to his work as an encyclopedist. Interestingly, it is from one of his disciples, writing around 650, that we find one of the earliest links between Saint James and Spain, when that disciple claimed that Isidoro was Santiago's successor in Iberia. Nonetheless, his relics in Seville became critically important to the Christians living in the city under Muslim rule, and it constituted a coup when Ferdinand secured their translation to Seville. Most commonly, we see Isidoro as a healer, helping the blind, the injured, the enfeebled, and even the land itself, when he ended a prolonged drought. People of all backgrounds, whether wealthy or poor, from within León or far afield, were saved by his munificence.

One of the most memorable miracles, though, goes back to that rivalry between church and cathedral. Bishops were not used to playing second fiddle, and for the better part of a century, that was certainly the case in León. Bishop after bishop sought to bring the Basilica of San Isidoro under their authority, only for Pope Alexander III to stifle such ambitions in 1163, when he declared that the church would fall directly under papal authority. Once San Isidoro's relics made it within the basilica, its significance was secured.

For that reason, then, it follows that every effort must have been made to re-route those relics to the cathedral. Let's turn back to Lucas of Tuy, then, who relates that as the relics of San Isidoro, along with the body of Alvito, Bishop of León, approached the city, it was agreed that the bones of each man would be placed on horseback, and from that point the horses would be allowed to carry them unmolested to their ultimate place of burial—wherever that happened to be. Alvito went to the cathedral, while Isidoro ended up in the royal church.

Years later, Lucas shares, another attempt was made to displace the basilica, when the queen of Fernando II sought to have San Isidoro made the seat of the bishop, which would result in the displacement of the basilica's canons with cathedral officials. The queen conspired to persuade the king of this action, and he conceded, sending a messenger to the pope who also agreed to the change. That papal bull, however, went astray in the market of León, and disappeared into the hands of people loyal to San Isidoro. Even that, though, wasn't the end of it. Bishop Mancio, Lucas explains, sent his archdeacon to Rome to denounce the abbot and canons of San Isidoro to the pope. At this point, San Isidoro intervened directly, arranging for the archdeacon's ship to be captured by pirates; along the way, the man was also struck blind. It wasn't an entirely bleak ending for the man; after making his way back to San Isidoro, and apologizing to the canons, he partially regained his sight. Lesson learned.

And yet, what couldn't be achieved in the short term would play out over the centuries. For most pilgrims today, the cathedral is the unquestioned star of the city. But its rise, one must acknowledge, is a tribute to the successes of Urraca, Lucas, and Isidoro, who made this city's star shine all the more brightly.

Keep reading...

Lucas de Tuy, Juan de Robles and Julio Pérez Llamazares (trans.), *Los Miraglos de San Isidoro*, 1992

Michael Lawrence Hollas, *Lucas of Túy and Thirteenth Century León*, 1985

Therese Martin, *Queen as King: Patronage at the Romanesque Church of San Isidoro de León*, 2000

Therese Martin, "Recasting the Concept of the "Pilgrimage Church": The Case of San Isidoro De León," *La Corónica: A Journal of Medieval Hispanic Languages, Literatures, and Cultures*, 2008

The Pursuit of the Masculine Ideal

Stage 20: León to Hospital de Orbigo

In my view, one of the most dramatic sights on the Camino is the entrance to Hospital de Órbigo. The 13th-century Gothic bridge just keeps on going, spanning nineteen arches in all. It's a testament to resilience, as most of the arches have been wiped out or blown up at some point, but each time they have been rebuilt in keeping with the original style, maintaining a semblance of continuity. As you make your crossing, pause at the monolith in the middle, commemorating ten names. It's a testament to what Henry Edward Watts, translator of Don Quixote, called "The most splendid and famous tournament ever held in Europe," and what David Gitlitz and Linda Davidson suggest "may have been Europe's last true medieval tournament."

So important was the tournament that Watts opted to include a description of the event as an Appendix to his translation. "As the most solemn and important of all the chivalric functions ever held in Spain," he writes, "in the age when chivalry was in its very prime, and as an event frequently referred to as the great precedent and exemplar of knightly usage," he deemed it essential context for understanding Quixote. The year was 1434, the event became known as the Paso Honroso, and the knight-hero at the center of the story was Suero de Quiñones.

At the root of the event, in Watt's re-telling, was unrequited love. Suero had long declared himself vassal to a lady, who goes unnamed in this narrative, and as a symbol of that affection and binding he bore a chain of iron around his neck. In order to deliver himself from this condition, either by winning over the love of the woman or being unshackled from his devotion, he declared that he would break three hundred lances in a jousting competition. He received King Juan II's endorsement and proceeded to invite the bravest knights from across Europe to join him in Hospital de Orbigo. Nine friends joined him in this challenge, swearing to defend the bridge together.

Before the tournament began, a dance took place in the king's hall, at which point the 22 terms of the event were spelled out for all participants. Armor, weapons, and horses were to be provided to all knights who participated, though they could certainly use their own; in the event that a knight's horse died in the competition, Suero swore to cover the expense personally. (The disdain reserved for a knight who deliberately harmed a horse–the rules condemned the "foulness" of such an attack–was reflected in the fact that any knight who aimed for a horse could be knocked out of the tournament with a single strike to his armor.) In the initial rounds of the tournament, all jousting matches were anonymous, until after completion of battle. Once a knight defeated three opponents (known in this context as "breaking lances"), he could challenge anyone. Suero declared that no knight would suffer vengeance for defeating him or one of his nine colleagues, and any knight who suffered a wound would receive medical care. Pilgrims who happened to stumble across the event, meanwhile, were guaranteed safe passage.

The other rules involved women. Every lady of honor within range of the event, the guidelines established, should put forward a knight to joust on her behalf, or forfeit her right-hand glove—a symbol of her affection. Suero identified three ladies beyond the one who had left him enchained, and he declared that he would give any knight who claimed one of their gloves a diamond. Most important, though, was the twenty-second term, which established that "the lady to whom Suero de Quinones himself belongs, should she pass that way, shall not be subject to lose her right glove, and that none shall joust on her account except he himself." As one final statement, Suero "beseeche[d] all those who love their ladies to come to his succour, to release him his vow." The following morning, they all proceeded to attend early mass, before the jousting began.

Suero cut a striking figure on the jousting list, with scarlet breeches (a color only allowed to knights), a matching hood, and an olive jerkin, all while sitting astride a powerful charger. Three pages shadowed him, each in matching outfits, while his nine colleagues followed, all dressed in scarlet as well. The king's trumpeters played as they marched to the field, joined by at least 68 other knights, including at least one German and three Italians. The first match of the tournament belonged to Suero, of course, and he met that German knight, Herr Arnold of the Red Forest, achieving a clean victory. Afterwards, Suero took Arnold to dinner. An honorable display all around, and a model of what chivalry could be. The most dramatic clash involved a larger battle matching Suero and his nine with Gutierre de Quijada and his knights. As Gitlitz and Davidson describe, Suero's crew came out on top, and Quijada departed in a foul mood, "swearing vengeance."

Every generation, it seems, is confronted with the challenge of constructively defining and channeling masculinity. Today, we have no shortage of headlines–a quick survey of the past year found stories in The Washington Post, The Guardian, The Telegraph, The Economist, and Vox, among many others–bemoaning the "crisis of masculinity" and struggling to find viable solutions. At the heart of this is the long-established link between men and violent crime. In the United States, statistics offered by the FBI in 2012 revealed that roughly three-quarters of all violent crime in the country is perpetrated by men, and the most extreme manifestations of that, murder and forcible rape, are almost singularly the acts of men.

Similar concerns raged in the Middle Ages. In George Payne Rainsford James's *History of Chivalry*, he paints a bleak picture in describing the reality on the ground in a post-Charlemagne Western Europe. As the feudal system developed, he writes, the "weak were oppressed on all sides; the powerful and wicked were unchecked," and the "world was weary of barbarity." Richard W. Kaeuper, in his introduction to Geoffroi de Charny's *A Knight's Own Book of Chivalry*, examined the same problem from the top down, noting that, "Rulers and intellectuals worried over the disruptive violence to which males were prone." A similar acknowledgement has often been associated with Pope Urban II's interest in organizing a crusade; even if the Holy Land wouldn't be liberated in the end, at least it would put the roving bands of militant men to a more constructive use for a time.

Having established these concerns, it makes sense then that the idea of chivalry emerged at this time, as a strategy for refocusing violent men towards the better angels of their brutal natures. And indeed, those chivalric ideals, Kaeuper argues, "surely went far toward solving the historical problems represented by vigorous masculinity in the Middle Ages."

The first attempts at formalizing the early conceptions of chivalry didn't emerge until the 11th century, and the reformist movement found its warmest reception in France and Castile-León. Nonetheless, its meaning inevitably shifted from place to place, and as with all initiatives organized around virtuous ideals, the lived reality often fell short of the goal. We can see this quite clearly, as it turns out, in the differing portrayals of Suero and the Paso Honroso, each of which emphasizes a different aspect of the chivalrous knight.

In James Michener's classic, *Iberia*, we see Suero de Quiñones portrayed as the warrior par excellence, the biggest badass on the Camino block. Michener first learns of the knight while in conversation with Don Angel Suárez Ema over lunch in León. It begins with confusion: "For some unfortunate reason I thought that Quiñones were something to eat and I replied that I hadn't tasted them yet." Once they established that they were discussing a man and not a snack, though, Suárez Ema launched into a lengthy description of the Paso Honroso.

"You understand that in the old days many evil men," he begins, "especially from Germany and France, infested this road, so that bands of knights were required to patrol it, protecting the innocent. For this reason, the Order of Santiago was established, composed of Spaniards. But fine knights from foreign countries formed their own order to protect pilgrims, too, so that along the way there grew up a congenial fraternity." Right from the beginning, then, we see the centrality of the pilgrimage to this discussion.

For all the virtues of this system, Suárez Ema continues, there was one significant problem. It's not what you think, whatever you might imagine. No, the system broke down because a "garrulous knight, say at Estella, could sit in the tavern, knowing that any competition might be miles away in León, and shout, 'I am the strongest and bravest knight on the Way of St. James,' and get away with it, while another knight here in León could bellow, 'I am well known as the strongest and bravest knight on the Way.'" It's like the most unsatisfying sports league in the world, never bringing together the best of the best to settle it on the field.

This unjust dynamic, above anything else, compelled Suero to "put an end to this nonsense." As such, with the king's blessing, he declared that "he was going to stand for thirty days at a bridge over the Río Orbigo and fight every knight who approached from either direction, which could mean thirty or forty fights a day, until it was made clear who was the champion of the Way of St. James." While Suárez Ema proceeded to acknowledge the role of unrequited love, this was just one of a set of ideas proffered by Suero "that were equally heroic." Ultimately, though, the point was to win, and Suero accomplished exactly that: "Quiñones seemed to have won every joust he entered, and it was some years along this road before any loud-mouthed knight dared to announce that he was the most powerful, for all knew Quiñones was."

While a knight's responsibilities certainly required military acumen, of course, many others would emphasize the religious aspect of chivalry. As Kaeuper explains, from its earliest emergence, chivalry was grounded in the Church. Before an accomplished square earned admission to the knighthood, he confessed, prayed, and fasted, spending hours in vigil. In the ceremony itself, he would be flanked by knight and bishop; the latter would bless his blade, consecrating it into virtuous service. In the final gesture, when the knight would receive three "blows" of the sword across his neck or shoulders, he would hear: "In the name of God,

St. Michael, and St. George, I make thee knight; be loyal, bold, and true."

Ramon Llull offers us the best look at this particular manifestation of chivalry. In the introduction to Llull's *Book of the Order of Chivalry*, Noel Fallows notes that the young Llull was "a carefree knight, seneschal and courtier," who "was composing a troubadour canso" when "he experienced a series of visions of Christ that precipitated a transcendent conversion." A far more serious man emerged, part scholar, part evangelist, and part theorist. After the disastrous Second Crusade, he decided to write his book on chivalry in the hope of sustaining the battle against Islam, in both the Holy Land and Iberia. Key to that, he believed, was a complete reform of the Order of Chivalry, rooted in a clearly defined hierarchy and code of conduct. Knights, Llull believed, needed to expend as much energy upon their internal development as their external pursuits, and he struck a deliberate parallel between the knight and the cleric. This represented a spiritual mission: "Unto the knight is given a sword which is made in the shape of a cross to signify that just as our Lord Jesus Christ vanquished on the Cross the death into which we had fallen because of the sin of our father Adam, so the knight must vanquish and destroy the enemies of the Cross with the sword."

While other priorities would overshadow these spiritual obligations in the major narratives of Suero de Quiñones and the Paso Honroso, we see glimpses of it in the aforementioned attendance at the early mass, and the special care shown to pilgrims. Even Michener's account includes a vignette in which Suero ensured that a knight who died in the tournament would be buried on sacred land.

By contrast, though, the romantic ideal stands out in most popular representations of this knight's tale. At the core of this, Kaeuper notes, was the goal of elevating "love above the passions of the brute," through which it "dignified women" and "gave purity to enthusiasm." James explores the sort of pure and dignified love that was integral to chivalry. As a starting point, he notes, "Each knight, as a part of his duty, either felt or feigned himself in love." This took on a ritual function in tournaments, as the knight's labors on the mock battlefield were framed as singularly driven by the hope that "his lady might descend from the high state to which the mystic adoration of the day had raised her" and "bestow upon her favoured champion a glove, a riband, a bracelet, a jewel."

This chivalrous love did not necessarily demand chastity. For all his "clerically inspired exhortations about virginity," Geoffrey de Charnei, Kaeuper writes, found "discreet love affairs" to be appropriate. A knight was measured by his prowess, and a woman's love, he recognized, could elevate that prowess. It was essential, though, for a knight "to think less about the pleasure of his body and more about his soul and his honor."

On the last day of the Paso Honroso, Watts writes, Suero and his companions—only eight, as one of them had been seriously wounded—joined together in the field, before two judges. Suero declared their victory and the completion of his vow. And with that, he "prayed for deliverance from his penance of wearing the iron collar on Thursdays." The judges agreed, and thus the King of Arms removed the iron collar from Suero's neck.

Interestingly, while the historical record is unanimous about Suero's martial accomplishments, the picture is much blurrier when it comes to his beloved. Gitlitz and Davidson conclude by noting that he achieved freedom from his "secret lady," after which he rode to Santiago as a pilgrim. (The truth of that can be seen in the presence of that collar in the cathedral museum.) The unnamed woman doesn't even receive that much acknowledgement in Watts's account. The implication in both is that the unrequited love remained permanently so, and our poor Emo Knight moved forward alone. Such an account, perhaps, reinforces that pure, chaste sort of love that appears in some portrayals of chivalry, making Suero an ideal representation of it. And yet, elsewhere, we discover a name to associate with the knight's great love, Doña Leonor de Tovar, and we also learn that the two married and had two children together.

For all the order, integrity, and nobility associated with the ritualized violence of knights in the age of chivalry, though, it couldn't entirely eliminate the baser impulses that so often lurk below the surface. 24 years later, Gitlitz and Davidson tell us, Suero happened to run across Gutierre de Quijada, still nursing a grudge. In their account, this culminated in one last duel; María del Rosario Falcó y Osorio, by contrast, tells us that instead Quijada's "peons" did the work. Regardless, the end result was the same. Suero de Quiñones, the one-time biggest badass on the block, lay dead in the field. And along with him passed the age of chivalry.

Keep reading...

Geoffroi de Charny and Richard W. Kaeuper, *A Knight's Own Book of Chivalry*, 2005

George Payne Rainsford James's *History of Chivalry*, 1830

James Michener, *Iberia*, 1968

Luis Alonso Luengo, *Libro del passo honroso: defendido por el excelente caballero Suero de Quiñones*, 1970

Miguel de Cervantes, Henry Edward Watts (trans.), *Don Quixote*, 1895

Noel Fallows, *Jousting in Medieval and Renaissance Iberia*, 2010

Ramon Llull, *The Book of the Order of Chivalry*, 2013

Thick, Sweet, and Hot

Stage 21: Hospital de Orbigo to Astorga

What museums offer in educational value and seriousness of purpose—offer in abundance, really—is sometimes offset by what they lack in the fun quotient. Look, I'm not opposed to seeing another roomful of vestments in a random Diocesan Museum, or a medley of torsos and potsherds in an Ancient History Museum, but I understand if you need to be in *just* the right frame of mind and extra caffeinated to commit to a visit. But chocolate? There's always room for chocolate.

It's the incongruity of Astorga's Museum of Chocolate as much as the quality of the collection itself that draws attention. A passion project launched by one Astorgano, José Luis López García, who decided to make his private collection a public institution, the museum is humble, with the limited visiting hours to match, and it's potentially most valuable as a reminder. Chocolate, here? In the hills of Northwest Spain?

In the next chapter, you'll learn about the Maragato people, who lived in this region for centuries. The men were well known as muleteers, transporting goods across the country in a world without trains or semi trucks. One of the most common routes ran from Galicia to Madrid, passing through Astorga along the way, and this meant that trade goods returning to Spain from the New World passed through here.

That's where chocolate comes in, quite literally. The first documented European encounter with chocolate came in reference to Columbus's fourth voyage to the Americas in 1502, when the crew encountered a Mayan trading canoe just off the Honduran coast. A much more detailed discussion of chocolate can be found in Hernán Cortés's letters to Charles V; in the second, in particular, he observed that cacao beans were employed as currency, and that, once ground up, they comprised a popular beverage. Popular that drink might have been, but for the earliest Europeans it wasn't love at first sip. The Milanese traveler Girolamo Benzoni reflected that it "seemed more a drink for pigs, than a drink for humanity," though he added that "it satisfies and refreshes the body, but does not inebriate." Can't have it all!

Two men have earned credit for spreading the gospel of chocolate, Francisco Hernández de Toledo and Juan de Cárdenas (additional credit goes to Marcy Norton for her wonderful overview of this subject), and their writings also reveal the particular ways that cacao was processed and consumed in the Mesoamerican world. First, it's important to underscore that the primary application came in liquid form; chocolate in those days was for drinking, not inhaling an entire bar in a half-hour or less when nobody is looking. The cacao beans were prepared through a process of fermentation, toasting, and grinding, resulting in a product that, in Cárdenas's words, "fattens and nourishes man, giving him salubrious and praiseworthy sustenance." While a simple preparation could follow, combining ground cacao with water and nothing more, the mixture was quite commonly embellished with spices and other ingredients. Perhaps surprisingly, the spices–there are references to gueyna-caztle, mecaxochitl, tlixochitl, achiote, and chiles–were, shall we say, *picante*, and the writers argued that the heat of these balanced out the "coldness" of the cacao, making it suitable for drinking in any climate. Sources also mention ground corn, barley, cinnamon, pepper, anis, and sesame being integrated into the chocolatey concoctions.

Indigenous use of chocolate extended to functions that made some Europeans quite uncomfortable. The Aztecs, for example, were known to make use of hallucinogenic plants, including the ololiuqui, the teonanácatl ("divine mushrooms"), and peyote, and it was quite popular to mix those in with cacao. Meanwhile, records from the Spanish Inquisition speak to the application of chocolate in "erotic magic." To offer one salacious example, a creole woman in Tlaxcala, Juana de Sossa, plied men she desired with spiked chocolate before sleeping with them, like the butcher's apprentice (according to the butcher's apprentice's daughter). In an unrelated contemporary study by Beatrice Golomb and Brinton Berg, women today who eat more chocolate report less interest in sex.

Cárdenas informs us that extensive debates were unfolding related to the health impacts of chocolate. Everyone had their own take on the subject: "some despise chocolate, considering it the inventor of numerous sicknesses; others say that there is nothing comparable in the world, that it fattens, elicits appetite, imbues the face with good color, makes the sterile woman pregnant, and (drunk with atole) makes the new mother overflow with milk; so there is no one who does not present their judgement to the populace." The heavy emphasis on pregnancy and motherhood extended to common accusations of a link between chocolate consumption and painful menstruation, with Cárdenas noting reports of "bloating, obstructions, coldness, and the abundance of thick humors in the womb." (Again, contemporary studies might have some relevance here, as there is some indication that, contrary to Cárdenas's assertion, the consumption of dark chocolate can help to alleviate menstrual pain, thanks to the high levels of magnesium.)

The burgeoning popularity of chocolate created a surprising problem, one that ultimately received papal attention. Like everyone else, the priests were soon hooked. Bartolomé Marradón, a botanist and doctor who traveled through Mesoamerica, recalled that "I once saw in a port town where we disembarked to purify water a priest saying mass who was obliged by necessity–being exhausted–to sit on a bench, and drink a tecomate full of chocolate, and then God gave him the energy to complete the Mass." Was the bedeviled Indian culture seeping into the Men of God, one cup at a time? Many knew, after all, that cacao had been a key feature of indigenous ritual life, central to many of the rites and ceremonies practiced prior to European arrival. A more pressing question soon arose from this. Ecclesiastical fasting is a key practice within Catholicism; by 400 AD, it had become customary to fast on Saturdays, along with Lent and the holidays. While food was banned during these times, observers were permitted to imbibe beverages. Did drinking chocolate violate the fast? The concerned Procurador of Chiapas decided to run the question up the flagpole in 1577, leading to a papal opinion from Gregory XIII, via Azplicueta Navarro, that it would not. Our friend Cárdenas, a killjoy if ever there was one, took issue with this, arguing just the opposite in 1592, but Cardinal Francisco Maria Brancaccio put his foot down in 1664, reiterating the pope's original judgement in *De chocolatis potu diatribe*. Our old friend Fr. Bernardino de Sahagún would be glad. A true choco-phile, he wrote that, "When an ordinary amount is drunk, it gladdens one, refreshes one, consoles one, invigorates one. Thus it is said: I take cacao. I wet my lips. I refresh myself."

He wasn't the only Spaniard taking pleasure in the drink. By the end of the 16th century, cacao had already become a trade staple, filling an ever more prominent spot in the barges shuttling back across the Atlantic. The 2700 pounds shipped in 1598 exploded to over 400,000 pounds just fifteen years later. By 1775, estimates suggest that Madrid's population alone consumed 2.3 million pounds of it annually. Chocolate is a helluva drug. Beyond the assorted medicinal applications, it thrived as a pleasure drink, one that gradually shifted from a treat for privileged elites to one enjoyed by the masses, at least on occasion. Its popularity derived in part by how it was adapted to better suit European tastes, swapping out the *picante* for sweetness, by integrating the much more familiar combination of sugar and milk.

The much-appreciated Astorgan chocolate was characterized in 17th-century chronicles in three words: thick, sweet, and hot. Beyond the advantages offered by its location on a major trade route, the city's climate also suited chocolate production well, especially as a taste developed for more solid offerings. Artisans employed a labor-intensive technique quite similar to Mesoamerican practices, known as *a la piedra* or *a brazo*. Cacao beans were first roasted over a wood fire, after which the beans were shelled by hand. The nibs were then rolled with granite stones, while heated over a fire, through which a liquor would be produced. Sugar and other ingredients could be added at this point. Next, the mixture was poured into moulds, before finally being left to cool on the ground. This is where Astorga's climate came into play, as the consistently cool and dry conditions allowed for that process to play out swiftly. That method prevailed until the 19th century, when mechanization finally transformed the industry.

Cristina González Pérez's short history of the city's relationship with chocolate cheekily observes that, as it was "the capital of a very large and densely populated diocese, with a large number of priests and monasteries" it therefore contained an equally large number "of chocolate consumers." The industry grew steadily over the subsequent centuries, rising from eight registered chocolate factories in 1752 to 23 workshops in 1920, and its reputation throughout the region followed apace. An article from 1873 notes that "the most valuable export consists of the considerable number of boxes of the famous chocolate and tasty shortbread from Astorga, which are invoiced daily to Madrid and many other provinces, and even to foreign countries and overseas."

It couldn't last forever. The monopoly that Spain enjoyed over New World goods in its early imperial period was first circumvented and eventually dashed. Competition expanded, and at the same time quality declined. Even the production of cacao shifted dramatically, moving away from Mesoamerica and towards West Africa, where some 70% of the global supply is grown today. Despite the decline, contemporary pilgrims will have no difficulty buying chocolate in Astorga, as three chocolate artisans remain in operation in the center. Each has a different selling point. If you like your chocolate plain and unvarnished, head to Hojaldres Alonso, where you can balance out your meal with some highly regarded puff pastries. Peñín Chocolatier, meanwhile, is famous for its orange chocolate, an unusual treat worth savoring. For something completely different, El Arriero Maragato offers chocolate with smoked meat, though their popular *mantecadas* might be a safer bet. Finally, consider starting your day at Churrería Flor de Trigo or Bar Juanín, where you can enjoy chocolate in the traditional way, the way that first made it a global phenomenon, though maybe leave the hallucinogens on the side.

Keep reading…

Margaret A. Graham and Russell K. Skowronek, "Chocolate on the Borderlands of New Spain," *International Journal of Historical Archaeology*, 2016

Marcia Norton, *New World of Goods: A History of Tobacco and Chocolate in the Spanish Empire, 1492-1700*, 2015

Cristina González Pérez, "El Museo del Chocolate de Astorga," *Cuadernos de Etnología y Etnografía de Navarra*, 1999

Terence Yew Chin Tan, et. al., "The Health Effects of Chocolate and Cocoa: A Systematic Review," *Nutrients*, 2021

The Maragato Tourism Industry

Stage 22: Astorga to Foncebadón

Today, the Maragato are probably best known as a lunch special, the Cocido Maragato. A carnivore's delight, built around a pile of salted beef and spicy chorizo, with some chickpeas and stewed vegetables on the side. Keep your eyes peeled and you might also notice portrayals of the distinct dress associated with the Maragatos. This appears most famously on the clock situated above Astorga's town hall, where statues of a Maragato man and woman toll the bell each hour.

Those are hints, reminders, of a people who once populated this region, about which precious little is known today. Unlike some of the other mysterious groups we have to reckon with in our journey across Spain, including the Knights Templar and the indigenous Iberians who may have shaped the Iron Age castro cultures, the Maragatos are far more recent, having maintained prominence in this region well into the 20th century.

One of the most lasting portrayals of the Maragatos comes from Concha Espina de la Serna's novel, *Mariflor,* or

La Esfinge Maragata, published in 1924. It's not flattering, which seems to be of a piece with the author's oeuvre, which tended to feature female protagonists enduring tragic disappointment. A review published by C.C. Glascock in the same year, put it thusly: "A book so devoid of all the joy of living, so persistently gloomy in the portrayal of ghastly brutalizing poverty among these Maragatan peasants, the tightening of the toils about the aspiring spirit of this lovely girl who is forced to abandon all of love's young dream." Sounds like a page-turner!

Let's dive right in. We meet the titular character, Mariflor, right away. She's traveling by train with her grandmother. That in and of itself is noteworthy; as Courtenay de Kalb points out, the train can be viewed as a symbol of loss for the Maragato people, and so it immediately establishes a dour tone. This is not a pleasure journey. Mariflor moved away from the *Maragateria* as a child. Her mother was a native of Bayona, on the Galician coast, and she never took well to the rugged landscape of the interior. Her father, meanwhile, had taken to the seas, in pursuit of wealth in the New World. But now, her mother was dead, her father was struggling in Argentina, and Mariflor was taking shelter in her birth land, Valdecruces, hoping to offer her grandmother some support.

Mariflor's grandmother's life is bleak. Over the course of her life, she bore thirteen children, but only two remain. Even after a brief moment of fond reminiscence, she is crushed back down: "after having given way for a brief space to a senile flight of the imagination, [she] again compressed her heart within the rigid walls of her cruel existence." Most Maragato men sought employment on the road, leaving the women to run the show in their absence. Independence, though, didn't offer any semblance of liberty. On the contrary, as she explains, "In our land there are no queens. All the women are slaves there."

Mariflor is barraged by the bleakness throughout her journey. When they pass from León into the traditional *Maragateria*, it seems "as if civilization stops abashed and hesitant at the threshold of the hostile region." Astorga itself, so loved by pilgrims today, appears "deserted and forsaken." Mariflor is appalled; "How desolate and petrified the city which was once the Roman Asturica Augusta!" She and her grandmother continue westward, taking the "route of the pilgrims" through Murias de Rechivaldo and Castrillo de los Polvazares, during which Mariflor "was suddenly overcome by a sensation of dismay, a heart-sinking in which fear and sorrow mingled with unexplainable poignancy." In quick succession, we learn that Mariflor felt "so small, so incapable, and so weak," not to mention "chilled and terrified."

There are two flickers of hope in the narrative. The first is Rogelio Terán, a young and romantic poet who shares the train compartment with Miraflor and her grandmother on their journey to the interior. His immediate attraction to Miraflor is sparked in part by her personality but perhaps more so by the vision it inspires in Terán of being a heroic figure, liberating the young woman from her "unhappy fate." The second is her female relatives in Valdecruces. After such a discouraging journey, Mariflor arrives "tremulous and fearful," only to be "greeted by warm, moist kisses, and embraced by strong, welcoming arms."

Mariflor bravely decides to meet the bleakness with determination. Despite having been "the girl accustomed to ease and to adulation," she would face "these privations and sacrifices with fortitude and courage." She embraces the role of a "redeemer," believing that "God had placed in her delicate hands the tiller of the family ship, which was drifting rudderless in the poverty of the land." Visions of Terán are never far from her mind; the reward for such salutary behavior, she hopes, might be God "triumphantly elect[ing] her the wife of an artist, the ideal of a poet."

The noose only tightens further as the plot unfolds. Mariflor's father, her great hope in Argentina, reports ever more dire conditions; no great wealth will be crossing the Atlantic and restoring the young woman to her once-comfortable life. In the meantime, her family in Valdecruces is neck-deep in debt; her grandmother is on the verge of losing her house, while the younger women face decades of arduous labor and despair. Mariflor, however, has the keys to their collective salvation. If she agrees to marry her cousin Antonio, he has the financial capacity to relieve the pressure upon her family. But at what cost? A life sentence in such a rugged country, where "already she thought she could detect an impairment of her beauty, the trace of the invisible claw of sacrifice causing her features to assume a sunken appearance, making them less firm, dimming their youthful radiance"? The abandonment of such true, pure love as she felt for Terán?

Well, surely our poet-hero will come to her rescue, right? The author warns us early on to avoid placing our collective eggs in that rhyming basket, in what ranks among the most gently scathing condemnations of the profession ever written: "Poets are usually like children: voluble and cruel. They play with the emotions through mere curiosity, without fear of destroying a heart, whether their own, or another's, and sometimes, with the best intentions in the world. Perhaps of all men, poets, because of their childish mental condition, most deserve the compassionate words: 'Forgive them, Father, for they know not what they do!'" Terán leans right into this framing later in the novel, when he writes to the priest of Valdecruces—because of course he couldn't convey this directly to Miraflor—that he will not be able to wed the woman. As he writes, "I contritely confess to you my sin of inconstancy, my useless eagerness for emotions, for tenderness, and for change. This sorrowful circumstance pains me deeply enough; of all my crimes, I myself am not only the criminal, but the chief victim." The chief victim! He adds that, "I now realize the pettiness of my spirit which, enamored of dreams, cowardly surrenders when it comes to face realities." The poor man!

There is no white knight; no dramatic plot twist; no deus ex machina to be found anywhere in the Maragatería. Miraflor reads the letter and offers a lone sentence in response: "You may write my father that I will marry Antonio." That's it. That's the novel. Apologies for the spoilers.

As a source for gleaning insights about Maragato culture, it is not without value. Concha Espina assembles some of the common theories and rumors about their origins, "unknown and obscure," suggesting that they "reveal the gloomy dreaminess of the Celts, they possess the stern courage of the Moors, and the frigid seriousness of the Bretons." The Maragatos were first referenced in writing in the 15th century, and over the years they have been associated not only with the groups highlighted above, but also Carthaginians, pre-Roman Aboriginals, Jews, and Germanic peoples. Most European peasants were bound to their land, rarely traveling far beyond their birthplace. By contrast, the Maragato men were muleteers, conducting goods over long distances, most commonly between Madrid and Galicia. In their absence, the women engaged in subsistence agriculture, extracting what they could from the challenging soil.

We can see those gender dynamics at work in the text, though it's impossible to appreciate the prevalence of the judgements rendered by Concha Espina. We are constantly reminded of the grueling, mundane lives endured by the women. Ramona, "barely forty years old," inspires an "unutterable terror" in Mariflor because of her withered, gaunt bearing. Felipa is even more jarring; instead of the 45-year-old imagined by Mariflor, she is actually 23, having already brought two children into the world. Maragatan women, Mariflor—or perhaps it would be better to identify Concha Espina's voice here—quickly understands, "must bear a child each year, mechanically, fearlessly, aged by brutalizing work, in order that the miserable race of slaves and emigrants will not run out."

Mariflor, the outsider, is deeply offended by these dynamics, but her female family members are largely untroubled. When Mariflor asks why no men remain in the town to assist with plowing, her grandmother rebuffs the query: "Why should there be, child! The only men who would think of staying here would be utterly worthless, of no use except for herding." Proudly, she continues, "The Maragatan men... are very clever, and they occupy themselves in other and more profitable work." The praise continues, with the men being labeled "excellent fathers, industrious citizens, economical, faithful, and pacific." Their treatment of their wives is a mixed bag, but it could always be worse! "If it is not their habit to beam upon their wives, or to take pity upon them, neither do they deceive nor corrupt them: they treat them neither well nor ill, because they scarcely have anything whatever to do with them." Again, it's difficult from a distance to parse the value judgements, but it's certainly true that the Maragatan men, through their extensive time spent on the road, eked out a much more profitable existence than men born into similar social circles during their era, and Maragatan women held down the homefront with remarkable devotion. It should be added that Mariflor's pairing with her cousin Antonio is consistent with our understanding of Maragatan society as well, which kept wealth local through high levels of endogamy.

It wasn't all drudgery. When the men return to Valdecruces in August, a large dance is held, filling the main street between the parish house and the church. They first perform the *baile corrido*, with couples joined together in a slow movement, "languid and genteel." A dance called the *dulzaina* followed, in which the women, standing in pairs, rotate in a circle. The men take their turn with the *entradilla* next, after which the men and women join together. The music, we know, would have likely involved the Maragato lute, the zanfoña (also known as a hurdy-gurdy), and the dulzaina (a double reed instrument, like an oboe, and not to be confused with the dance), along with the acclaimed Maragatan drummers.

And, of course, there is the still-admired Maragatan dress, which Concha Espina describes in vivid detail. While the daily wear of the women is "crude" and seems "to oppress and overburden her delicate form, and to distort her hips with its thick folds," the "rich garments" brought out for special occasions feature woolen petticoats, skirts, scarfs, and earrings. Antonio, when he makes his call to court Miraflor, cuts a particularly fine figure, with a "smocked shirt, red-flowered waistcoat with silver buttons, reddish brown breeches, a coat with skirts, fastened tight about his waist with a silken cord, cloth leggings with garters [...], and a fanciful belt."

While the mostly-unremitting bleakness makes for a gloomy read, the timing of the novel contributed to that, and has to be factored into any assessment of its authenticity. Concha Espina sets the table in this way: "For entire centuries have [the Maragatos] survived the desolation of the desert waste, alone in the integrity of their rare purity, stranded upon the plain like a helpless ship grounded and sinking, which is abandoned and forgotten in the turbulent sea of civilization." The arrival of the train in 1860, though, proved too large a wave for the ship to survive, bringing an end to generations of muleteers. A Maragatan diaspora followed between 1870 and 1930. Miraflor's father wasn't alone by any means; many traveled to the Americas, in pursuit of new opportunities. Over the same time period, the Enlightenment drive towards nationhood, combined with the Francoist prioritization of Spanish unity, meant that distinct cultures within the peninsula were marginalized.

The Maragatería moved into a period of steep decline. Between 1900 and 2015, it lost 82% of its population, with an average population of 53 people across its 57 villages. In the meantime, the distinct cultural qualities of the region ebbed, between the ever more crippling poverty and the arrival of non-Maragatos into the emptied spaces. And yet, counter-intuitively, the Franco regime opted to promote Maragato folklore, though perhaps "co-opted" would be a better word. Franco sought to promote traditionalism and attachment to the soil, along with Catholic fervor, embedding the core values of his administration within the deeper history of Iberia.

Since the 1990s, the Maragatería has experienced a resurgence, but the same can't be said for Maragatos. The region was marketed to urban Spaniards as a quaint heritage space, one with plenty of property available at bargain rates. In time, that triggered a process of rural gentrification. Castrillo de los Polvazares in particular, located just off the Camino (and well worth the detour) has been absolutely transformed, with housing prices jumping to the half-million euro range. Other towns along the Camino, like Murias de Rechivaldo, Santa Catalina de Somoza, and El Ganso, have experienced developmental booms thanks to pilgrim traffic. Along the way, some Maragatos have returned to the region in retirement, so it's not purely a marketing ploy; traditions persist in some form. But that only adds to the complexity. In

Santiago Millas, the other Maragato town that has seen substantial redevelopment as a tourism hotspot, resentment has surfaced related to the Maragato Museum and related cultural events. In the words of Pablo Alonso González, this process speaks to "the appropriation of a 'given heritage'–in other words, community and social life as a whole network of relationships–and its recasting as an 'abstract performance.'"

This is the maddening challenge posed by tourists. We are drawn to authenticity, hoping to come in contact with something unique, timeless, and aesthetically gratifying, but our very presence tends to dilute or corrupt whatever authenticity once existed. Without that interest, without the value of those traditions to local tourism, what would survive of the Maragatería today? There is already so little! It is something to consider, perhaps, during a leisurely, meat-filled lunch in Castrillo de los Polvazares.

Keep reading...

C.C. Glascock, "A Portrayal of Spanish Life," *Texas Review*, 1924

Concha Espina de la Serna, *Miraflor*, 1924

Pablo Alonso González, "Heritage and rural gentrification in Spain: the case of Santiago Millas," *International Journal of Heritage Studies*, 2017

Pablo Alonso González, "The heritage machine: the neoliberal order and the individualisation of identity in Maragatería," *Identities: Global Studies in Culture and Power*, 2015

Pablo Alonso González, "Race and ethnicity in the construction of the nation in Spain: the case of the Maragatos," *Ethnic and Racial Studies*, 2016

The Hidden Templar Life in Europe

Stage 23: Foncebadón to Ponferrada

In the end, I failed in achieving my goal for this chapter. Let's get that out of the way up front. We can still, though, learn a thing or two from failure.

In my defense, the Knights Templar is one of those subjects about which the signal-to-noise ratio is wildly out of whack. It would fit snugly on the History channel between shows devoted to ancient aliens and Sasquatch; the majority of the countless books available on Amazon are more likely to peddle esoteric gossip than credible evidence. (The sad part is that the market has rendered its verdict, and the myth is in greater demand than the fact.) As a consequence of this, while it's certainly still possible to enjoy the hulking Castillo de los Templarios in Ponferrada–I mean, I don't know how you *couldn't* enjoy a giant castle–it's far more challenging to get a solid grasp of what happened within those walls.

Nonetheless, we can reconstruct the broad brush-strokes of the Templars without too much difficulty, but it first requires a little context. In 1085, the Byzantine Emperor

Alexius initiated a war with the Seljuk Turks, in response to their conquest of Jerusalem. A decade later, as the threat of Turkish intrusions upon Byzantine lands grew more palpable, he reached out to the other half of Christendom, seeking Pope Urban II's support in a war to bolster the faith. For Urban II, this had immediate appeal, though it's too easy to focus on the Christian vs. Muslim aspect of it today, even if Urban paid lip service to it. The papacy, rarely as steady on its feet in those years as we imagine from a distance, needed strengthening, and a large-scale military operation offered a possibility of bolstering its sovereignty. More pragmatically, the burgeoning ranks of armed men roaming through mainland Europe were causing headaches. All those strong arms needed to be pointed in a more constructive direction.

And so, on November 27, 1095, Pope Urban II changed the course of history, by making his call for what would be the First Crusade:

> "...your brethren who live in the east are in urgent need of your help, and you must hasten to give them the aid which has often been promised them. For, as most of you have heard, the Turks and Arabs have attacked them and have conquered the [Greek empire] as far west as the shore of the Mediterranean and the Hellespont, which is called the Arm of St. George. They have occupied more and more of the lands of those Christians, and have overcome them in seven battles. They have killed and captured many, and have destroyed the churches and deva-stated the empire. If you permit them to continue thus for awhile with impunity, the faithful of God will be much more widely attacked by them. On this account I, or rather the Lord, beseech you as Christ's heralds

to publish this everywhere and to persuade all people of whatever rank, foot-soldiers and knights, poor and rich, to carry aid promptly to those Christians and to destroy that vile race from the lands of our friends" (from the account of Fulcher of Chartres)

The impact was immediate. While the more formal armies, organized under royal initiative, would take time to coordinate, the peasantry required less strategy. Behind the leadership of Peter the Hermit, thousands marched (well, ambled in disorganized hordes) on foot from France to the Holy Land. It didn't go well. The *real* First Crusade arrived in the Holy Land via sea, and the initial results were nearly as fruitless as Peter's. Once they cleared the initial, interminable siege of Antioch, though, the waters cleared for a march on Jerusalem that took less than a year. And the siege of Jerusalem itself was a bloody breeze, ending in massacre after just five weeks. Jerusalem, at last, was in Christian hands.

The floodgates opened on pilgrims to the Holy Land. One acute problem, though, was the fact that, while a not insignificant share of the region now comprised the Kingdom of Jerusalem, most pilgrims would be traveling over land, through often hostile terrain. They needed protection. And so, the story goes, in 1118 (or thereabouts) a French knight, Hugues de Payens, joined together with eight fellow knights to create the Poor Fellow-Soldiers of Christ and of the Temple of Solomon. Of course, that wouldn't fit on a business card, so in common parlance that distilled down to its more compact, lasting form.

The Knights Templar quickly grew into a force, earning recognition and significant privileges within the Church. Bernard of Clairvaux, a driving influence behind the Cistercian Order, embraced the Templars, providing them with a

Rule to govern their daily life and practical assistance. Later, Pope Innocent II awarded them significant liberties, including freedom from all authority besides the pope's, relief from tithing and taxes, and the right to appoint their own chaplains and build their own churches. These were substantial boons, and they almost certainly inspired envy in some circles.

By most accounts, the Templars conducted themselves with honor, but the ground in the Holy Land constantly shifted under foot. On Christmas Eve, 1144, Edessa fell to Seljuk forces on the Northeast frontier–the first defeat experienced by the Christian kingdom. This triggered calls for the Second Crusade, which ended poorly for all involved. Embarrassingly enough, most Christians never even reached the Holy Land, instead getting entangled in so many conflicts between Greece and Turkey that anti-Greek propaganda circulated in Western Europe, calling for a different crusade on their fellow Christians. Only the Templars emerged with their reputations unscathed from the debacle, having earned praise for helping to bring some organization and discipline to the struggling forces. Even still, they could only do so much, and in the decades that followed, the opposition only grew more imposing. The rise of Saladin, legendary warrior and Sultan of Egypt and Syria, culminated ultimately in the fall of Jerusalem in 1187. The Kingdom of Jerusalem persisted, weakened and without its capital, and the Templars maintained their efforts.

More crusades followed. The Third is the last one bearing any semblance of honor or principle, with Saladin facing off against three Christian kings: Richard the Lionheart of England, Philip II of France, and Frederick Barbarossa, the Holy Roman Emperor. While the Christian forces won some worthwhile victories, and Richard at one point rode within 12 miles of Jerusalem, they eventually yielded the city without even making an attempt, on the advice of the Knights Templar. The reality on the ground was that while they might win it, they couldn't reasonably hope to hold it. Instead, a truce signed with Saladin reopened the Holy Land to peaceful travel for all pilgrims. The Fourth found a way to outpace the Second in shame and embarrassment. The most notable event was the sacking of Constantinople, the Byzantine capital and a Christian city, by the Crusaders. Christian-on-Christian violence then reached a new level when the Albigensian Crusade launched in Southern France in 1209, targeting the so-called Cathar heretics. All of this represented bad news for the Templars, as European interest in the Holy Land ebbed, and with that interest went funding and military support. Of course, the bar can always go lower, and so it did in the Sixth Crusade (the Fifth, suffice it to say, was ineffectual *and* boring). The Holy Roman Emperor organized the Sixth Crusade, but was excommunicated by Pope Gregory IX for not doing it soon enough, and then excommunicated for going on crusade while excommunicated. The Knights Templar were stuck in a Catch-22, sworn to protect all pilgrims to the Holy Land, but also to obey the Pope and avoid excommunicants. They took refuge in semantics. When they rode with the Emperor's forces, they weren't part of his army; they just happened to be traveling in the same direction. When they obeyed orders, they didn't obey *his* orders, but rather served in the name of God and Christendom. Conditions only deteriorated further in the Holy Land. With little blame to be shouldered directly, the Templars saw it through to the bitter end, with the fall of Castle Pilgrim in 1303, the last Christian holding in the Holy Land.

That wasn't, however, the end of the Knights Templar, though it may well be considered the beginning of the end. After all, they had holdings in Europe, like the castle in Ponferrada. Extensive holdings. After just a decade, they had already been bequeathed a significant network of houses, castles, and fields across Europe, making the order, one officially espousing poverty, among the wealthiest organizations in the world. Indeed, that network contributed to one of the Templars' lasting innovations, as it became an international banking service, allowing travelers to draw upon funds without having to carry them–with the accompanying risk–at all times. (In lieu of charging interest, which would have been frowned upon as an act of usury, they essentially devised the service fee. Jerks.) This, too, would become a major source of envy.

So let's (finally) get back to where we started: what were the knights doing on those estates, so far from the Holy Land and their core mission? Have you ever encountered a book that seemed like it was written just for you? That's how I felt when I discovered *The Everyday Life of the Templars* by Helen J. Nicholson. While she didn't go as far as I did in this chapter, declaring failure from the jump, she nonetheless acknowledged the severe constraints within which she operated. At the forefront of that challenge is the air of secrecy that surrounded the order. As she explains, "During the twelfth and thirteenth centuries, when the Templars were at the height of their fame, more and more individuals were recording their experiences of the world–but the Templars did not." They didn't document how they lived, what they did outside of their military commitments, or much of anything else. This didn't just confound the work of historians; it also poured fuel on the envy, already engendered by their wealth and influence.

Despite those challenges, Nicholson successfully cobbled together enough evidence–particularly from the United Kingdom–to lend some insight into the Templar practices on the homefront. One of the most useful sources is the Templar regulations themselves, modeled after Augustinian rule, which provided the broad brushstrokes of their daily lives. The keyword was simplicity–the knights and their other community members were mandated to eat simple food, wear simple clothing, and obey commands from their superiors. Simple food meant that, in their two daily meals (save for Friday, when they only received a lone meal), meat was available thrice weekly, with vegetables and grains only on the other four days. A snack was permitted in the afternoon, served with water or warmed wine. Knights ate in pairs, but weren't allowed to talk; instead, Bible readings were offered over meals, to make better use of the time. Simple clothes involved a woolen, white mantle, with a red cross adorning the left breast, set over a dark tunic, and with a soft cap over the head. Pointed shoes, laces, and long hair were all banned.

Days were structured on canonical lines. The Templars were roused by bell and expected to dress and proceed straight to chapel for matins or lauds. In the summer, this happened as early as 3:30am. From there, prime occurred at 6am, terce at 8am, sext around mid-day, nones in early afternoon, vespers at 6pm, and compline at 8pm (all times specific to the summer season). When Templars were on the road, and thus couldn't adhere as closely to this schedule, they were expected to compensate by reciting the Lord's Prayer a certain amount of times.

The Knights were held to a high standard and discipline was commonplace. Lesser offenses, like disobeying a command, resulted in a period of penance, during which the guilty Templar would eat their meager meals–just bread and water–off the floor. More significant infractions earned a knight public flogging or incarceration. The most severe punishment, expulsion, came as a consequence of a surprisingly wide range of misbehavior, from revealing Templar business to outsiders and leaving a castle through something other than the main gate to heresy, sodomy, killing a Christian, and fleeing from Muslims in battle.

Their primary focus, beyond living pure and simple lives, was to make a profit from running their estates, in order to funnel those funds towards the mission in the Holy Land. Around Europe, they managed farms, livestock, vineyards, olive groves, and other assorted industries, while also providing important services to the wealthy and the powerful. At the same time, they were often responsible for administering justice within their community and maintaining the parish church.

Was there any joy to be found in all this earnest labor and rigid structure? They weren't allowed to play chess or backgammon, though other board games were permitted, provided that no gambling occurred. No hunting was permitted, either. They were explicitly banned from kissing women (don't even ask about men), including aunts and sisters. There's some indication that pets may have been permitted, which could have offered valuable companionship. Some suggest that hopscotch had its fans.

While those insights are helpful, an additional problem is posed by the distinct case of Spain. Because, while today's Spain qualifies as mainland Europe, in the Middle Ages the picture was much muddier. Even if we reject the idea of the *Reconquista*, it doesn't change the fact that Pope Urban II and his successors worried that they would be robbing Peter to pay Paul if their call to crusade stole warriors from Iberia. In 1096, Urban II appealed to a group of Catalan counts, asserting that "it is no virtue to rescue Christians from the Saracens in one place only to expose them to the tyranny and oppression of the Saracens in another." That said, it wouldn't be before 1123 that Christian military struggles on the peninsula would carry the papal imprimatur of crusade, when Pope Calixtus referenced, "those [...] who are known to have placed crosses on their clothing either for the journey to Jerusalem or for that to Spain." Along with this, of course, there were non-military pilgrims to protect–the pilg- rims of our ilk, walking to Santiago de Compostela, a service that fit squarely into Templar goals.

So what do we actually know about the Templar Castle in Ponferrada? Judit Garzón Rodríguez offers us some tempting tidbits. Ferdinand II of León first donated properties to the Knights Templar in the region, in recognition of their efforts to the south in Extremadura. This included Ponferrada, in 1178, with the accompanying expectation that the knights would maintain security in the area, though that primarily meant guarding against bandits, not Muslim armies. While Alfonso IX withdrew the gift in 1204, he returned it in 1211, and it remained in Templar hands from that point until 1308. The imposing castle that we admire today didn't exist at that point. An early Iberian fortification was first established here, and later converted into a Roman manor house (the northernmost part of today's structure). When the Templars inherited the site a millennium later, practically no defenses were installed, so they spent the next century expanding the walls.

Beyond that, we have a legend. The story goes that after the Templars arrived in Ponferrada, and the construction was well underway, they discovered an image of the Virgin situated within an oak tree. The knight who first discovered the Virgin had fought in the disastrous defeat in the Battle of Alarcos, in which the Castilian forces lost Trujillo, Montánchez, and Talavera. More crushing, though (and this is firmly in the realm of the legendary), was the knight's loss of the True Cross in the battle. The Virgin consoled him and instructed him to return to her the following day. He did, bringing his colleagues with him, and they discovered the cross in the Virgin's hands.

With apologies to the Virgin, I wasn't entirely satisfied with this picture of life in Ponferrada during Templar times, so I reached out to the folks at the castle, in the hope that they might have access to higher quality sources. They were kind enough to respond. Here's what they wrote, following translation: "there are only two specific publications about the Templar castle: A book from the 1980s by a certain Luengo with countless historical errors (among them he claims that the Taus of the castle are Templar when they belong to the Count of Lemos) and another book written by the architect of most of the castle reconstructions that we have for sale at the ticket office of the same, but it talks more about the architecture of the castle and the construction phases than about the Templars themselves." That's it. That's all we've got.

It's important to note that there's one last reason for the dearth of evidence. Things didn't end well for the Templars. All of that envy that had percolated over the course of their rise to prominence? It transformed into a full-fledged green-eyed monster after the Holy Land fell, and the Templars suddenly didn't seem to have a legitimate purpose any longer. Philip IV, newly raised to the French throne in 1303, made it his mission to bring about their demise, with the ulterior motive of appropriating their vast wealth.

First, he made a series of public accusations against the Templars, which included clandestine behavior; denying Christ; kissing each other on the mouth, navel, and anus; and bowing before a head-shaped idol. He was just getting started. On September 14, 1307, all officers in his kingdom received a sealed mandate, with orders not to open it until October 12. At dawn the following morning, every single Templar in France was arrested. Just eleven days after that, four Templars, including the grand master, Jacques de Molay, confessed to the charges. Few outside of France found the confessions credible, including Pope Clement V, who intervened at this point. In a second round of interviewing, overseen by the pope, the Templars retracted their confessions. Philip responded by accusing the pope of siding with heretics. While the pope tried to move forward with an even-handed trial that would provide the Templars with every opportunity to make a robust defense, Philip continued to force the issue, individually trying any knight he got his hands on. Matters were complicated by the fact that, if the Templars retracted their confessions but were found guilty, they would actually be punished as heretics, which meant that they faced burning. As a result, many opted to re-confess, in order to escape the flames.

While the papal commission determined that the case against the Templars was not proven, it acknowledged that the order maintained some unorthodox (though undefined) practices. That was more than enough for Philip, though, who swiftly moved forward with capital punishment for many Templars. And really, despite his public posturing, it was good enough for Clement V as well, who proceeded to claim Templar holdings for the Holy See.

As noted, one of the major challenges and frustrations when trying to learn about the Templars is the abundance of misinformation that circulates about the subject. Sometimes, though, those rumors are too good to be true, too satisfying to be ignored. So forgive me if I compromise on principle, by bringing this chapter to a close with the juiciest rumor at all. On March 18, 1314, Jacques de Molay and another Templar official, Geoffrey de Charney, were burned at the stake, on Philip's orders. The legend goes that, as the flames lapped at his body, de Molay spat a curse upon both Clement and Philip. He implored Jesus to prove his innocence by ending Clement's life in 40 days and Philip within the year. Why those particular numbers? Who knows! Don't ask questions.

In any case, as it happens, Clement died 33 days following the execution, and Philip after five months.

And in the meantime, despite the Council of Salamanca declaring Spain's Templars innocent of their crimes, they were stripped of their powers and holdings soon after. The castle, meanwhile, passed first into the hands of the Crown of León, before moving through a long series of owners and an extended decline phase. Finally, in 1924, it earned distinction as a National Monument, setting in motion–slowly, so very slowly–the preservation efforts that have culminated in its much more recent restoration.

Keep reading...

Dan Jones, *The Templars: The Rise and Spectacular Fall of God's Holy Warriors*, 2017

Euan Beveridge and Kevin O'Gorman, "The Crusades, the Knights Templar, and Hospitaller," *Tourism and War*, 2013

Helen J. Nicholson, *The Everyday Life of the Templars*, 2017

Judit Garzón Rodríguez, "Templarios en El Bierzo: El castillo templario de Ponferrada como reminiscencias del pasado," *ArtyHum*, 2016

Stephen Howarth, *The Knights Templar*, 1982

John Moore's Terrible, Horrible, No Good, Very Bad Trip to Spain

Stage 24: Ponferrada to Villafranca del Bierzo

No matter how badly your Camino goes, there's no way your trip to Spain could be worse than Sir John Moore's.

Even when he was retreating to Villafranca del Bierzo, sprinting westward along the Camino Francés, he had cause for mild optimism, a tenuous confidence that disaster might be averted. But after the firing squad cut loose, mowing down a single soldier beneath a lone tree in the Plaza Mayor, the brutal truth was laid bare. A full-fledged sprint to A Coruña followed.

In 1808, the Peninsular War was a year old. What had started with a swift French invasion and occupation of Portugal, by way of its flaccid Spanish ally, expanded in 1808 as Napoleon cut the puppet strings and installed his brother Joseph on the Spanish throne. British fears of a lost continent surged, though flickers of hope sparked around Iberia, as small resistance movements ignited. An opportunity existed, British military leaders surmised, to land a fleet in Portugal, march eastward, and rally the local Spanish forces to halt Napoleon's progress.

The magnitude of the challenge cannot be overstated. For all their aspirations, the British could only bring 30,000 men to Portugal, along with some 12,000 to A Coruña, a force that could hope for little more than to bloody the nose of Napoleon's nearly 300,000 troops on the peninsula.

Those hopes rested, to a significant degree, on the shoulders of an exceptionally capable, if politically controversial, leader. Sir John Moore, born in Glasgow in 1761 and first commissioned in 1776, had assembled a wealth of experiences in the field by 1808, including tours of duty in Corsica, the West Indies, Ireland, Netherlands, and Egypt. Most recently, he had led operations around Sweden, at least until he ran afoul of King Gustavus IV, after which he returned briefly to England. In between those military operations, he also served as a Member of Parliament, though his Whiggish political views would hold him back in a period of decline for his party. He similarly made some enemies, as Christopher Hibbert so delicately characterized it, for having "the displeasing capacity for being almost never wrong" as well as having "something of the prig" about him. And yet, such loyalty and adoration did he inspire among his immediate subordinates, such competence did he display to his superiors, that he represented an obvious choice to take a leadership role in this most vital of operations.

Right from the beginning, Moore and his men were in a race against time, facing forces beyond their control, and operating with far less reliable intelligence than any commander would like. The British forces that had preceded Moore to Portugal had grown soft and disorganized from idleness, and demanded precious time to reorganize. At the same time, the rainy season rapidly approached, threatening to bog down the army along the subpar roads crossing into Spain. And for all the promise heralded by the encouraging stories of a Spanish uprising, their forces proved to be fragmented, poorly organized, and capricious. Moore rarely knew where they were, where they were moving, how large their numbers were, or how well they were equipped. Worst of all, their regional disposition impeded any sort of national coordination, as each localized force resisted any sort of subservient position. The buy-in from other locals was often lacking as well, and Moore's meager warchest—just £25,000—left him without the funds necessary to coordinate transportation and other supplies. And Moore didn't only have men to contend with. A significant number of women and children had traveled with the army to accompany their husbands and fathers, far in excess of the acceptable number, further compounding the logistical challenges facing the command.

The initial journeys inland for both Moore's main force, as well as his secondary contingent traveling from A Coruña under Sir David Baird's leadership, were miserable in nearly every regard. A driving, ceaseless rain battered their faces, while bitterly cold nights compounded the discomfort. The English soldiers found Spanish peasants to be suspicious, arrogant, and unsupportive; Sir Charles Napier condemned the common folk as "cruel, dirty, cheating, proud and crafty. They ought to be exterminated for their treatment of animals, and flogged for laxness." A chaplain was caustically dismissive of a Spanish city he passed through, noting that "nothing can surpass their abominable filth, nor could I describe it minutely, without exhibiting the most disgusting pictures."

Then matters worsened. Upon arrival in Salamanca, Moore met with the Marqués de Cerralbo, president of the Junta, who informed him of a series of disastrous defeats experienced by the Spanish forces. Most alarming was the routing of the Army of Estremadura, which had yielded Burgos to the French forces. Now, those French forces were rolling on towards Valladolid; within a week, they would hold the city that had previously been suggested to Moore as a rallying point. Also bad, General Joachim Blake's Army of Galicia had been twice thumped and sent retreating over the Cantabrian mountains with its tail firmly ensconced between its legs. Meanwhile, as Baird's forces arrived in Astorga, they received equally alarming news. Two contingents of French forces were far too close for comfort, with Marshal Lefebvre on the banks of the Carrión and Marshal Soult at Reinosa, only 100 miles away. Anticipating that the French might be gearing up for an advance on León, Baird planted his flag in Astorga to await word from Moore.

The hopelessness of the situation weighed on Moore; his growing bitterness flowed forth in a letter to Lord Castlereagh: "The enthusiasm of which we heard so much nowhere appears... I am at this moment in no communication with any of their generals. I am ignorant of their plans or those of their Government." Or, to put it more bluntly, "We are here by ourselves." They had ridden headfirst into an imminent disaster, and it now rested squarely on Moore's shoulders to extricate them. The stakes were high. As Moore had learned from a friend prior to his departure from England, "'The army, which has been appropriated by His Majesty to the defence of Spain and Portugal, is not merely a considerable part of the dispensable force of this country. It is, in fact, the British army... Another army it has not to send." If victory was already out of reach, the key now was to secure the least crushing defeat possible.

In the meantime, Napoleon and his Imperial Guard marched into Madrid, taking the city. News also arrived of a crushing defeat of Spanish forces on the Ebro River near

Tudela. In the face of such miserable tidings, a dour Moore prepared to execute a retreat from the continent.

Two developments changed his mind. First, two Spanish leaders, 3rd Brigadier-General Augustín Bueno and Don Ventura Escalante, Captain-General of the Kingdom of León, arrived in Salamanca to implore Moore to stick around. They insisted that 60,000 Spanish troops remained available to rebuff French advances. Moore was skeptical, but ultimately he came around to the idea. His ambitions remained modest. Again, an unmitigated victory was beyond the realm of the possible. But if he could draw Napoleon's attention and lure him into the northwest, he might buy the Spanish enough time and space to achieve a sustained resistance.

The second development was more dramatic, almost cinematic. A French officer had traveled alone into a Spanish village near Segovia. As Hibbert puts it, "this had not prevented him from behaving in an insolent manner to the unfriendly villagers, and in particular to the postmaster, who had, in accordance with the implacable code of Spanish peasant behaviour, arranged to have him murdered." A search of his possessions revealed communications from Marshal Berthier in Madrid to Marshal Soult on the Carrion. Berthier, under the belief that Moore's forces were already in retreat, encouraged Soult to march on León, claiming that he would face no resistance along the way. This marked the first positive break of the entire operation for Moore. Marshal Soult had only 18,000 men and this faulty intelligence might encourage him to pursue a more reckless approach than he might otherwise take.

Marshal Jean-de-Dieu Soult, it should be noted, posed more than a match for Moore. First commissioned in 1792, he was already a general by 1794. Napoleon called him the "ablest tactician in the empire." Even the British soldiers who faced him in this war emerged impressed. As William Napier later wrote, "I take this opportunity to declare that respect which I believe every British officer who has had the honour to serve against him feels for his military talents."

Moore led his forces onto Sahagún, now nearly 29,000 strong. Despite the promise of support from abundant Spanish forces, Moore's entire command structure remained skeptical and dismissive. One liaison officer declared that, "It is morally impossible that the Spanish troops can stand before a line of French infantry. A portion of, at least one third of, the Spanish muskets will not explode." Lord Paget was more spiteful. "Such ignorance, such deceit, such apathy, such pusillanimity, such cruelty was never before united. There is not one army that has fought at all. There is not one general who has exerted himself. There is not one province that has made any sacrifice whatever."

The British forces were more than sufficient in their initial skirmishes with French soldiers, during which they enjoyed a decisive victory that cleared Sahagún of the enemy. Moore established his headquarters in the Benedictine convent, which the Camino still passes through along its exit from town. It must have been a relief, to finally taste success, to feel like they might be able to make a positive contribution in support of the larger cause.

Of course, it couldn't last. Word soon arrived from the Marqués de la Romana, the most capable of the Spanish military leaders, that Napoleon was sprinting northward from Madrid, with advanced forces already emerging into the Castilian plain. Moore quickly recognized that any aspiration of landing a firm blow on Soult had been dashed; if he and his men had any hope of escaping Napoleon, they needed to retreat immediately.

Napoleon, for his part, wasn't just looking to chase them off. "If only these 20,000 [English soldiers] were 100,000," he wrote in the midst of his advance. "If only more English mothers could feel the horrors of war." One almost imagines the drool dribbling down his chin. Nonetheless, before long he delegated full responsibility to Marshal Soult, and turned his own attention elsewhere.

It's difficult to capture just how appalling the retreat proved to be. The conditions, crossing the Cordillera Cantábrica in the midst of winter, were miserable enough. But the British forces, never a model of discipline in the first place, became nearly ungovernable. They were angry and ashamed, having never received a proper opportunity to face the French head-on. They were starving, wet, and freezing, in gear that was falling to pieces amidst the bleak conditions. When they crossed the bridge over the Esla in Mansilla de las Mulas, when they sprinted through León, Soult was hot on their heels. Initial plans to cross the mountains at Pajares were scuttled due to snow, which left Moore's forces largely on the Camino Francés as they pushed onward to Astorga.

The city would suffer from their brief presence. The Spanish contingent led by the Marqués de la Romana was also there, and had been without food for three days already. Many of them were ill from typhus; ragged bands of English and Spanish soldiers combed the city to find sustenance, literally tearing it to pieces. Any hope the military leadership might have held to make a strategic stand here were quickly dismissed; starvation would do Soult's work for him.

Reports indicated that Villafranca del Bierzo, 50 miles further westward, offered the nearest large food supply. The march to that point, through snow-covered hills, was the stuff of nightmares. Abandoned carts and frozen animals lined the way; haggard remnants of Romana's army were, as Hibbert puts it, "howling like dogs with the maddening ache of hunger."

Villafranca offered the lone hope for a last stand. Pilgrims know the geography well. With only a narrow pass pushing westward, and steep mountains flanking both sides, it offered an ideal geography for a defensive position. With a solid stockpile of supplies, they might dig in their heels and hold off Soult. But you know what to expect at this point; it all went terribly wrong. The town was ravaged by rioting soldiers, who pushed aside villagers and military commissaries alike in pursuit of food and drink. The artillery wagons were set ablaze, all ammunition being tossed into the river. Horrified, Moore managed to strongarm his regiments into the Plaza Mayor. A lone soldier, who had robbed a house and struck an officer, was made an example, facing execution by the aforementioned firing line. It was a drop in the bucket. The soldiers had shamed themselves; the only remaining question was whether they had doomed themselves as well. Floggings began. Floggings continued. Morale did not improve.

The images of the onward retreat through the mountains are horrifying. Bloody footprints, from man and beast, lining the snow-clogged track. Women staggering along, dragging their moribund children. Hibbert relays how Commissary Schaumann "saw a woman fall up to her waist in a bog and as she was sucked down by the slimy, ice-cold water, the men behind her walked over her head." More remarkable and less horrifying, a pregnant Irishwoman halted her march when contractions began, gave birth, and then caught back up with her husband and his regiment. The baby would ultimately grow up hale and hearty in England. Moore briefly gave thought to making a stand in Lugo; the armies paused just long enough to kindle hopes that they might finally, just maybe, get to confront their French rivals. Instead, Moore recognized that the supplies were insufficient, and a defense utterly impracticable. They marched on, all the more sour for the false summit.

From the Camino Primitivo's Lugo, they worked their way to Betanzos on the Camino Inglés. Winter's worst gave way to more mild conditions which, combined with sights of the sea, brightened the mood. The British engineers enjoyed their greatest success of the trip, blowing the bridge in Burgo to absolute smithereens, and buying their forces a little more breathing room en route to A Coruña, which they finally reached on January 11, 1809. Even then, however, disappointment lurked, as a large portion of the British transport ships were still stuck near Cape Finisterre.

Nonetheless, those ships would arrive, and the loading process began. On the morning of 16 January, after a long day spent overseeing these operations, Moore remarked to his Military Secretary that, "if there is no bungling, I don't see why we should not all be off safely tomorrow." Cue the fateful music.

Unfortunately, the French found a different way to cross the river and soon encircled A Coruña, setting in motion one last battle, which kicked off shortly after dinner on the 16th. Moore was transformed; Thomas Graham characterized it as "a transition from fixed gloom bordering almost on despair, to a state of exaltation." Suddenly, Moore was everywhere, riding breathlessly from one contingent to the next, barking orders and offering encouragement. Charles Napier, in particular, conducted himself with such remarkable heroism that an awed French captain ordered his soldiers not to fire on the man. As night fell, the battle wore on, but the outcome was largely determined. The British would successfully fend off the French advance, ensuring a successful retreat with the following morning's tides.

And at that moment, as he circled with Colonel Graham, Henry Percy, and Captain John Woodford, Moore fell suddenly from his horse—the victim, it turned out, of a round-shot that ripped a massive hole through his left shoulder, exposing a lung and smashing his ribcage and collar-bone. A prolonged and painful death followed. Moore's men frantically sought some sort of treatment, but Moore rebuffed it all, only seeking assurance that the French had been beaten. "You know," he said to Colonel Anderson, "I have always wished to die this way."

While 8000 British soldiers were lost in the aborted conflict, it would be erroneous to characterize it as an unmitigated failure. By distracting Napoleon and drawing his forces deep into the northwest, Southern Spain remained free, and resistance efforts continued to grow. And many of the soldiers that were saved would emerge as the backbone of the force that returned under the Duke of Wellington's command a few months later. Thinking back on Moore's impact years later, the duke would remark to a friend that, "You know... we'd not have won, I think, without him."

Keep reading...

Christopher Hibbert, *Corunna*, 1961

Janet Macdonald, *Sir John Moore: The Making of a Controversial Hero*, 2016

Philip Haythornthwaite, *Corunna 1809: Sir John Moore's Fighting Retreat*, 2001

The Three Miracles of O Cebreiro

Stage 25: Villafranca del Bierzo to O Cebreiro

Myth permeates every meter of O Cebreiro. The scene is etched in my memory: early in the morning, ensconced in fog, the thatched roofs of the *pallozas* barely visible in the hazy sky, the aroma of woodsmoke in the air, and a pervasive silence, save for the muffled patter of pilgrim feet. You could easily convince me of any number of esoteric mysteries having their roots in these hills, which gleam like emeralds when the sun finally makes a token appearance in the late afternoon. I'm not the only one, apparently; the town is linked with three miracle stories, each of varying degrees of credibility.

The first is the wildest. Indiana Jones made a terrible mistake. (The Monty Python crew was so badly off the mark we need give them no attention.) The Holy Grail, we learn, was stashed nowhere near the old Republic of Hatay in contemporary Turkiye. Instead, it found safe-keeping in a small, Galician mountain village—our very own O Cebreiro! The Holy Grail has a long history, inextricably linked with the Holy

Chalice, the same cup used by Jesus at the Last Supper to share wine with the Apostles, during which he affirmed that it formed a covenant in his blood. It was from this act, and his accompanying statement–"Do this in remembrance of me"– that the Eucharist derives. The same cup, some stories go, was then used by Joseph of Arimathea to collect Jesus's blood at the Crucifixion. The grail itself appeared for the first time in Chrétien de Troyes's *Perceval, the Story of the Grail*, firmly embedding this within the long tradition of Arthurian myths.

The Spanish nationalist poet, Ramón Cabanillas, is credited with forging the connection between O Cebreiro and the Holy Grail. In his poem, "O cabaleiro do santo Grial," first read on Saint James's Day in 1926, Cabanillas begins with the legendary Breton King. Arthur, he explains, commanded his knights to find the Holy Grail, in order to imbue his reign with spiritual glory. Galahad, the pure and loyal knight, is specially chosen by Arthur to pursue the relic in Galicia. One legend, relayed by Edward Stanton in *Road of Stars to Santiago*, suggests that Joseph of Arimathea was one of the people involved in the transport of James's body to Galicia, and that he subsequently could have deposited the Grail in O Cebreiro. Regardless, Galahad completes his journey to the village, where he encounters a lone, humble hermitage. Cue the miracle: "And then the hermitage filled with the glow of moonlight and of blond angels dressed in twisting white linen, one with the spear of the Passion, the other swinging a censor, soldiers of the Lord, both with the sign of a red cross on their breast and a white lily in their hand." His eyes turn to the altar: "A clamor of bells breaks out, the earth flowers with roses, and the dove of the new covenant comes down from heaven to renew the mystery, holding the green branch of peace. Around it, in a circle, twelve stars shine, and remain, hovering quietly above the Holy Grail."

Joaquin Rodriguez Campos offers a fascinating discussion about the larger context behind this poem, explaining that Galician nationalists like Cabanillas were striving in the early 20th century to distinguish their region from the dominant Castilian identity. If that Castilian identity was linked to the Carolingian tradition and exemplified by knightly figures like El Cid and Don Quixote, then Galicia needed a different model. For that, Cabanillas and others found succor in the region's traditional Celtic ties (more on this in Stage 29), in which Arthur and his knights provided their own set of heroes to emulate and ideals to follow. In lieu of the corruption and domination they associated with Castilians, then, the Galicians sought spiritual purity, fidelity, and love. In any case, Mathew Kuefler (who deserves credit for the above translation of Cabanillas's poem) confirms that no other reference linking O Cebreiro to the Holy Grail exists prior to the 20th century. He suggests that Richard Wagner's opera Parsifal, which debuted in 1882, triggered a resurgence of Arthurian narratives, which then fed the imaginations of men like Cabanillas.

More documentation exists in support of the second miracle linked to O Cebreiro, and the one that fully established the village's reputation within the Christian world. Our best source for this story is Fray Antonio de Yepes, a Benedictine monk who lived in the late 15th and early 16th centuries. He relates that around the year 1300 (some accounts suggest 1212), in a characteristically brutal winter, the village of O Cebreiro was getting blasted with blizzard-like conditions. A burned-out, cynical monk, all but devoid of faith, was nonetheless preparing to celebrate Mass in the most perfunctory fashion, assured that none would brave the storm to attend on such a miserable day. On the contrary, though, one dedicated peasant from the neighboring village of Barxamaior, Juan Santín, braved the elements, and when he finally arrived in the church he was soaked and chilled to the bone. Far from impressed, the condescending monk wondered who would make such a hazardous journey, "just to gaze upon a bit of bread and wine?", and proceeded to admonish Santín for his foolhardiness.

And then the miracle happened. The Lord, Yepes tells us, decided to open the eyes of his embittered, arrogant monk, while also rewarding the devotion of his humblest of servants. As such, at the moment of consecration, when the monk uttered the prayers, "the host in his hands became flesh, and drops of blood fell upon the corporal below. At the same time, the wine in the chalice became blood." The monk fell to his knees, his belief restored, and the peasant revelled in the glory of the blessing. Even the head of the wooden statue of the Virgin Mary seemed to tilt forward in adoration.

Fast forward nearly 200 years to 1486. As Ferdinand and Isabella made their own journey along the Camino de Santiago, they spent a night in O Cebreiro at the old monastery, at which point they learned of the miracle and were quite moved by the sight of it. The following morning, they decided to bring the relics with them, as the isolated village, so susceptible to harsh weather, was hardly a place for safekeeping. Their horses, however, dug in their heels and refused to leave O Cebreiro, until the entire entourage returned the relics to the small church. The story goes that Ferdinand and Isabella subsequently gifted the reliquary in which Jesus's blood and flesh remain to this day. The miracle received papal recognition soon after, with papal bulls issued by Innocent VIII in 1487 and Pope Alexander VI in 1496 that acknowledged it.

Mathew Kuefler has a fascinating theory that links together these two miracle stories. It begins in 1072, when Alfonso VI granted the lands on this mountaintop to a group of French monks from the monastery of Aurillac. And actually, we need to go back even farther to establish that monastery's history, as it's relevant to the larger discussion. In the 9th century, the Aurillac monastery was founded by Gerald, a nobleman who would become "one of the first male saints who achieved holiness not by abandoning his position and wealth for the cloister or cathedral but simply by doing good as a layman." There was, it should be noted, a legend linking Aurillar, Gerald, and a chalice, formerly owned by Saint Peter. Regardless, the years passed, the monastery declined, and eventually the connection to Aurillac severed. Only after the miracle of the Eucharist occurred did attention return to O Cebreiro.

Here's the clever theory: Saint Gerald of Aurillac is known as Saint Géraud in French and San Giraldo in Spanish. Back in his day, though, the language of choice in Aurillac was Occitan, and within that he was known as Sant Guiral. In Galicia, that condensed down further, to Sant Gral. As Kuefler asks, "Is it really that hard to imagine that some, shown a chalice they were encouraged to revere in a church named for Sant Gral, about whom they had never heard, mistook it for the Holy Grail?"

In any case, Saint Gerald maintains one foothold in the village of O Cebreiro today, and it's a credit to our third miracle–the man, the myth, the legend: Elías Valiña Sampedro. We have Laurie Dennett to thank for much of what we know in the English-speaking world about the priest, as she spent time with him in O Cebreiro in the 1980s, shared stories from that time in her book *Waybread*, and translated Luís Celeiro Álvarez's biography, *Pilgrim Spirit: Elías Valiña and the Revival of the Camino 1959-1989*.

Elías Valiña Sampedro was born in 1929 in a small village near Sarria, where he attended school as a young child, passing along the Camino de Santiago every day. At 12, he enrolled in Lugo's Diocesan Seminary; by 1957, he was an ordained priest, waiting on an assignment. When an opening emerged for a new priest in O Cebreiro, the first three candidates turned it down; the conditions were just too bleak. A 30-year-old Don Elías, however, accepted the assignment in 1959 and threw himself headfirst into the role, working not only to save souls, but also to save O Cebreiro itself.

By that time, O Cebreiro was a crumbling, isolated village, absolutely ravaged by poverty. The *pallozas*, with their circular stone walls and arching thatched roofs, so striking and evocative today, were the primary habitations in those days, split between humans and their livestock and still limited to dirt floors. The village lacked electricity, plumb- ing, and telephone. Most of the villagers were illiterate, their diets mostly composed of root vegetables and meat and dairy from their livestock. The church and old monastic complex were, if anything, in even greater disrepair than the rest of the village. The former's roof had collapsed, its walls crumbling, largely abandoned since the Civil War. The latter, meanwhile, had mostly been converted into housing for mules, cows, and a colony of bats.

Within just three years, Don Elías managed to set in motion a profound transformation. At the heart of this was his successful recruitment of the Dirección General de Arq- uitectura in Madrid to preserve and repair the village, which resulted in the restoration of the *pallozas* and the con- struction of new housing for the residents—complete with plumbing, electricity, and phone lines. He also oversaw the planting of native trees and the rehabilitation of the church, as well. As for the old monastery? It was converted into accommodation for travelers. It still exists: the Hospedería San Giraldo de Aurillac.

If Don Elías's accomplishments were limited to O Cebreiro, that alone would justify his lasting recognition.

However, his reputation today is even more closely tied to his pivotal contributions to the resurrection of the Camino de Santiago in the second half of the twentieth century. The most tangible impact of his ceaseless efforts was felt in reestablishing the route itself, through his painting of yellow arrows and authoring of the first modern guidebook. Equally significant, if harder to quantify, was his work in advocacy and organization. Time and again, Don Elías managed to persuade regional and national groups to support his initiative, as when he convinced the Spanish Secretary of State for tourism to commission a guidebook in 1980, or when the Diputación of Lugo agreed to install stone markers in 1988. He also played an integral part in spearheading the first national and international meetings of Camino associations, in 1985 and 1987 respectively, out of which emerged agreements on the pilgrim credential and guidelines for *refugios* (as albergues were originally called). Throughout, he labored to preserve ruins along the way, persuade farmers to restore lost paths, and encourage priests to offer hospitality to pilgrims.

Perhaps it's an exaggeration and a misrepresentation to characterize a man as a miracle. Antón Pombo of Gronze has certainly articulated his concerns about the mythicization of Don Elías. There are colorful stories that circulate about the man–such as his declaration to the Guardia Civil, when confronted about painting those yellow arrows, that he was "preparing for an invasion"–about which no real evidence exists to confirm. Beyond that, the singular elevation of Don Elías risks eliding the many other contributors who played important parts in this lengthy process. Had there been no Elías, would the Camino have experienced a resurgence? It's difficult to imagine anything but an affirmative response.

But the story of Don Elías, O Cebreiro, and the Camino de Santiago is a classic case of right person, right place, and right time. When nobody else would come to O Cebreiro, like Juan Santín in that snowstorm, Elías came. And once he arrived, like the miraculous Eucharist, he remained, dedicated to the village for the remainder of his all-too-short life. The best way to secure its persistence, its long-term relevance and significance, was through the restoration of the Camino to its once-great role in Spain. That work proved integral to his core mission, and through that effort he helped to resurrect a powerful force for good in the world, bringing peace, joy, and renewed health to millions. It's not the Holy Grail, but I suspect Galahad and Arthur would be proud.

Keep reading...

Joaquín Rodríguez Campos, "Ideas on Atlantic Culture in the Northwest Iberian Peninsula: 'Myths' and 'Realities,'" *Journal of the Society for the Anthropology of Europe*, 2002

Laurie Dennett, *Waybread*, 2023

Luís Celeiro Álvarez, *Pilgrim Spirit: Elías Valiña and the Revival of the Camino 1959-1989*, 2024

Mathew Kuefler, "How the Holy Grail Ended up in O Cebreiro, Galicia," *Brocar: Cuadernas de investigación histórica*, 2012

Galicia's *Hórreos*

Stage 26: O Cebreiro to Triacastela

Here's a challenge: during the peak of walking season, in the spring or summer, log into one of the big Camino-focused Facebook groups. Keep your eyes peeled. At some point, someone is going to share a photo of a small stone or wooden structure, along with a question, something like: "I keep seeing these everywhere! What are they?" If a full week passes without you encountering this question once, I owe you a café con leche.

But if you've completed a Camino through Galicia (and neighboring Asturias), you already know the answer. It's an *hórreo*. And I could just as easily challenge you to walk a kilometer in Galicia without seeing one, feeling equally secure that I won't have to pay out. You simply can't have a typically quaint Galician village, its granite houses sprinkled around seemingly haphazardly, without *hórreos* perched somewhere in the surrounding yards.

Because *hórreos* are quintessentially Galician, though, and the limited writing that exists on the subject is mostly in Galego, the Galician language, people in the English-speaking world know little about them beyond the simple translation: corn cribs. It's admittedly easy enough to leave it at that–mystery solved, story completed. If you've ever read anything about European forays into the "New World," though, there's an inconvenient fact rattling around in the back of your brain. Corn, or maize, didn't originate in Europe. It was introduced far later, after its discovery in Mesoamerica.

The Asturian admiral Gonzalo Méndez de Canço gets the credit. He lived a fascinating life. He first traveled to America at age 17, and in time contributed three of his own ships (one of which was named *El Apóstol Santiago*) to the royal navy. In 1595, elevated by that point to the rank of admiral, he was called to Puerto Rico to help defend the island (and a significant treasure stashed there) against the notorious bane of Spain, Sir Francis Drake. De Canço acquitted himself quite well. In the first clash, a cannonball shattered the mizzenmast of Drake's flagship, while a further 28 balls blasted his cabin to bits. After licking his wounds, Drake ordered a counter-strike, and de Canço thwarted him once more, sinking nine English ships and killing 400 Englishmen in the process. This would represent one of only two defeats in Drake's prolific career. Building off this success, de Canço was soon awarded the role of governor of La Florida, arriving in St. Augustine in June 1597. In between heated clashes with the Guale tribes, de Canço's attention increasingly turned to corn. He promoted intensive cultivation all over Florida, sharing tools and seeds with settlers and indigenous people alike, while also building a mill to process the grain. Finally, when Philip III opted to replace him in 1603, de Canço made the long trip home, but he did so with two packages of seeds, destined to be planted in his birthplace (Tapia de Casariego) and his wife's (Mondoñedo), both on the Camino del Norte.

Corn transformed agriculture in Northwest Spain. Before its arrival, cereal harvesting flowed in annual cycles, with wheat or rye growing in the winter and millet predominating in the summer. Corn quickly became the summer crop of choice, planted in late April and harvested in October. Despite its dominance, it permitted some crop diversity. Space is required between rows of corn for optimal growth, but things like beans and pumpkins could be raised in those areas, and often were. The shift to corn allowed farmers to abandon the fallow periods that once marked the months between winter and summer, and encouraged the draining of wetlands to promote even greater growth. In comparison to millet and rye, corn enjoyed a superior agricultural yield, which represented a boon to local landlords, who over time were able to raise rents by 300-400%.

For all that, its early implementation was a borderline disaster. As the poorest inhabitants of Galicia and Asturias replaced millet with corn as their primary source of cheap calories, their health was lost somewhere in the maize. The problem has subsequently been diagnosed as niacin (Vitamin B) deficiency, or Pellagra. Indigenous farmers in the Americas had long understood how to best prepare the grain. A critical step in the process is called "nixtamalization," which allows for niacin and tryptophan to be absorbed by the consumer. Early Europeans in the Americas were taught to soak the corn in calcium hydroxide, which accomplished this goal. Unfortunately, their peers back in Spain didn't get the instruction manual, just the seeds. While Pellagra was diagnosed in Spain in 1735, it was endemic in Southern Europe for two centuries, and it would later, according to Karen Clay and colleagues, cause "more deaths than any other nutrition-related disease in American history" in the American South in the early 1900s.

Nonetheless, the corn train had left the station, and there was no stopping it. With corn, Galicia was now ready for corn cribs. As spotty as the historical record is, though, we have some evidence that indicates that the latter actually preceded the former. In 1219, King Alfonso XI transferred ownership of present day Betanzos (on the Camino Inglés). That doesn't matter to the present discussion. What does, though, is this line from the document, delineating the property under discussion: "and on the other side, on the path leading to your *hórreo*, except the same *hórreo* with its yard..." In the same century, we also find the first visual representation of an *hórreo*, in the Cantigas de Santa María. The small drawing features three *hórreos*, quite similar to the structures we see today. What's the deal?

To answer that question, we have to turn to Veronica Lorenzo-Luaces Pico's work, *Agricultural Temples in the Iberian Landscape, Larders from the Past*, which offers an invaluable overview of the *hórreo's* evolution. Well before corn, as we know, cereals were grown throughout the region; even the Iron Age castro culture is linked to millet production. And certainly, some sort of structure would be required to preserve and protect the harvested grain. In those early days, a proto-*hórreo* structure, known as a *cabazo*, served this purpose. Constructed from small, interwoven branches, and shaped more like a barrel, these deteriorated and decayed over time, leaving little evidence. They haven't been forgotten entirely, though; some modern *cabazos* can still be found in Galicia today. In time, the more familiar, rectangular-shaped structures emerged, such as we see in the Cantigas, mostly built from wood in those early days. Pico's close analysis is helpful here, because similar doesn't mean identical, and there's a crucial design difference in those 13th-century *hórreos*: they lack cross-ventilation slots.

This is an easy–but critical–design element to appreciate about contemporary *hórreos*. For a long time, I couldn't understand why *hórreos* became a staple in Spain, and yet were entirely absent from the United States. Why didn't we develop similar corn cribs in my home country? There are, of course, plenty of factors that come into play here, and certainly corn storage facilities did develop. The key difference, though, is the climate. In the United States, corn can complete the ripening process in the field; the conditions are dry and warm, allowing for this to play out naturally. By contrast, Galicia's climate is not so accommodating. Corn has to be picked when the humidity level is still quite high, meaning that a different process has to be followed for drying out the grain. This is the beauty of *hórreos*. Corn is stacked deliberately within, divided into sections using cross-planks, which provide channels for air to pass through consistently. The *hórreo* itself is typically positioned in open areas or on elevated slopes, where it can better catch a breeze. Agrarian researchers have studied this. O. A. Perez-Garcia and colleagues measured the effect. When the outdoor humidity is at 90% or higher–hardly a rarity in Galicia–the indoor humidity, within the *hórreo*, is more than 5% lower. By contrast, when the outdoor humidity drops below 65%, the interior humidity actually climbs by 3%. The *hórreo*, it turns out, has a stabilizing effect, maintaining a more consistent temperature and humidity level within which the corn can be better preserved.

Pilgrims on the Camino del Norte, walking through Asturias, will discover some key differences between the Asturian and Galician *hórreos*. Unlike their rectangular peers, Asturian corn cribs tend to be square-shaped, with few openings in the walls, and they typically feature broad porches. Form follows function; in Asturias, corn is dried on the porch before being moved inside for storage. By contrast, *hórreos* in Portugal tend to be even narrower rectangles than what is found in Galicia.

That is, of course, just one of many design differences. Part of what makes *hórreos* so charming to visitors is their aesthetic qualities. The Spanish geographer Ignacio Martínez Rodríguez did critical work here, developing a typology of *hórreos* to helpfully classify the significant varieties. Class, it should be noted, is bound up in this richness. Once corn established itself in the region, a curious phenomenon developed. While *eating* corn became associated with poverty, given the abundance of more nutritious (and pricier) alternatives, *harvesting* corn was a mark of wealth and distinction, a testament to the amount of land owned by the estate. As such, it wasn't enough to simply establish a functional *hórreo*; it needed some panache!

To become a more discerning *hórreo*-phile, start by considering the materials. Is it made out of wood, stone, or a mixture of the two? Mixed-material *hórreos* are most common, representing roughly 70% of all *hórreos*, usually combining stone frames and wooden sides. Stone varies by region, but is typically either granite or slate; the wood is primarily chestnut. Next, consider the base. Is the structure supported by legs or sheer walls? Some method was necessary, of course, to keep mice and other pests from the grain. The legs alone were not enough; look closely and you'll likely see small channels inscribed around the base of the legs, which fill with rainwater to better fend off ants. Sheer walls became desirable when storage spaces were added beneath the *hórreo*, maximizing the real estate value, or to further elevate the structure to improve airflow. If stairs are required to reach the corn, they are nearly always detached from the heart of the structure, to protect its integrity.

For many, the most appealing element of *hórreos* is the ornamentation that embellishes the structures. Crosses are, without a doubt, the most common feature, but Pico has found that they appear on less than half the extant *hórreos*, and are more common on stone than wood. Mixed-material *hórreos*, on average, are more sparingly adorned, but when they do feature decorations, they can be quite diverse. Keep an eye out for bell towers, sundials, weathervanes, animals, and saints. Older folk beliefs sometimes survive on *hórreos* as well. These often manifest as phallic symbols, speaking to fertility. The symbols of the snake and the cosmic tree are also important, though; the former embodied the annual life cycle in ancient Galicia, while the latter formed a conduit between earth and sky, through which the spirits might move.

As effective as *hórreos* are, modern technology certainly offers alternatives, making *hórreos* less critical than they once were. Despite that, though, Galicia has embraced the structure. The region's tourism website declared it "the land of the 30,000 *hórreos*," reflecting a common estimate for the total number of corn cribs in Galicia. Spain went a step further, passing a law in 1973 mandating the protection of all historic *hórreos* in Galicia and Asturias. Even if their primary function declines in usefulness, their secondary function–shining brightly as a distinct cultural marker–is sure to thrive for centuries to come.

Keep reading...

Ignacio Martinez Rodriguez, *El Hórreo Gallego*, 1979

Ron Dulaney Jr., "The Galician Hórreo and its Cultural Fields," *The International Journal of Design in Society*, 2013

O. A. Perez-Garcia, et. al., "Evaluation of traditional grain store buildings (hórreos) in Galicia," *Spanish Journal of Agricultural Research*, 2014

Veronica Lorenzo-Luaces Pico, *Agricultural Temples in the Iberian Landscape, Larders from the Past*, 2011

Live By Monastic Isolation, Die by Monastic Isolation

Stage 27: Triacastela to Sarria

I confess that when I first walked the Camino Francés, I yielded to temptation. Departing Triacastela, pilgrims have two options: a shorter, 18-kilometer walk to the large Galician town of Sarria, or a more meandering, 25-kilometer approach that loops through the old monastery of Samos. What can I say? I was tired and sore! I took the short route. On future walks, I remedied that grievous error.

The inconvenience of Samos's location is kind of the point. While its origins date to the 6th century, making it the oldest inhabited monastery in Spain, most of what we know about the place comes from the 10th century onward, from which point the abbey embraced Benedictine rule. As Estefanía López Salas succinctly explains, the monastic movement was intrinsically linked to the principle of isolation, separating from the world and submitting to a fixed rule in order to escape the perils of the secular world and promote a life of prayer. The Benedictines brought even greater structure to this, imposing a series of guidelines for all monasteries to follow.

It's hard not to be stunned when first arriving in Samos. The religious complex is nestled snugly within a lush, green valley, tree-covered hills forming a ring around it. The quiet Sarria River flows past, along the northwest side of the monastery. Look past the beauty, though, and instead appreciate the strategic merits of this position. When first established, Samos–known at the time as Sámanos–was a stone island in a sea of green, cut off from the outside world by those hills. An ancient Roman road passed close by, but it didn't connect directly to the site, offering the best of both worlds. And while the valley was certainly modest in size, sufficient land existed to meet the agricultural needs of the monastic community.

Indeed, a multidisciplinary study of the landscape found evidence of prehistoric terracing here, dating to the Iron Age–one of the few in Northwest Spain to include cereal pollen evidence. Given the unusually high density of Iron Age hillforts, or *castros* (more on that in Stage 29), in the immediate vicinity, that speaks to the need for maximizing agricultural production in those early years. Additional terracing was installed in the 8th and 9th centuries AD, during the peak of that first incarnation of Samos. A third round followed in the 12th and 13th centuries, around the same time that the Romanesque church was built, while the most significant of all land transformations followed in the 17th century. The land sufficed to sustain an independent community, but technological advances were required to achieve that.

Even today, when the world has encroached upon the monastery's once splendid isolation, the complex maintains an air of secrecy. Again, that's by design. Benedictine rule required separation and self-sufficiency. As outlined in Chapter 66 of the Rule, "the monastery ought to be so organized [...] that all necessaries, that is, water, a mill-house, a garden and various crafts may be forthcoming within the monastery, so that there may be no necessity for the monks to go beyond the gates, because that is by no means expedient for their souls."

Samos diligently adhered to those guidelines. Take a look at the monastic complex on Google Maps, using the satellite view. You'll immediately notice the two cloistered sections– grassy courtyards surrounded by buildings. As monks were intended to be cut off from the outside world, these cloistered areas provided access to nature and served as a locus for the religious complex, while still protecting their privacy. Windows on the exterior walls are limited, minimizing the degree to which outsiders can look in, or vice versa. Within the walls, all necessary facilities were installed, including the kitchen and dining area, the church and library, and first shared dormitories but then later individual cells for the monks. Over the years, other small industries took shape within the monastery, with dire consequences.

In those early years, though, the monastery thrived, and its importance necessitated careful management of contacts with the outside world. It established a separate guesthouse, as dictated by the Rule, within which foreign visitors could be kept removed from the monastery's daily operations. Benedict was particularly explicit about minimizing contact, writing that, "By no means let anyone, unless appointed thereunto, either mix with, or speak to the guests, but if he shall meet or see them, after humbly saluting and asking their blessing, he shall pass on, saying that it is not lawful for him to talk with a guest." The monks of Samos did, on occasion, need to venture forth into the outside world–with the abbot's permission, of course–but they were mandated to follow a Las Vegas-esque set of guidelines in those cases. What happened in the secular world needed to stay there: "Let no one presume to relate unto others what he has seen or heard outside the

monastery, because therefrom arise many evil consequences."

As the centuries passed, the outside world encroached
to an ever greater degree upon the monastery, which
required additional measures. Walls were established
surrounding the monastic lands, which extended roughly 2.5
kilometers outward from the complex, in the 17th and 18th
centuries. Within those walls, business thrived, with farming,
cattle breeding, orchards, and timber harvesting all taking
place. The formation of Samos town, which first took root at
the intersection of the main road, posed another challenge.
Only 100 meters separated the town from the monastery, but
that distance was enforced, and the abbot exercised
significant influence over developments within the town,
limiting the placement and size of houses.

Isolation and self-sufficiency were integral to the life of
Samos for more than a millennium. Ultimately, though, those
factors nearly conspired to bring about its demise. A major
source of income for the Samos monks in the 20th century
was the production of the Benedictine liqueur "PAX," which
prompted them in the 1940s to establish a storage space
below the abbey chamber, adjacent to the staircase closest
to the Nereid Cloister. At the time, as many as 90 people
lived within proximity to the space. This was a large operation, with tanks capable of holding 20,000 liters of alcohol,
along with all other relevant equipment and ingredients.

What happened next would almost be comical, if the
consequences weren't so severe. On September 24, 1951, a
typical morning unfolded in the liquor business. The monk
Benito González and a pair of students were working on one
of the alcohol tanks, when they discovered that one of the
taps appeared to be blocked. Unfortunately, the lighting in a
medieval monastery often leaves much to be desired, so
they decided to strike a match to better illuminate the

operation. Alas, the open flame came too close to the alcohol, and... boom. A powerful explosion cascaded through the
heart of the abbey, erupting straight through two floors and
onto the roof. It wasn't the first fire to feed upon Samos; an
early 16th-century blaze made its mark. But this would be far
more devastating.

And here is the downside of isolation: the closest
firefighting crews were based far from the monastery. It took
nearly two hours for any help to arrive, with the first firemen
coming from Lugo, and later crews traveling from Ferrol and
Monforte de Lemos. Monks and local residents did their best,
prioritizing saving the lives of elderly monastic resi- dents
and the most precious images and objects of worship, while
also stacking sandbags at the entrances to the church and
library, but the fire spread at a merciless pace. The one
saving grace is that the fire never reached the gasoline
stored in the monastery, though the alcohol combined with
the old chestnut structures provided plenty of fuel. The next
day, *La Voz de Galicia*, offered this bleak summation: "The
Royal Abbey of Samos destroyed by fire."

Maybe it wasn't *quite* that bad. The stone walls and
vaulted areas emerged largely unscathed, preserving the
bones of the monastery. The church, as well, experienced
only limited damage, thanks to the heroic efforts of the
rescue team. However, the acclaimed Nereid Cloister was
nearly obliterated, and the Great Cloister and sacristy were
similarly ravaged. The wooden staircases were gone, as
were 380 windows and more than 200 doors. Enough
survived, though, to keep hope alive that Samos might rise
again, and local governments quickly rallied behind the
initiative. Their efforts bore fruit. Perhaps, like me, you are
surprised to learn that just 75 years ago the monastery faced
such destruction. Few signs of the immolation are evident to
contemporary pilgrims passing through.

In the center of the Great Cloister today stands a statue to Samos's favorite son, Father Benito Jerónimo Feijóo. Born near Ourense in 1676, Feijóo entered the Benedictine order at the Monastery of Samos at the age of 12. While there is no reason to question his faith, the pursuit of a life devoted to learning was likely a more powerful motivator; he later reflected that "no other pleasure in the world [was] capable of enthralling as much" as study. Few in Spain at that moment were similarly inclined; on the contrary, Feijóo was consistently appalled by the overwhelming ignorance of his time. Dual purposes emerged: to elevate the clergy around him, while also combatting the foolishness of the common people. To this day, Feijóo is acknowledged as one of the leaders of the Spanish Enlightenment, and his philosophical outlook still carries weight today. As he wrote, "The greatness of discourse is to penetrate and persuade the truths; the lowest skill of wit is to entangle others with sophistries."

For all its understandable focus on isolation, Samos's greatest figure is one who reached far beyond the monastery to reshape Spanish thought, while the monastery's persistence was only made possible by the extensive financial support of the surrounding towns.

Keep reading…

Estefanía López Salas, "Las causas y las consecuencias del incendio de 1951 en el monasterio de San Julián de Samos. Nuevos datos para su estudio," *Cuadernos de Estudios Gallegos*, 2016

Estefanía López Salas, "The Monastic Citadel of San Julián de Samos as an Affirmation of Isolation," *8th International Conference CIRICE*, 2018

Estefanía López Salas, "The Reform of Samos Abbey between 1491 and 1637," *Imago Temporis, Medium Aevum*, 2017

José Carlos Sánchez-Pardo, et. al., "Dating and Characterising the Transformation of a Monastic Landscape. A Multidisciplinary Approach to the Agrarian Spaces of Samos Abbey," *Environmental Archaeology*, 2024

The Traumatic Relocation

Stage 28: Sarria to Portomarín

When I first crossed the bridge over the Minho River into Portomarín, perhaps I could be forgiven for focusing more on the steep flight of stairs immediately in front of me, as opposed to the scenery around me. Still, my guidebook had provided me with the broad brushstrokes of the town's history. In particular, I knew that its position on the hill, reached by those onerous stairs, was a relatively recent phenomenon. The original Portomarín was situated lower down, alongside a humbler Minho, until a dam was built upstream in 1963, necessitating the town's relocation.

The most vivid story I encountered at the time involved the transfer of the *Igrexa de San Xoán* (also known as the *Iglesia de San Nicolás*). Each and every block of the church was individually numbered, to ensure that its reassembly would go as smoothly and with as much fidelity to the original as possible. For years after, one could still discern those chalk marks on some of the interior stones. Another church, the *Igrexa de San Pedro*, was similarly moved, as were two historic manor houses: the 16th-century *Conde da Maza* and the 17th-century *Pazo dos Pimentales ou de Berbeteros*. A single arch survived from the medieval bridge.

Only on a later visit did I come to understand what happened to the rest of the original Portomarín. It's still there, beneath the river's surface. If you happen to be on the Camino Francés during a drought-ridden summer, take a close look as you cross the bridge. You just might see some of the old buildings poking through the surface.

I liked the story of Portomarín. It was equal parts charming and haunting; a noble effort to preserve history, mixed with the mild creepiness that always accompanies ghost towns. I enjoyed staring into the depths, trying to tease out the lurking structures. As the years passed, though, I finally came to learn something much more important about Portomarín's history.

The residents had no say in the dam; no voice in the move. It was forced upon them.

After assuming power, Francisco Franco set out to transform the country into what has been characterized by Bibiana Duarte-Abadía and Rutgerd Boelens as a "regenerationist hydraulic utopia," and what Franco himself saw fitting within a larger "ideology of mastery over nature." The 180 reservoirs in the country in 1939 surged to 800 by 1975. In the process 500 towns, like Portomarín, were flooded, their surrounding valleys swamped, the adjacent forests destroyed. Estimates suggest that 50,000 people were displaced along the way. Forced labor from political prisoners was integral in many of these construction projects. There's no way of knowing how many people died. We have some data from isolated events, like the 144 people who died in Ribadelago in 1959 when a dam broke. Suicide as an act of resistance occurred in the face of numerous evictions. Pedro Arrojo and Javier Martínez Gil deemed it a "hydrocaust."

Franco pitched this as a paternalistic gesture in service to the depressed countryside, offering "redemption" through these "modernizing" projects. At the same time, though, it fit within a larger series of corporation-friendly initiatives that expropriated communal lands for timber production and consolidated agricultural tracts. The rural-to-urban migration process, already long underway in Galicia, was only accelerated by these reforms. While it's easy to frame this as economic inevitability, such an oversimplification elides the impact of these decades of deliberate environmental transformation.

While hydroelectricity surged as a key energy source in Spain throughout the 20th century, and it still accounted for nearly 10% of the country's total energy generation in 2023, the tide is turning against dams worldwide. Over time, we've come to recognize the downsides of dams—their deleterious impact on biodiversity, the ways they impede the flow of sediments and nutrients and the accompanying erosive consequences, and the risk they run of undercutting the recharge of underground aquifers. The impact on many fish populations has been particularly alarming. A major research project conducted by Barbara Belletti and her team in 2020 determined that Europe has at least 1.2 million instream barriers. Not all dams, by any means; some are quite modest in height. And certainly, some are essential, and should be maintained. But Dam Removal Europe studied the issue in 2021 and found that at least 150,000 of those impediments are obsolete, serving no useful purpose. To this point, the organization has documented the removal of 8146 barriers across Europe. Spain has been one of the leaders in dam removal, with over 200 dams eliminated thus far.

Will the movement someday reach Portomarín? Should it? The more immediate concern in the town seems to be the cone of silence that has hovered over the forced relocation, from its earliest days. The persistence of silence, the lack of open dialogue, is one of the most lasting consequences of the Franco years–it's no accident that the underlying history of the Portomarín dam is absent from most accounts–but some tentative efforts have been made by sociologists and educators, like Belén Castro Fernández and Ramón López-Facal, to break the ice.

Those initial attempts at dialogue have offered us a richer picture of what unfolded in Portomarín. A significant generation gap exists within the town's current population. The small, aging group that lived through the forced relocation is around 75 years old today, meaning they were between 16 and 25 at the time of the event. They carry a palpable sense of loss. A major contributor to that feeling is the fact that, when the original town was flooded, many residents opted to leave. That created an initial rupture, breaking many long-standing friendships, something that has been only lightly reckoned with by those who remained. The survivors also bemoan the loss of their homes, connecting this to a loss of memories linked to family that were embedded within those physical structures. More broadly, the move triggered a fundamental change in the way of life for those in Portomarín, altering the town's rural nature and its residents' relationship with the river, while severing local traditions.

The survivors acknowledge that there were material benefits to the move. They received modern houses in new Portomarín, and updated services and infrastructure were available to the townspeople. However, it ultimately didn't offset the profound loss. As one resident said, "We were very poor people, my parents had seven children... the money was welcome at the time because two of my brothers were married and had no job... but it did not compensate at all for the suffering of my parents."

The generation gap's accompanying perception gap is most tangible when it comes to those material benefits.

Younger people living in Portomarín today are far more likely to see this as a fair exchange, and for that reason the older residents eschew dialogue. They find it difficult to imagine that the younger people might understand the price paid for their more comfortable accommodations.

Those different viewpoints also manifest when discussions arise surrounding the ruins of old Portomarín. For the survivors, the crumbling remains are a reminder of their collective trauma: "We would have preferred never to have seen the ruins of Portomarín ... they bring back to me a thousand memories of my parents, of my grandparents, who suffered so much because of the reservoir." By contrast, the ruins are a curiosity to the town's younger folk, who see potential for the structures to be preserved and promoted as a tourist attraction.

The Camino de Santiago is connected to this larger discussion. For those who think fondly about the relocation, the dam, the new Portomarín, and the Camino are all of a piece, speaking to the region's redevelopment and modernization. As one resident observed, "We owe everything to the Way. That's why the word Portomarín is synonymous with the Way because without it the heritage we are speaking of would not have existed in Portomarín." And yet, to some the Camino is a double-edged sword. It reorients the entire town economy towards serving pilgrims for half the year, meaning higher prices, businesses geared towards passing tourists, and a seasonal population. One resident claims that the benefits offered by the Camino are used as an excuse by regional leaders to deny Portomarín other services. "They say, 'They have enough with the Way.'" Another bleakly sums it up this way: "The Way of Saint James is going to do more to put an end to the town than the move."

A coldly cynical evaluation of Portomarín, taking this all in, might conclude that this problem will resolve itself. Just give it another decade or so. The unfortunate victims of the forced relocation will pass on, and the more amenable, younger generation will embrace the opportunities that were created. And who knows, maybe another door will open, with the dam's removal and the recovery of old Portomarín as a novelty.

But history casts a long shadow, and it's all too easy to fall prey to its darkness when we deny its presence. The tourism industry believes that we want shiny, upbeat stories, and it works to feed us such rose-colored narratives. By instead recognizing the region's recent, painful past, too long ignored, perhaps we can make a modest contribution to bringing it back into the light.

Keep reading...

Ana Fernández-Cebrián, "Roots Under the Water: Dams, Displacement, and Memory in Franco's Spain," *A Companion to Spanish Environmental Cultural Studies*, 2023

Belén Castro Fernández and Ramón López-Facal, "Portomarín, la memoria herida de un desarraigo," *Revista Electrónica Interuniversitaria de Formación del Profesorado*, 2019

Belén Castro-Fernández, et. al., "Emotional conflict and trauma: the recovery of stolen memory using a mixed-methods approach," *Humanities & Social Sciences Communications*, 2021

Helena Miguélez-Carballeira, "The traumatic rural unconscious in contemporary Galician culture: hydropolitical violence in literature and film," *Journal of Spanish Cultural Studies*, 2024

The Castro and the Celts

Stage 29: Portomarín to Palas do Rei

When two guidebook authors both agree about a can't miss sight, it's probably worth listening. In July 2020, I spoke with Beebe Bahrani and Rev. Sandy Brown, authors of two of the major guidebooks on the Camino Francés, about why guidebooks still matter. At the risk of oversimplifying, their answer could be summed up in one word: Castromaior.

"So, my wife and I were walking together in 2018," Sandy reminisced, "and I said, you know, I've never gone to the Castro at Castromaior, so let's do it. We turned left on the path and we walked up to the berm. And I looked down and I thought, oh my gosh, I can't believe I have neglected this all this time." As Sandy stood and admired the low walls of the ancient hill fort, he looked down "on the right and there are all these pilgrims that are just walking by because you can see the trail not more than 50 meters away. And I'm thinking these poor people, they're probably only going to get here once."

Beebe enthusiastically agreed, noting that "when I first came upon it I became an evangelist." As "everyone was walking by, I was like, no guys, come here, come here, you have to see this. It's one of those things... It could be life-changing."

Pilgrims passing through this stage before 2006 could be forgiven for walking past this hill fort, given that it hadn't yet been excavated. Over the next four years, an archaeological team, though, brought this site back to the light, revealing a fort that had thrummed with life between the 4th century BC and 1st century AD. Like other castros from the era, it enjoyed an elevated, hilltop perch, affording its residents ample visibility, to better track potential threats from the surrounding countryside. In the near future, pilgrims will be able to visit not only the ruins but also a still-developing interpretive center, to better appreciate what they're seeing.

Of course, the interpretation of such ruins is already part of a larger narrative coursing through Galicia, highlighting the region's long-rumored Celtic roots. It's right there in the name; the "Gaelic" jumps right out.

In *Ghosts of Spain,* Giles Tremlett paints a vivid picture of this connection: "Gallegos are proud of their supposedly Celtic origins. They have legends of *meigas* and *brujas,* good and bad witches. There are mysterious beings called *mouros,* who hoard treasure under the abandoned castros (iron age settlements) that sit on hilltops and promontories. Death, the afterlife and Purgatory are particular obsessions. A band of tortured souls from Purgatory known as the Santa Compaña, for example, wanders remote country roads at night, awaiting a chance for redemption [...] The bestiary of Galician folklore is large and scary. It includes *lobishomes* (werewolves), deceptively beautiful *nereidas* (fishwomen) and mouchas, melodic owl-like spirits whose calls announce the coming of Death." The Xunta de Galicia asserts that hill forts, like Castromaior, "are vestiges of the Celtic culture and were in use for over one thousand years." Pilgrims who have completed their journey into Santiago de Compostela will fondly remember the *gaita*, or bagpipe, player just before entering the Praza do Obradoiro. That's no accident; the bagpipe has been embraced across Galicia as a symbol of those Celtic roots. Over 5000 registered *gaitas* are in the city of Ourense alone, while an entire festival dedicated to Celtic music is held in the coastal town of Ortigueira, on the Camino del Mar, each summer.

Heck, we could stop where most people start, with Wikipedia: "The Gallaeci were originally a Celtic people who for centuries had occupied the territory of modern Galicia and northern Portugal; bounded to the south by the Lusitanians and to the east by the Astures. The Gallaecians lived in fortified villages now called castros (Latin: castra / hill forts): ranging from small villages of less than a hectare (more common in the north), to great hillforts with more than 10 hectares, named "Oppida" or "Citânia", which were more common in the southern half of the traditional settlement area." Celtic, Celtic, Celtic.

The problem, though, is that many contemporary historians have come to the conclusion that the story of Galicia's Celtic origins is a load of bunk.

A 1998 article by Patrick Sims Williams captures the shift in mood, "from celtomania to celtoscepticism." As historians and archaeologists brought modern techniques to bear on the subject, the traditional narratives surrounding Celts couldn't withstand such scrutiny. In his 2003 book, *The Celts: A Very Short Introduction*, Barry Cunliffe cheekily refers to the Celts as "All things to all men." Micheal Morse offered a similar judgement, writing that "the Celts are, and always were, a creation of the human mind." John Collis is even blunter, flatly asserting that Celtic society "merely represents a mishmash of information from different times and different places which is often of little value for understanding the societies being described. Descriptions, or rather caricatures, of societies cannot be transposed in time and space under an invented concept of the 'Celts'; indeed the whole use of the terms Celt and Celtic is something which should be avoided as it distorts our understanding of the archaeological record."

What's the deal? A core part of the problem is a linguistic one. Throughout ancient history, names like the Keltoi, Celtae, Galli, Galatai, and Galatae were used almost interchangeably across the Mediterranean, generally applied by individuals in the "civilized" center to the "barbarian" hinterland. To make matters worse, given that many of these peoples were non-literate, we have precious little evidence of their cultures, relying heavily on emerging archaeological discoveries to supplement the dubious Mediterranean sources. Those archaeological discoveries offered up some evidence in support of the pro-Celtic narrative. As Sharif Gemie explains in his *Concise History of Galicia*, graves dating as far back as the 5th century BC have revealed objects with the "swirling motifs" and "intricate curls" so distinctive of Celtic artifacts. And yet, they also include regionally distinctive swords, torcs, fibulae, as well as their own distinct patterns on pottery and other jewelry. For a long time, archaeologists saw similar physical evidence across different sites as evidence of a shared culture. However, that view has subsequently been challenged. Through trade or other forms of exchange—and we know such acts occurred—ideas, techniques, and objects could spread, without a singular "ethnic group" being established.

Constanze Witt sums up the current state of the field quite eloquently: "Thus, the ancient authors give us many fragmentary but vivid, often stereotyped, often propagandistic, sometimes contradictory, always constructed glimpses. Archaeology shows us an artistically innovative, lavish, stubbornly abstracting, colorful, and gorgeous craft production. In the preserved material culture, in burials, deposits, and settlements, we find unique and powerful expressions of local identities. Burials, bones, pots, coins, weapons, minor arts, tools, textiles, metals, plant and animal remains, traces of architecture, inscriptions, and above all their contexts and relationships help to flesh out our picture of the Iron Age Europeans. Whether, in any single case, they are among peoples who would have called themselves 'Celts' is a question we cannot answer, and which is probably irrelevant."

The larger issue, though, is that while the answer might be academically irrelevant, it is politically very relevant. As KA McKevitt has documented, the Celtic myth is at the root of modern Galician identity. The 18th and 19th centuries saw the birth of the nation all across Europe, as modern notions of Frenchness, Italianness, and the like percolated across the continent. This process was complicated by the fact that such countries were not monoliths; they contained many distinct cultures within their borders. As a consequence, the construction of one dominant identity often necessitated the erasure of others.

In Spain, the Castilian identity held prominence, and even today we can still see the lingering tension engendered by its national elevation at the expense of strong regional identities, especially in Catalonia, the Basque Country, and Galicia. The persistence of that Galician culture, though, didn't happen by chance; it was the work of intellectuals in the 19th century. After James Macpherson lit the spark, inspiring a continent-wide fascination with the Celts that shaped the Romantic movement, Galician writers found ways to embed this within their regional identity. This occurred first in 1838, when José Verea y Aguiar introduced the connection to Celticism in his *Historia de Galicia*. The movement picked up steam a few decades later, when two other historians, Benito Vicetto and Manuel Murguía, deliberately set out to manufacture a Galician golden age, a purpose for which the supposedly Celtic origins were found-ational. Later historians, Justo Beramendi and Xosé Manoel Núñez Seixas, dismissed the historiographical value of such works as "almost null," but the impact was substantial. This is where the Galician-Celtic link took firm root.

The goal wasn't solely to craft a distinct path for Galicia; it was, in truth, to establish an identity that was superior to the rest of Iberia, and particularly to Castilian Spain. By the 20th century, this became justification to demand political autonomy.

In 1986, the Galicia-Celtic connection reached its apogee, when the region joined Ireland, Scotland, Wales, Cornwall, Brittany and the Isle of Man as the seventh member of the Celtic League, an NGO dedicated to promoting modern Celtic identity and culture. This didn't end well; as *The Economist* notes, the decision "caused shrieks of protest" from the other members, claiming that it "wrecked the 'linguistic criterion' of membership." Within a year, the Celtic League reversed course, and Galicia got the boot.

If the Celtic connection is spurious, then, what do we actually know about Castromaior? The evidence is clear that the site was continuously occupied. Built in the Iron Age, around the 6th-5th centuries BC, it lasted until its first contacts with Rome, in 1st century AD. The structures that survive today are primarily from that last, most elaborate, period, though some remnants of the earlier phases are visible in the foundations. In the earliest stage of occupation, there were likely only two walled enclosures; the homes themselves were constructed from more perishable mate-rials, and thus little remains of those. The first significant stage of remodeling resulted in stone houses (combining slate and quartzite) with thatched roofs. The walls rose as high as four meters, with the roofs climbing still higher. The second round of transformations made the fort feel even more like a town, with the notable addition of shared public spaces and transversal streets branching off the main promenade. Evidence of cereal crops has been discovered in the surrounding hills, dating from the earliest stage of occupation.

The most striking discovery from the excavation has been a set of 13 Roman coins, most of which were found in a room subsequently interpreted as a kitchen, because of the presence of a fireplace. Those coins are advantageous because they allow for more precise dating. All 13 come from Rome's Republican and Augustan periods. It's rare to find such coins in Northwest Spain; they didn't appear in the region until the Cantabrian and Asturian Wars, between 29 and 19 BC. Thus, it's fair to conclude that these are linked to Castromaior's final stage.

What brought the hill fort to such a definitive ending? We can only speculate. The evidence suggests that it was abandoned rapidly; the renunciation of belongings, like the coins, certainly hints at a rushed departure. Was this another step in Roman conquest and assimilation? Roman conquest of the region was achieved by 19 BC, but provincial rule and integration were gradual processes. As new settlements were established, were the populations of castros encouraged to relocate or forced to make the move? Did communities seek to escape Roman dominance? Greater clarity may come with time and a lot more shovels.

For now, though, it's enough to note that the real shame of the Celtic myth is that it obscures the fact that the truth of Galicia's past is remarkable enough. The "castro culture" that dominated the region in the Iron Age, likely influenced by the native Iberian population, was a more distinct Atlantic presence, differentiating it from most of the peninsula. The hill forts were the lone type of fortified settlement used in the region for a millennium. As larger towns gradually coalesced in the *meseta*, these smaller communities, often no larger than two hectares, remained the only game in town in what became Galicia.

We just know so, so little about what life was like in these communities. One major problem is the dearth of funerary evidence. As C. Alonso del Real pithily put it, the people in these castros "lived, but did not die." Between the Late Bronze Age (9th century BC) and the beginning of the Roman period, there is a near-complete absence of burial sites. And we rely on those for developing our understanding of ancient cultures! Another challenge is that the hill forts, particularly in their early stages, lacked any sort of large-scale storage spaces. Such areas existed in the Late Bronze Age, but again, they slipped from the picture in these Iron Age communities. This exacerbated the challenges of finding material evidence that could speak to the cultural habits of these castros. Some evidence exists of their agricultural practices; by the late Iron Age, we see deeper, more fertile soils surrounding many of the forts and gentler surrounding slopes. A crop rotation strategy seems to have existed, allowing for the alternation of cereals and legumes. Ultimately, though, the dearth of physical evidence and written records, along with the sudden imposition of Roman rule, has left us with precious little to work with.

But we have those forts! Castromaior on the Camino Francés. Castro Chao Samartín on the Camino Primitivo. Castro de Fazouro, among so many others, on the Camino del Mar. Celtic or not, a lasting, consequential culture thrived here, for the better part of a millennium. It is something worth acknowledging. It's certainly worth a 50-meter detour to visit.

Keep reading...

Almudena Orejas Saco del Valle, et. al., "Roman Denarii from North-Western Hispania, Findings from Castromaior," *Sonderdruck aus Madrider Mitteilungen*, 2016

César Parcero Oubiña and Isabel Cobas Fernandez, "Iron Age Archaeology of the Northwest Iberian Peninsula," *e-Keltoi: Journal of Interdisciplinary Celtic Studies*, 2004

Constanze Witt, "The 'Celts,'" *A Companion to Ancient History*, 2009

Giles Tremlett, *Ghosts of Spain*, 2006

Kerry Ann McKevitt, "Mythologizing Identity and History: A Look at the Celtic Past of Galicia," *e-Keltoi: Journal of Interdisciplinary Celtic Studies*, 2006

Miguel Ángel López Marcos, et. al., "Arquitectura defensiva en el Castro de Castromaior" *Arqueología de la Arquitectura*, 2016

Sharif Gemie, *A Concise History of Galicia*, 2006

Emilia Pardo Bazán's Masterpiece

Stage 30: Palas do Rei to Arzúa

Galician villages share certain qualities. Narrow roads converge at odd angles, in no semblance of order. Wizened cow eyes gleam from darkened interiors. A pervasive vacancy reigns, challenged only occasionally by a lone elderly man, ambling along with a walking stick. And in the midst of that, all of that, stand outsized stone buildings, composed of large chunks of cut granite, whispering secrets of times past. All too often, those whispers are all we can hope for.

A deeper story lurks, though, just off the Camino Francés, about an hour after Palas do Rei, near the village of A Ponte Campaña. Head south for a kilometer and you'll reach yet another large stone estate, seemingly no different from the scores of other similar structures already passed. This one, though, has a story. Perhaps the greatest Galician story ever told.

It is the story of four lives converging, colliding, in the novel *Los Pazos de Ulloa*.

The Marquis of Ulloa, Pedro Moscoso: On paper, he was the most powerful man in the area, a land-owning noble upon whom many peasants were dependent for survival. Single and young, he spent his days alternating between hunting and idleness, living roughly and drinking hard. Strolling around his estate, the "last scion of the Ulloas wandered with his hands in his pockets, whistling distractedly, like someone who does not know how to kill time." An abusive relationship with his head servant's daughter, Sabel, had resulted in a son, who ran wild around the estate, while that head servant, Primitivo, managed all operations. In a rare moment of self-awareness, Pedro denounced them all, declaring to the priest Julián that "They're plundering me, they're eating me alive."

The Priest, Julián Álvarez: From the beginning, we are made aware of Julián's softness, his inexperience, his lack of preparation for the real world. Raised in Santiago de Compostela, immersed alternately between his training for the priesthood and his cousins' home filled with young women, Julián emerged as a sensitive and deeply devout young man. A nearby abbot went further, calling him a "sissy," and bemoaning his "effeminacy, pure effeminacy." As he transitioned into the Ulloa estate, assigned to serve there as chaplain, he was shocked by what he discovered. Through his eyes, we see the decline of the once-grand *pazo*, or manor house. All glass had been broken from the windows, replaced with paper patches. The once vibrant paint had been ravaged by humidity. The wooden floors had fallen prey to the onslaught of moths. The delicate priest was troubled deeply with the disrepair of his own bedroom: "All this filth and crudity stirred in him a great longing for order and cleanliness, a wish for neatness in life as well as purity of the soul." While he started out working to bring order to the decadent estate, originating with the haphazard archives, he soon turned to the marquis himself. What the man needed, Julián determined, was a wife. A good, noble, moral wife.

The Wife, Nucha: It never should have been Nucha. When Julián and Pedro traveled to Santiago de Compostela to visit Señor De la Lage's family, the understanding was universal—the marqués had come to take a wife, and that wife would be chosen from one of the patriarch's four daughters. All attention was drawn early to flirtatious and lively Rita, the eldest of the four, who quickly established rapport with Pedro. The match seemed obvious, indisputable. However, the insecure marqués grew nervous about Rita's friendly, outgoing nature, declaring, "I'd swear she's fair game." When pressed, Julián advocated for Nucha, giving away his own forbidden feelings when he noted that she "borders on perfection." Nucha's goodness immediately came in conflict with Pedro's brashness, and he derived a twisted pleasure from the hunt. "When he made Nucha blush, he felt the pleasure of a child determined to open a rosebud with his fingers, scratching the skin of her soul with impudent jokes and crass familiarities that she rejected energetically." Nonetheless, Nucha did her duty; she married Pedro; in time, she bore him a child. It wasn't enough.

Primitivo, the Head Servant: Pedro's decline ran parallel to Primitivo's ascent, as he expanded his base of power throughout the region. We see little of his deeper motivations; he mostly exists in the shadows of the larger narrative, a murky figure that inspires fear. But he was always there. When Julián first arrived, Primitivo "scrutinized the newcomer with his little dark eyes." As Julián sought to execute essential reforms, Primitivo obstructed and obfuscated, impeding all changes. When Julián encouraged even the most modest changes, Primitivo's intense reaction laid bare the reality to the priest, as "Primitivo did not even bother to hide his furious glare, sizing him up with a look that amounted to a declaration of war." Disturbed, Julián turned to the marquis, and exhorted him to cast the usurper aside. Pedro, however, was blunt and fatalistic in his assessment: "The truth is that Primitivo is no steward, and it's worse than if he was, because he dominates everybody, including me." This engendered a different kind of fatalism in Julián, who determined that, "One had either to kill Primitivo or to deliver oneself into his hands: the priest realized that there was no way out."

Of course, a fifth life demands the spotlight here: Emilia Pardo Bazán, the author of *Los Pazos de Ulloa*, and (with apologies to Rosalia de Castro) Galicia's most acclaimed writer. Born into a noble family in A Coruña in 1851, she was privy to a dramatic period in both Spanish and Galician history. On the national level, the liberal revolution failed in 1868; five years later, the First Republic formed. This sparked the Third Carlist War, resulting in the restoration of the Bourbon monarchy. In Galicia, the relics of Santiago, hidden in 1589 under threat of invasion by Sir Francis Drake and subsequently forgotten, were finally rediscovered in 1879 and verified by papal decree in 1884. After only 40 pilgrims had attended the cathedral on Saint James's Day in 1867, this helped to breathe life back into Compostela, beginning with a special jubilee year in 1885.

Pardo Bazán was a trailblazer in her own right. The first woman president of Madrid's leading literary society as well as the first female professor of Romance languages, she bluntly declared that "I am a radical feminist. I believe that women should have all the rights that men have." In a notably backhanded compliment, fellow writer Juan Valera commented that, "She has a peculiar and rare talent... for all her perversion of taste, morality, and theodicy, Doña Emilia is quite a novelist."

In *Los Pazos de Ulloa,* Pardo Bazán worked to capture the decline and fall of rural Galicia. As Sharif Gemie describes in *A Concise History of Galicia*, we have to challenge our assumptions about what the rural nobility was like in these years. Once Galicia was absorbed into the larger Spanish state, the wealthiest elites relocated to be in proximity to the court, and many others could afford to pursue university training in urban centers. Still others pursued colonial endeavors, or emigrated to Portugal. Minor nobles—perhaps 11,000 in all by the mid-18th century—were left behind. To make matters worse, in the late-15th century, Galicia's nobles had sided more with the Portuguese throne than Ferdinand and Isabella, and the consequences of that alignment would be felt for centuries to come. In fact, between 1520 and 1858 no official royal visit was made to Galicia. The political structures imposed by the Spanish Crown largely bypassed those nobles.

The idleness and indolence of Pedro Moscoso was no mere work of fiction; it reflected the lifestyle of so many of these country nobles. Work was disparaged; people of standing were expected to keep clean hands, to not sully themselves with labor. Despite owning extensive lands, then, they gained little return from these holdings. While agricultural reforms improved the productivity of fields across Europe, Galicia remained stuck in the past. Equally challenging was the population boom that occurred throughout the region, as it surged from 300,000 in 1500 to 1.3 million in 1750. The highly-inefficient, small-scale farms worked in old-fashioned methods eked out barely enough to maintain the growing base.

The aforementioned political turmoil across Spain made its mark on Galicia as well. In the midst of those dramatic shifts in power, two positive reforms emerged: the return of constitutional monarchy in 1875 and the introduction of universal manhood suffrage in 1890 (women wouldn't gain the right to vote until 1931). The fear of further civil conflict, a consequence of the recurring Carlist Wars across the 19th century, resulted in collusion between the Liberals and Conservatives, who agreed that future elections would only involve their two parties. To further water down Spain's democratic principles, they also established a system of *caciquismo*, in which local bosses–caciques–would independently decide which party would receive their area's votes. Rural areas like Galicia typically skewed ultraconservative, but Pardo Bazán's portrayal of Primitivo also highlighted a cacique in the making who might shift the political winds in a different direction.

It would be easy to dismiss Pardo Bazán's portrayal of rural Galicia as the judgemental condemnation of an urban elite, but her perspective is more nuanced than that. In her portrayal of pilgrimage and the Camino de Santiago, as documented by Maryjane Dunn, Pardo Bazán finds great virtue in the "primitive soul" and the simplicity of "humble and sincere faith." As she traveled to Rome via train in 1888 as part of a Spanish delegation to honor the jubilee year, she reflected that, "I'm almost angry that in this journey the train is divided into first, second, and third class cars, for I would like us all to be equals, like brothers and sisters." She even found beauty in the aged village, noting that throughout Spain "the thinker may find beautiful places, which speak out through their eloquent monuments, with their haughty decaying stones, and the silent majesty of their neglect." By contrast, even Santiago de Compostela itself doesn't escape scrutiny in her writing. Pedro Moscoso, a rural dandy made uncomfortable by urban refinement, still found it fit to condemn the cathedral for its shabbiness. The Portico de la Gloria itself was, in his estimation, "very badly sculptured, and the figures on it looked as if they all had been squeezed through a sieve. Craftsmanship must have been terribly rudimentary in those days." And Pardo Bazán's narrator underscores how the city was a hotbed of gossip, hardly rising to a more noble and distinguished standard.

Today, the old manor house remains in private hands; only its exterior can be appreciated by a visitor. Unlike in those decadent days of Pedro Moscoso, it is far better maintained; the garden itself has been trimmed back, a tangible reassertion of civilization in this quiet corner of Galicia.

And yet, the weight of history prevails. In the final chapter of *Los Pazos de Ulloa*, Julián considers this: "But certain places, like certain people, let a tenth of a century pass unnoticed. There stands the house of Ulloa to prove this truism. The massive lair, defying time, appears as heavy, gloomy, and forbidding as ever." Emilia Pardo Bazán, as a novelist, was not bound by fact; she had the luxury of conceit, of dramatization, of a too-tidy narrative arc. Within the pages of her great novel, though, she captured a piece of the deeper truth, something louder than a whisper, that underlies this landscape that is so utterly idyllic to its visitors today.

Keep reading...

Emilia Pardo Bazán, *Los Pazos de Ulloa*, 1886

Maryjane Dunn, "Nationalism, Regionalism, and Faith in the Works of Emilia Pardo Bazán: St. James and the

Pilgrimage to Santiago de Compostela, 1880-1920," *Ad Limina*, 2018

Sharif Gemie, *A Concise History of Galicia*, 2006

The Eucalyptus Revolution

Stage 31: Arzúa to Pedrouzo

There's a timeless quality that permeates the walk through Galicia. Maybe it's the well-trodden trail, flattened smooth by so many pairs of pilgrim feet. Perhaps it's the stone bridges spanning gurgling creeks, carrying the appearance of having fallen into place quite naturally, without human intervention. For me, though, it's the eucalyptus, towering high above the trail, and contributing to an air of silence that hushes the chatter of passing pilgrims.

I once saw a pilgrim write that he deliberately chooses not to read about the places he's walking through, so that he can make meaning of them with his own eyes, as opposed to having his perspective shaped by what others tell him to see. It's the kind of statement that carries its own internal logic; on the surface, I find it largely unobjectionable. Upon reflection, though, it seems more troubling, and the euca- lyptus has a lot to do with that.

After all, some cognitive dissonance occurs when one actually pauses to consider the presence of those eucalyp- tus trees within this 'timeless' landscape. It doesn't take a botanist to know that such trees (like corn) aren't native to Europe, instead originating far away in Australia.

The first Europeans to encounter eucalyptus were Captain Cook and his crew on their first voyage across the Pacific Ocean between 1768 and 1771. At one point, Cook's ship, the Endeavor, became ensnared amidst the Great Barrier Reef, suffering such damage that seven weeks of repairs were required. While the ship was beached, crew members made their initial forays into what became Australia, discovering the eucalyptus, among many other natural phenomena. The tree's name was inspired by its unusual flowers, which are wrapped in protective shells (in the original Greek, "eu" means "well" and "calyptos" means "covered").

It would take nearly a full century for eucalyptus to take root in Spain. Fray Rosendo Salvado, born in Tui, Galicia in 1814, entered the Benedictine Abbey of San Martiño Pinario in Compostela when he turned 15. After initial postings in Southern Italy, he achieved his goal of serving on a foreign mission, sailing to Australia in January 1846. Along with his colleague José Benito Serra, he founded what became known as "New Norcia" deep in the bush of the Victoria Plains, in honor of Saint Benedict's birthplace.

In the years between Cook's initial contact and Rosendo's arrival, exploration continued around this unique region, leading to the discovery of numerous species of eucalyptus. The E. globulus variant, first encountered by French explorers in Tasmania 1792, ultimately took Iberia by storm, thanks to this humble monk. In 1863, Fray Rosendo sent seeds of the E. globulus to his family in Tui, and within decades the Galician landscape would be profoundly transformed.

There were many aspects of eucalyptus that proved to be immediately enticing in many different places around the world. First, the tree is highly adaptable to different kinds of soil and climate, and spreads rapidly. Second, it filled the

274

mining industry's ravenous hunger for fuel. Eucalyptus grows in high density and features a high heat capacity, making it exceedingly valued in such contexts. Third, eucalyptus is a thirsty, thirsty wood, and its planting can help to solidify swampy terrain. While this wasn't as relevant to Galicia, in some areas it helped to combat malaria, offering a boon to public health.

Its Galician onslaught began in earnest in 1908, when the Spanish government's forestry administration initiated its first experimental eucalyptus plantings. Demand for wood in Spain's burgeoning industries continued to outpace supply, necessitating national reforms. The prolific eucalyptus seemed like the answer.

Of course, the demands became only more urgent in the wake of the Spanish Civil War (1936-1939), when much of the country's infrastructure suffered from destruction or neglect. While it had been founded in 1934, the Patrimonio Forestal del Estado (PFE) effectively launched in 1939, tasked with executing the General Plan of Reforestation in Spain. In its first decade, the PFE reforested 28,003 hectares in Southwest Spain, and nearly a third of that was eucalyptus. In those early years, eucalyptus served primarily as a source of energy, though the demand for this ebbed by the 1960s. For a time, a significant demand also emerged for essential oil, with this first emerging during World War I, and then peaking in the 1950s, with an annual production of roughly 300 tons distilled. Ultimately, though, it became most valued in Spain for its use in the manufacture of cellulose pulp. After some initial experiments in the early 1950s proved promising, the Spanish National Institute of Industry launched the National Cellulose Companies (ENCE) of Pontevedra, Huelva and Motril in 1957. From an initial annual capacity of 36,000 pulp tons, this has surged to nearly two million tons in the early 21st century.

It's easy to overstate how prominent eucalyptus has become on a national level. While nearly 275,000 hectares were planted with eucalyptus by the government between 1940 and 1982, that comprises only 9.3% of the total reforestation area. In recent decades, some under-productive eucalyptus forests–primarily in Andalucia–have been replanted with native species, further reducing its footprint.

But it's a starkly different story in Galicia, as pilgrims know well. Even setting aside the eucalyptus for a moment, the region was already experiencing dramatic changes throughout the 20th century. By the 1950s, significant portions of the rural population were moving into urban areas; not coincidentally, a decline in agricultural production followed apace. Between 1985 and 2005, agrarian lands dipped by 15%, leaving them abandoned and unused. Tree plantations became a tempting alternative, not only because of the varied demands for lumber, but also because an absentee landlord could extract some profit from the land with minimal supervision. The numbers tell the story: in 1973 there were roughly 28,000 hectares of plantations in Galicia; by 1973, those had jumped to nearly 400,000. While pines were promoted early in the Franco years, in time these were largely replaced with eucalyptus, especially in coastal areas. Eucalyptus trees grow to maturity in just 15 years; a single hectare's worth will yield up to €2,500 annually.

Rural Galicians have not always responded kindly to the tree. Agrarian workers rebelled against new plantations in the 1980s, tearing up trees and setting fire to property. In more recent years, municipal governments have joined the resistance, declaring themselves "Eucalyptus-Free-Zone Municipalities." Less formalized "de-eucalyptus brigades" have also been organized throughout Galicia since 2017, striving to replace the trees with native species.

What's the difference between native and invasive species, anyway? Maybe it's not quite as contentious as pilgrim vs. tourist, but it's also not as black-and-white a distinction as it first appears. Diego Cidrás and Marien González-Hidalgo have laid out the underlying tensions quite well. They highlight the International Union for Conservation of Nature's (IUCN) definition of invasive alien species (IAS), characterizing these as "animals, plants or other organisms that are introduced into places outside their natural range, negatively impacting native biodiversity, ecosystem services or human well-being." Cidrás and González-Hidalgo add, though, that IAS are often also distinguished by their adaptability, rate of reproduction, and pace of growth. By contrast, they cite Antonsich's definition of native species as "occurring within their natural range and whose dispersal is independent of human action."

On the surface, then, this sounds as intuitive as one would have expected; the Galicia eucalyptus is obviously an invasive alien species. Despite that, when the Scientific Committee for the Environment recommended that the eucalyptus be declared invasive, both the Xunta of Galicia and the Asturian Government rejected the proposal and then defended their decision in the Spanish courts when the municipality of Teo appealed. The Spanish High Court of Justice ruled that "there is no scientific evidence [...] to catalogue E. globulus as IAS." None?!

Economic concerns certainly undergird this political resistance. In Galicia today, eucalyptus is responsible for 60% of the income enjoyed by the region's private forest owners—and given that nearly all the forests are privately owned, many of them by small landowners, this encompasses almost a tenth of the Galician population.. Half of all wood cut in Spain comes from Galician forests, and roughly half of that is eucalyptus.

And yet, opponents of eucalyptus frame this increasingly as a matter of life and death. The same issue that made the tree so desirable in its initial migration to Europe–its flammability and high heat potential–makes it particularly susceptible to wildfires today. Indeed, as a pyrophyte species, eucalyptus isn't just susceptible to fires; it is reliant upon them in order to spread and thrive. Over the course of the dry season, crispy tinder–fallen leaves and bark–accumulates at the base of these trees, an all too welcoming host for a spark, any spark. From there, it accelerates. Fire spreads twice as quickly through a eucalyptus forest as it does through native oak. Even worse, it keeps going. Eucalyptus is the only species in Galicia capable of spreading fire over long distances. A vicious cycle follows, as the fires wipe out remaining native species, while the eucalyptus rebounds, making the just-burned land even more vulnerable to a future fire.

In 2024, vicious wildfires swept through Northern Portugal, briefly shutting down the Camino Portugués. That was, of course, one of its less damaging consequences; after all, nine people were killed in these fires. Look beyond the headlines, though, and you'll see a familiar problem at the root of these fires. The eucalyptus plantations, along with pines, to a lesser extent, provided the primary fuel. CNN framed its discussion of this phenomenon around the far more mundane subject of toilet paper, noting that the eucalyptus globulus's pulp is a key source for such materials.

As we follow the Camino through Galicia, and particularly in what I find to be its most enchanting stretch around Pedrouzo, it's worth recognizing that there is nothing timeless or eternal about this landscape. It is human made, transformed almost entirely within the last century. And in the decades to come, another dramatic shift could unfold, whether by human choice or cataclysmic wildfire. It is, admittedly, less enchanting to confront the reality instead of living the myth, but there is power to be found in recognizing the dual resilience of our landscapes and our lives. After all, walking through native oak won't be so bad.

Keep reading...

Álvaro Merino and Abel Gil, "Eucalyptus fever: speculation and wildfire in Galicia," *European Data Journalism Network*, 2023

Diego Cidrás and Marien González-Hidalgo, "Defining invasive alien species from the roots up: Lessons from the 'De-eucalyptising Brigades' in Galicia, Spain," *Political Geography*, 2022

Federico Ruiz and Gustavo Lopez, "Review of Cultivation History and Uses of Eucalypts in Spain," *Centro de Investigación Forestal ENCE*, 2010

Making Santiago

Stage 32: Pedrouzo to Santiago

With apologies to Kevin Costner and Ray Kinsella, just because you build it, that doesn't mean anyone will actually come. For every great pilgrimage shrine, there are hundreds of crumbling, forgotten ruins; for every Santiago, there are scores of forgotten saints, their reliquaries coated in dust.

The first time that people learn that there were three great Catholic pilgrimage destinations in the medieval world, they're quite understandably surprised to discover an obscure city in Northwest Spain placed on equal footing with Rome and Jerusalem. But the ascent of Santiago de Compostela was never an inevitability. While the pilgrimage began almost immediately after the discovery of what were identified as the relics of Saint James, with King Alfonso II of Asturias traditionally acknowledged as the "first" pilgrim to the shrine, its early appeal moved in fits and starts. By the late 11th century, far from a mecca, the religious center of Santiago de Compostela was understaffed, underfunded, and unrefined. The canons, limited as they were in number, were criticized for their appearance, simultaneously unkempt and overdressed, and theologically they were undistinguished, to say the least.

And then, suddenly, everything changed. More than any other single individual, Diego Gelmírez, who would eventually become the first archbishop of Santiago de Compostela, deserves credit for its ascent to international prominence. Richard Fletcher, meanwhile, demands ack nowledgement as the historian who made Gelmírez best known to the English-speaking world, in his seminal work, *Saint James's Catapult*. While we don't know precisely when or where Gelmírez was born, it seems fair to plot his birth in the mid-1060s, and he was certainly a native Galician, part of a family of some prominence. Educated in the cathedral school of Compostela, he was fast tracked to success within the Church. What he might have lacked in intellectual dynamism or originality was resoundingly offset by the man's steadfast devotion to Santiago de Compostela. In Fletcher's assessment, "The key to an understanding of his career lies in his intense ambition for the glory of Saint James."

Gelmírez was elected bishop of Santiago de Compostela on July 1, 1100, thanks in no small part to his elite networking skills. Early on, he had proven himself to Raymond of Burgundy, the eventual Queen Urraca's first husband, when the couple administered Galicia. During those years, Gelmírez was elevated to the role of administrator of the temporalities of the church of Santiago, which placed him in a position of significant power within the city, overseeing the administration of justice, the maintenance of the city's defense, and tax collection. When the previous bishop, Diego Peláez, proved himself to be too troublesome for his own good, Alfonso VI advocated for his removal, and for Gelmírez to take his place. Even with that endorsement, though, the matter remained in the pope's hands, and Gelmírez refused to leave that to chance. He traveled to Rome in late 1099, ostensibly on a pilgrimage, but also with ulterior motives. He made a positive impression on Pope Paschal II (and imparted no shortage of expensive "blessings" to papal authorities along the way), and returned to Santiago with the bishopric secured.

Now that he had the job, he needed to actually perform in the role, and the circumstances he faced were daunting. Beyond the problems outlined above, he also assumed management of an expensive building program, including a new cathedral, at a moment when one of the major traditional sources of funding—the tributes paid by Muslim *taifa* kingdoms, which then allowed Alfonso VI and his predecessors to demonstrate their largesse through significant gifts to the Church—had been lost, following the king's conquest of Toledo. That had also triggered the wave of Almoravid invasions into the peninsula, which must have adversely affected pilgrim traffic—and its concomitant income.

But Gelmírez would not be deterred. Over the course of his first few years in the role, he transformed the bishopric. From that low point of seven canons, he built the chapter to 72 canons, a remarkable size. For comparison's sake, Toledo— the center of the Church in Spain at this point—had only 30. He swiftly resolved the economic issues that had long plagued the chapter, ensuring that his canons would be properly fed and housed. At the same time, he elevated standards, particularly in the realms of education and dress. Gelmírez's dual authority in the city, over matters secular and spiritual alike, allowed him to empower ambitious and capable canons with desirable opportunities, which also reinforced their loyalty and commitment. The speed with which Gelmírez pulled off these changes is a testament to his qualities as a manager.

His boldness is best exemplified in his 1102 mission to the diocese of Braga. The city housed the relics of Saint Fructuosus, and they were as central to its identity as James's were to Compostela. Nonetheless, Gelmírez decided to secret away the relics, translating them to Santiago in a bold maneuver that was accomplished so swiftly that he faced no opposition. Again, Gelmírez's singular purpose was to aggrandize Compostela, even if it came at the cost of other communities within his domain. Part of the brilliance of this maneuver was the showmanship that he displayed in the final delivery of Fructuosus. From Milladorio onward, still a stop on the Camino Portugués today, a procession of clergy and townspeople, all barefoot, marched the relics into Santiago. As Fletcher describes it, this "was a collective act uniting bishop, chapter, clergy and people of the town. It was an occasion which focused, which fused together, in a ceremony which owed something to rituals of penance and also, very probably, to secular rituals in honour of royalty, an intense religious devotion, a communal pride and a warm social solidarity."

Far from blanching at the financial burdens associated with the cathedral's construction plans, Gelmírez doubled down. As art historian Marilyn Stokstad has written, he went far beyond the cathedral to also rebuild churches throughout the region. No corners were cut, no expense spared. He hired the best artists and invested as much energy and funding into the decoration and furnishings of the interior as he did to the architectural frame. While Diego Peláez deserves acknowledgement for initiating the rebuilding of the cathedral, thus setting in motion the development of the shrine so beloved by pilgrims today, it was Gelmírez's dedication and follow-through that ensured its successful completion, even if that wouldn't transpire until long after his lifetime. After all, as Barbara Abou-El-Haj explains, the project had already languished for the better part of a decade prior to Peláez's fall.

Beyond the cathedral, Gelmírez sought to build out the rest of the facilities required by a 12th-century bishopric. For starters, he rebuilt the canon's refectory and established a cloister. Outside the north transept, in what today is known as the Praza da Inmaculada, he oversaw the installation of an enormous fountain, designed by the cathedral treasurer Bernardo. As pilgrim traffic surged, the demands for water in the urban center strained the supply, but this fountain could accommodate up to fifteen filthy *peregrinos* at once. Gelmírez, of course, didn't neglect his own needs; a bishop needed an episcopal palace, after all.

Gelmírez's interpersonal skills, so essential to his rise to prominence, were tested even further over the succeeding years. Following the death of Alfonso VI in 1109, the political situation in Galicia deteriorated. As discussed in Stage 19, Queen Urraca, the first woman to rule independently in European history, was viewed with skepticism and hostility in many parts of the kingdom. In Galicia specifically, matters were complicated by the ambiguous role of her son Alfonso Raimúndez, who seemed to be positioned to supplant her as king if she remarried. Instead, she maintained authority over Galicia following her unhappy marriage to Alfonso 'El Batallador,' to the great disdain of many Galicians.

As such, Gelmírez suddenly had to balance the competing interests of Queen Urraca, with whom he had a relationship dating back to his service to Raymond, Alfonso Raimúndez, who he had tutored as a young man, and Galician nobles like Pedro Froílaz de Traba, who were militantly opposed to Urraca. This was a decidedly uncomfortable position, and Gelmírez didn't always cover himself in glory as he navigated his way through the conflict, sometimes pouring fuel on the fire. At one point, Gelmírez agreed to the crowning of Alfonso Raimúndez as king of Galicia; at another, Urraca plotted to arrest Gelmírez. Ultimately, though, Urraca and Gelmírez needed each other too much to fully split from one another. In particular, Urraca had

assets desirable to Gelmírez–lands and buildings throughout Galicia, along with royal privileges–while Gelmírez could offer liquid wealth in exchange, which she desperately needed to find her military operations.

Over the same years, Gelmírez maintained a full court press on the pope in pursuit of his most cherished goal: elevating the episcopal see of Compostela to a metropolitan rank, and thus making himself an archbishop in the process. As early as 1095, he pushed for this, arguing that every church in Christendom bearing apostolic relics was at least the center of an archbishopric, if not something greater, save for Compostela. Nonetheless, despite positive relationships with Popes Paschal II and Gelasius II, it was only when Gelmírez's third pope, Calixtus II, ascended to the papal throne in February 1119 that success would finally be within reach. As it happens, Calixtus II was born Guy of Burgundy, the brother of Raymond, with whom Gelmírez had cut his teeth so many years before. And Calixtus II did not disappoint; before long, he issued four papal bulls that, among other things, gave rise to Archbishop Gelmírez. In Fletcher's judgement, this "was the greatest triumph of his life."

Remember, though, that Gelmírez had both spiritual and secular authority in the city, and while he enjoyed these almost unblemished successes on the spiritual side, the secular matters continued to pose challenges. His efforts had brought unprecedented wealth to Compostela, but that didn't guarantee his popularity with the townsfolk. Urraca, during one of the low points in her relationship with Gelmírez, sought to capitalize on that percolating dissent, stirring up anti-Gelmírez hostility. In 1116-17, this would come back to bite her, in what stands out as the wildest sequence of events in the city's history. A group of towns-people rose up in rebellion and enjoyed some immediate successes, nearly imprisoning the bishop and driving him out of the city. Over the course of six months, his palace was destroyed, he lost all of his rental income, and his efforts to retake control proved entirely futile. At last, he yielded to Urraca. The toothpaste, however, was not enthused about its return to the bottle; regardless of the queen's expectations, a not insignificant portion of the rebels held forcefully to their gains. And if they could turn on the bishop, they could just as easily vent their spleens towards an unpopular queen. So in the spring of 1117, Gelmírez and Urraca found themselves cornered by a pack of rabble-rousers in the cathedral's bell-tower.

Stokstad relates that Gelmírez at this point sought to save the queen, telling her that, "it is I and my relatives that they consider enemies, and our death is what they really want." The horde seemed to confirm this claim, declaring: "Let the Queen leave if she wishes; we will give permission to leave and to live only to her; the others shall perish." Urraca then, believing that she had been guaranteed safe conduct, tried to escape, only to be badly abused. She was tossed to the mud, beaten, her clothes ripped to shreds, "until she lay on the ground on her breast for a long time shamefully naked and in sight of everyone." For Gelmírez, this provided a convenient distraction; having changed clothes and holding a crucifix directly in front of his face, he managed to pass through the crowd unmolested. While that extricated him from the fire, he was still very much in the frying pan. With three allies, Gelmírez climbed over walls and roofs, then passed through the window of a private home. From there, they made a small hole in the wall–by hand!–so that they could pass into the next house, and the next, and the next. Architectural standards were different back then! Finally, though, they made it back to safety. Once the queen and the bishop had escaped peril, they went on the offensive. As described in the *Historia Compostelana*,

"The Bishop after sending news of his liberty to the Queen from Iria proclaimed excommunication against all the inhabitants of Compostela and forbade them to enter the Holy Church, an act which terrified the citizens to the marrow of their bones and disheartened them entirely." At that point, the queen's forces besieged the city.

Why did Gelmírez face such animus in a city he had placed squarely on the map? For as much wealth as the archbishop had brought to Compostela, as Stokstad puts it, "Even a relatively benevolent dictator was still a dictator." Across Europe, free cities were taking shape, offering independence from royal government and the possibility of self-rule. In many regards, Gelmírez was accommodating; "as long as the archbishop saw that it was clearly in his best interests, he granted more and greater privileges." Inevitably, "he moved too slowly" to satisfy many of the townspeople. Nonetheless, even acknowledging the ongoing tension in the city, Gelmírez's effective management was, in many regards, beneficial to Compostela in the long run.

By contrast, Gelmírez's relationship with the monastic center of Cluny was far more harmonious. Cluny had been founded in France in 910, and by Gelmírez's time the order already had a foothold in Spain. Alfonso VI had become a major patron, granting four monastic houses to Cluny between 1073 and 1077, including the Monasterio Real de San Benito in Sahagún. A younger Gelmírez paid a visit to Cluny, gaining an audience with an aged Hugh, among the most famous abbots of the Middle Ages. His successor, Pontius, emerged as a steady ally of Gelmírez as well, reinforcing Cluniac support for Compostela.

This would bear fruit in many ways, but the most significant may have been the creation of the Codex Calixtinus, one of the world's first guidebooks. As Stokstad writes, "Without the extremely skillful propagandizing of the pilgrimage to the tomb of Saint James by the church, especially by the monastic orders, no great city would have developed." While we don't know a great deal about the background of the Codex, most historians agree that it originated in the first half of the 12th century, most likely inspired in part by Gelmírez. Despite the name, the book had no association with the pope; rather, it is most commonly associated with the French monk Aymery Picaud. While direct ties to Cluny can't be proven, the work concludes with an acknowledgement that it "is being written" in the abbey of Cluny. We're fortunate that the Codex survived into the present, as it offers an incredible window into the pilgrimage in all its medieval glory. In the Middle Ages, though, the book was instrumental for building the international reputation of Santiago de Compostela. Along with a concrete overview of the route, the Codex also features a collection of miracle stories, highlighting the power of Santiago.

For all his skill, Gelmírez was also fortunate. Certainly, he arrived in power at a complicated moment, not least of which because of the changes triggered by Alfonso VI's conquest of Toledo. That said, the timing was opportune for the ascent of Compostela in two critical ways. First, as Fletcher explains, "the impulse to undertake pilgrimages is stronger at some periods than at others," and between 950 and 1150, "the practice of pilgrimage [as] a journey to a miracle-working shrine" experienced a boom time. What explains that change? Among other things, Fletcher highlights a shift in the practice of confession. Over the course of those two centuries, instead of the traditional approach, which involved absolution being granted only after completion of penance, absolution was increasingly granted at the moment of confession. Importantly, though, absolution wouldn't save the individual from suffering in the next world as a consequence of that sin. This served to elevate the importance of penance, through tangible acts of contrition, and penitential pilgrimage emerged in these years as a particularly noteworthy manifestation of that.

Along with that, around the same time that Gelmírez became bishop of Santiago, the first crusade was getting underway. Initially, this raised some concerns in Iberia, as leaders feared that experienced knights might take their services to the Holy Land, when they were needed more urgently than ever to fend off the emerging Almoravid threat. In recognition of this, Pope Callixtus II sent a letter to churches across Western Europe in 1123, beseeching their care: "we beg, my sons, that you understand in your charity how important it is to go to Spain to fight the Moors and how many thanks will be given to those who voluntarily go there."

He then took it a step further, extending the incentives associated with crusading in the Holy Land to Iberia: "This same indulgence we ratify and confirm: that all those who go, as we said above, with the sign of the cross of the Lord on their shoulders to fight the infidels in Spain or the Holy Land, will be absolved of all the sins of which they have repented and confessed to their priests... and they will merit coronation in the celestial kingdom beside the holy martyrs who from the beginning of Christianity until the end of time received or are to receive the palm of martyrdom."

In those two developments, we can see the roots of Santiago Peregrino and Santiago Matamoros emerging side by side, and Gelmírez took full advantage of such fertile terrain.

Having now arrived in Santiago de Compostela and completed your pilgrimage on the Camino, you undoubtedly have many people to thank. Your loved ones at home who supported you in this journey. Your fellow pilgrims, including perhaps a Camino family, that enriched your daily walks and kept you moving through the hardest days. The hospitaleros who provided shelter and care on each and every night. And Santiago, perhaps, whether you think of him as the apostle who sacrificed his life in order to help spread the good word, or the myth that nonetheless served and serves as a galvanizing force, without which none of this would exist.

On top of all of them, though, save a word for Archbishop Diego Gelmírez. For whatever faults he certainly bore, he loved this city more than his life, and he spent every day laboring to create the place that remains so special today.

Keep reading...

Barbara Abou-El-Haj, "Santiago de Compostela in the Time of Diego Gelmírez," *Visual Culture of Medieval Iberia*, 1997

Marilyn Stokstad, *Santiago de Compostela in the Age of the Great Pilgrimages*, 1978

Richard Fletcher, *Saint James's Catapult: The Life and Times of Diego Gelmirez of Santiago De Compostela*, 1984

Acknowledgements

In June 2024, I did something grossly irresponsible. I quit my dream job in order to go for a walk. My initial attempt at crossing the USA on foot was interrupted by COVID and I felt a powerful pull to complete that journey. After nearly four months and 5,000 kilometers of walking in the USA, I reached my home in Portland, Oregon, and then dipped my toe in the Pacific. But that wasn't enough–not by a long shot. Italy came next. I set out to spend six months walking on pilgrim roads, heading up and down the peninsula. As I type, I've completed the first half of that trek, from Matera and Santa Maria di Leuca in the south to the Slovenian border in the northeast. The second half will follow in the fall.

Along with walking, my goal was to carve out sufficient space to dedicate myself to a series of writing projects. In time, those will include books devoted to the walks across the USA and Italy, but this one, *The Camino Compendium*, has been rattling away in the back of my head for years. It demanded to be at the front of the line.

It's an unsettling thing, taking the leap away from a comfortable, traditionally successful life and into the unknown. I'm a much better teacher than I am a writer; as such, I'm far more likely to experience failure and setbacks on a daily basis in this life than I did in my old one. Of course, that was part of the allure.

Given such uncertainty, it was a great comfort to receive the support of many friends, former students, colleagues, pilgrims, and hikers when I launched a Patreon in May 2024, and I want to extend my gratitude to them here. Thank you to Calissa, Andrei Stoica, Laura Perazzoli, Ben Z, Tom Coleman, Dirk EYBL, Allison Venuto, Scott Heiner, Eric Juhos, Jennifer Hanson, Tom Zepf, Scott, Robert Freitas, John Floyd, Bill Wrobleski, Rick and Frankie White, Gerard Forde, Shanna Yarbrough, Edie Sundby, Herman (Chuck) Watson, PeterO, and Mary, along with all those who prefer anonymity!

I'm also grateful to you for reading this. More incredible books are published in a year these days than any of us can hope to read in a lifetime. Thank you for devoting part of your all-too-limited reading time to my book. If you have an additional moment to spare, please consider posting a review–on Amazon, GoodReads, the Camino Forum, your Camino Facebook group of choice, or wherever else you like. These are the lifeblood of authors in 2025; they help more than you can possibly know. And along those lines, please reach out if you have any corrections, suggestions, or other feedback to this text. For all the work that goes into the first edition of a book, there's a reason that second editions exist. You can reach me at caminopodcast@gmail.com.

If you're interested in following along as I continue churning kilometers, you can find me online at www.davewhitson.com and www.patreon.com/davewhitson.

Dave Whitson
June 2025